The ido loves

BEER

♦ America's best—where they're made
and where to find them.

♦ Old world brews—the best imported brands
readily available here at home.

♦ The history of beer.

♦ The making of beer.

♦ All about pilsners, porters, Belgian ales,
bitters, stouts, wheat beers, lambics,
flavored beers, and more.

♦ The joys of homebrewing.

♦ Edited and with a foreword by a
Master Brewer.

And much more!

BEER

DOMESTIC, IMPORTED, AND HOME BREWED

EVE ADAMSON

Technical Editor, and with a Foreword by, ERIC NIELSEN, Master Brewer

Produced by Amaranth

HarperTorch
An Imprint of HarperCollinsPublishers

The author gratefully acknowledges the following for their kind permission to reproduce labels in the text of this book: Kalamazoo Brewing Company, Inc., for labels appearing on pages 269, 274, 282, 285; Lost Coast Brewery for labels appearing on pages 305, 308, 313; Merchant du Vin for labels appearing on pages 65, 66, 69, 72, 88, 91, 110, 111, 121, 122, 123, 301, 307; Millstream Brewery Co. for labels appearing on pages 268, 271; Sleeman Unibroue Inc. for labels appearing on pages 187, 188; and Three Floyds Brewing for labels appearing on pages 275, 277, 286. Further reproduction prohibited.

❦

HARPERTORCH
An Imprint of HarperCollins*Publishers*
10 East 53rd Street
New York, New York 10022-5299

Copyright © 2006 by Amaranth Illuminare
ISBN-13: 978-0-06-079611-2
ISBN-10: 0-06-079611-1

First HarperTorch paperback printing: July 2006

HarperCollins®, HarperTorch™, and ❦ ™ are trademarks of HarperCollins Publishers Inc.

Printed in the United States of America

Visit HarperTorch on the World Wide Web at www.harpercollins.com

10 9 8 7 6 5 4 3 2 1

Contents

Foreword

by Eric Nielsen, Master Brewer

During the preceding eight to ten millennia (give or take a week or two), the brewing of beer has consistently been the largest biotech industry on the face of our planet. During most of this period, beer has been a far safer drink than water. Boiling sterilizes beer, and the subsequent chemistry that occurs during the brewing process leaves the stuff essentially bulletproof to all known human pathogens. Beer is also not subject to contamination from open sewers, unlike water from the community well. Compared to beer, safe drinking water is a quite recent innovation.

Prior to Pasteur's microbiological discoveries in the mid-1800s, beer provided our civilization with the safest, cleanest beverage available. Historically, beer has also provided us with a cheap and efficient method of storing grains that vermin cannot infiltrate, unlike grains in their natural state. Today debate rages within the scientific community as to whether the brewing of beer or the baking of bread served as the initial kernel of civilization.

Neolithic history aside, contemporary brewing is arguably one of the most vibrant culinary scenes around today. The North American craft-brew revolution of the late twentieth century has been bolstered by an increasing international awareness, and the result is good for everyone. Today we have available to us a broad palate of distinctive brews no less than global in scope. Beyond beer as a mere beverage, recent interest in the culinary use of beer in the United States has ignited a new trend: specialty and import beers in the context of fine dining. The time for good beer is this evening in your glass. We invite you to tip this glass with us, saluting brews both from the past and in the future.

Although a full manual on craft-brewed beer could easily fill an entire bookshelf, this little book readily serves as an apt introduction to the wide diversity of beers available throughout the planet today. Apologies to the many worthy brewers and breweries that don't appear in this guide, which is by no means all-inclusive. We strongly encourage readers to delve into their local artisanal brewing scene to find out what's fresh, what's new, and what's being made right where you live. Please, support your small local breweries; these are the people who are keeping artisanal beer alive!

The talents of author Eve Adamson radiate through the pages of this text. Her enthusiasm, intelligence, attention to detail, and raw talent when evaluating beers have been admirably transferred to the pages you currently hold. She adds to this project a writing history that includes a strong culinary background; this has served as an ideal springboard for her work with this manual.

On a more personal basis, I am delighted to address you, the budding beer connoisseur, as one of your guides to this complex, varied, and utterly rewarding field. I have been involved in the home-brew and craft-brew industry for the last twenty-five years, stumbling into a master brewer's degree as well as a career in the specialty beer industry along the way. I find that this industry provides an insightful opportunity to use the entirety of one's brain: the analytical side drives the urge to tease apart the specific flavors, nuances, and even historical notes of a beer, while the artistic side luxuriates in the consumable culinary art that is the heart and soul of a well-crafted brew.

As you develop your appreciation of fine beers, open your palate and mind to the idea that beer can taste like almost anything. Beyond the initial and dominant flavors of malt and hops, let that analytical side of your brain and palate investigate and identify subtle notes of smoke, bubble gum, chocolate, nutmeg, toffee, or even grapefruit. Some of the best contemporary chefs argue that the nearly limitless range of flavor profiles available in beer make it a far more versatile dining (and cooking) companion than wine. Strive to develop a slow, relaxed, almost European deliberation, tasting beers gracefully in a quiet and relaxed atmosphere.

The conversational style of this text allows it to be expert, yet not pretentious; technical expertise has created a work that is concise without being watered down. These features come together to create a book that is an easy read, both joyful in spirit as well as packed with information. Cheers! And have fun!

Introduction

A girl, writing about beer? Wait a minute . . . girls don't like beer, do they? What does a girl know about beer? And why should you read what a girl has to say about beer?

First of all, as a person who enjoys good beer and the pursuit of gustatory knowledge, I've learned quite a bit over the last few years tasting beers from around the country and around the world. As a food writer, I am obsessively interested in *taste* and the sensory impressions possible from the things we choose to eat and drink. And finally, as a woman, I have the unique advantage of *not* growing up with some cultural idea that I should be swilling cheap pale lager like it was going out of style while watching football or mowing the lawn.

That's not to say that any stereotypes about men and women, football or lawn mowing, or especially *beer* apply to anyone reading this book. My point is simply that I love beer—good, complex, interesting beer in all its many incarnations, from lightest to darkest, sweetest to hoppiest, brewed all over the world from Belgium to Seattle. I love to taste beer and tease apart the nuances of aroma and flavor. The more I do this, the more I like to consider myself a beer evangelist, spreading the news that beer can be something truly delicious, interesting, complex, and appealing to anyone's taste, whether they like hop bombs or thick malty sweetness, whether they like fruit beers or pilsners, and, yes, whether they are a man or a woman.

In writing this book, I have attempted to transfer some of what I have learned about beer to you as you embark upon your own personal journey of tasting and enjoying the world's best beverage. Anyone can learn from this book, whether novice or aficionado, although the primary focus of this book is to introduce those mainly familiar with pale lager to the vast and fascinating world of beer available to you right here in your own hometown.

This book begins with some background about what beer is, how it is made, and why it is such a popular drink. Following that, find your own personal guide to how to taste beer and what different styles of beer should or typically will taste like. (This book is pocket-sized so you can take it with you to your local beer store or cozy pub.) Then we start our world tour, looking at different countries and the beers they have to offer, as well as different regions of the United States—what started where and who is doing what. Finally, you'll find short lists of beer organized by style and geographic region for you to try, so you can expand your palate and increase your awareness of what beer can be, with check boxes by each beer so you can mark them off as you try them. I'm hoping some of you might eventually try every beer in this book! If you do, be sure to let me know. You can find me through my website at *www.eveadamson.com.*

How to Use This Book

You don't have to read this book from front to back. If you want to know how beer is made, read Chapter 1. Interested in how to taste? Go to Chapter 2. Eager to learn more about good Belgian beers, or British beers, or great microbrews from the Pacific Northwest? Skip to those chapters. It's your book and your beer journey.

This book is designed for the novice beer drinker interested in trying new beer styles and refining his or her beer palate without having to travel the world. While I certainly wish I could spend a leisurely year (or decade!) touring the world in search of its greatest ales and lagers, I (like most) don't have the time or finances for such a trip. Fortunately, some of the world's best beers are available right here in the United States, and those are the beers that are the focus of this book.

In other words, this is not a travel guide. Instead, this book focuses primarily on learning how to appreciate the subtleties of the many great beers you can get in this country. Many great brewers produce amazing beers in other countries that are not available in the United States, but that would make for a much longer book. While you won't be able to get every beer listed in this book in every state, you should be able to get almost all of them in at least a few states. For the chapters covering other countries, I have listed only beers that I know or am pretty sure are available in at least a few states.

In these country and region chapters, for each beer style reviewed, I've included a simple scale that shows the color and flavor of each style of beer. For instance, a pilsner is rated on a scale between pale straw color and almost black, and also on a scale from sweetly malty to bitter and hoppy. Because some styles have a range of color and flavor—for instance, an amber ale can range from light copper to deep brown—this is also indicated. Brewing chemists are much more precise about such measurements and have their own number scales, but since most readers probably aren't brewing chemists, I feel these simple scales are easier to read and give you a clearer, if more general, idea of a beer style's typical color and maltiness versus hoppiness. I've also listed typical alcohol percentage for each style, which can also be a range. For instance, some strong ales are very high in alcohol, some not so high. Finally, I list an ideal serving temperature range for the style of beer, although your particular taste may differ, especially according to the season. A beer served outside on a crisp October evening should be served less chilled than that same beer on a hot, muggy summer day when it might turn tepid before you finish half your glass. Take this serving temperature listing as a general guideline.

Below this basic information about each beer style, you'll find a list of specific beers that fall into that style from the region or country relevant to that chapter. Because many countries make the same styles, these styles are often repeated in different chapters. However, a pilsner from Czechoslovakia isn't exactly like a pilsner from America, so the written descriptions of the styles sometimes differ slightly to take these variations into account. Sometimes the descriptions are similar or exactly the same, simply for your convenience so you don't have to keep flipping back and forth.

Also, I have made every effort to include a wide and interesting range of beers to try. I wish I had room to list all the great ones, so I hope nobody will be offended if

I have left out a favorite beer. It is not an indication that I don't or wouldn't like that beer. Obviously, I listed my own favorites and the favorites of other knowledgeable beer drinkers I know, plus many other breweries and beers I found to be significant, interesting, relevant, representative and instructional. The beer scene changes frequently, however, and while I have made every effort to keep this list updated, some of the beers listed here may no longer be available. And of course there will always be great beers emerging that didn't make it onto these pages. I offer sincere apologies to any worthy breweries or individual beers that aren't listed here. However, the beers listed here are many, and varied, and exciting.

Acknowledgments

So many knowledgeable beer connoisseurs helped with the research necessary for this book. The wonderful folks at the Heorot in Muncie, Indiana—a true beer pub with an astonishing selection—were full of helpful information. Thanks to Stan Stevens for the beer tasting; to Jeff Meyer for advice, counsel, and the Good Beer Show (*www.goodbeershow.com*); to Brian Fickle for letting me go back behind the bar and have a look around at the casks and hand pumps; to Mark Hoyt for international information; and to the various opinions, perspectives, and insights from Bob, Kenny, Spencer, April, Guy, and everyone else I've had the privilege of sharing beer with at the Heorot. Thanks to John's Grocery in Iowa City for its great influence on the beer scene in Iowa, and to the patrons at Dave's Foxhead for input. Thanks to Larry Bell at Bell's Brewery and the other breweries kind enough to contribute label art for this book, particularly Unibroue (thanks Angela!), Lost Coast, Three Floyds, and my local brewery, Millstream. Special kudos must be bestowed upon my extremely knowledgeable tech editor, Eric Nielsen, for his invaluable additions and corrections to this manuscript. The chapters on Belgium and on homebrewing, in particular, could not possibly have been written without Eric's expertise. Thanks also to my friends who helped me sample, taste, and generally enjoy the camaraderie and revelry that inevitably accompany an evening of good beer, particularly Shannon Gillette, Jason Ruyle, and Nick Martin.

Thanks are also due to the many seriously beer-invested participants on Ratebeer—in my opinion, the best and most informative beer website available—for their vast knowledge and willingness to answer questions. Anybody who wants to take his or her knowledge about beer to the next level should log on to *www.ratebeer.com* and start rating and reading and learning. What a fantastic resource you guys have created! I especially want to thank Eric Manning, who first introduced me to Ratebeer; to world-travelling beer connoisseur and style expert Josh Oakes; and to other Ratebeerians who took time out to contribute their thoughts and knowledge: Joe Tucker, without whom the site could not be; and also Jon Calafato, Jeff Clark, Brian Kinzie, Robert G. Standera, Aaron Goldschmidt, Eric Starnes, Michael Campbell, Phil Williams, Matt Simpson (*www.thebeercellar.com*), and Mark Roman. Thanks also to the folks at Beeradvocate (*www.beeradvocate.com*), another great beer information and rating site; the American Homebrewers Association (*www.beertown.org*), and the inimitable beer writer Michael Jackson (if anybody has influenced the contemporary perception of beer, it's this guy—find him at *www.beerhunter.com*) for their helpful and comprehensive resources. Thanks to the many breweries and bars all over the country, from Manhattan to San Francisco and many spots in between, full of friends and strangers eager to share their thoughts, knowledge, and intense passion about beer with me. Finally, thanks to Ben, for gamely sampling far more beers than he really wanted to sample, until finally throwing up his hands and returning happily to his bottle of Guinness Extra Stout.

From Eric Nielsen, technical editor:

Addressing you, dear reader, is a privilege that I have gained over years of beer study and beer touring in both the United States and Europe. I'm compelled to also thank those who have been pivotal in making this opportunity possible: Dr. Michael J. Lewis, Professor Emeritus of the Brewing Science program at the University of California Davis, not only a world-renowned scientist and captivating lecturer, but also a very much beloved and insightful instructor in the brewing sciences; Ashton Lewis and Tom Shellhammer (the best teaching assistants that anyone could ever ask for); and the deliciously diverse beer department at John's Grocery of Iowa City (and its staff), which have given me the opportunity to pursue my love of teaching within the context of beer. An appreciative nod goes as well to the numerous institutions at which I've taught *something* at the grades one through Ph.D. level, allowing me to hone my teaching and writing skills over the past couple of decades, as well as to the numerous brewers that have opened their doors to me over the years.

BEER

1
All About Beer

Say "beer" and most people know what you mean: that golden, fizzy stuff that goes so well with burgers, or maybe that dark, malty drink suited to cozy British pubs. "Beer" is an umbrella term that encompasses light lagers, dark rich ales, specialty beers flavored with coffee or fruit, porters and stouts, lambics and barley wines, even (arguably) nonalcoholic malt beverages. In other words, the term "beer" encompasses a much larger universe than can be summed up by the question, "Light or dark?" although color is one important aspect in the evaluation of a beer. Beer can refer to a cloudy pale wheat beer scented with orange peel and coriander, a rich chocolaty porter that almost tastes like a dessert all on its own, hearty bronze-burnished Scottish ales, and complex, multilayered Trappist ales with lingering flavors of banana, nutmeg, licorice, or honey. And that's just a beginning!

Learning about, tasting, even brewing beer will expose the curious to a wide range of flavorful, interesting, nutritious beverages brewed from that original staple of the human diet: grain. Trickier to make than wine but more versatile to pair with food, beer can potentially match any food or stand on its own as an aper-

itif, a thirst-quencher, an after-dinner drink; the stuff
that warms and cheers a group of friends, stimulates the
minds and palates of connoisseurs, or simply relieves
that deep-down thirst that comes from a hard day's
work.

Beer is one of the original sources of human nutrition. In fact, some people argue that the desire to brew
beer was the single driving force that created agriculture, since many of the first crops consisted of barley, a
grain not conducive to baking bread but ideal for brewing beer. Beer has long been an integral part of northern
European culture, where it evolved from a hearty, dark
ale to the pale lagers so popular all over the world
today. But over the past few decades, beer has continued
to evolve by circling in some ways back to its roots: ales,
some from ancient recipes, have become popular again,
and beer has blossomed into a multitude of forms—
sour, sweet, heavy, light, grainy, malty, viscous, bitter,
floral . . . the list goes on, and so do the types of beer
that beer connoisseurs can now sample and enjoy, not
to mention brew themselves. The recent profusion of
home brewers, microbreweries, and beer connoisseurs
forming clubs, societies, classes, and tasting events is
further evidence that beer is back in a big way and better than ever. The appreciation of the vast and diverse
world of beer may be a recent trend in America, but the
pleasures and subtleties of beer are nothing new. Just
ask anyone from Ireland, England, Germany, or Belgium about the beer "trend." In these countries, beer
has been a primary source of nutrition and life-
sustaining force for thousands of years. In fact, archeo-
logical evidence suggests that humans have been
brewing beer pretty much since we discovered how to

live together in organized societies and grow our own grain.

But what is beer, exactly? What goes into beer? How do you make it? What are the different types? How do you taste it, and how do you know what's representative of different styles? How can you tell if a beer is "off," and how can you tell when a beer is really, really good?

Understanding more about what beer really is will help you to better appreciate the evolution of beer all over the world, not to mention that pint glass sitting in front of you. Does it taste like a pilsner should? Is it a good example of a stout? Does it go with pretzels? Here's what you need to know.

What Is Beer?

Beer, quite simply, is a beverage made from four basic ingredients: grain, yeast, hops, and water. More specifically, most beers fall under one of two categories: ales or lagers. The difference between an ale and a lager has nothing to do with alcohol content or color or sweetness versus bitterness. The only difference is in the type of yeast and brewing method used. Ales use a certain species of "ale yeast" that traditionally fermented on the top of the beer at warmer temperatures. Lagers use a different species of "lager yeast" that traditionally fermented at the bottom of the beer vat, under colder temperatures. Lagers need to ferment and age longer than ales and were once aged in caves during the summer months to stay at the cool temperatures lager yeasts prefer.

These two subcategories—ales and lagers—are only the beginning of the vast variation of styles of beer pos-

Family Tree of BEER

LAGER
German
Cooler, longer fermentation

Pilsner
All bock,
doppelbock, etc.
Oktoberfest/Märzen
Schwarzbier
Rauchbier
Dunkel
Helles
Dortmunder
Baltic porter

HYBRIDS
Altbier
Kölsch
Steam

ALE
UK or Continental
Warmer, faster fermentation

Bitter, ESB
IPA
Red ale
Dry stout
Sweet stout
Porter
Barley wine
Strong ale
Old ale
Belgian ale
(dubbel, tripel,
Trappist, abbey, etc.)
French bière de garde
Scotch ale (all styles)

SPECIALTY

Materials
(often ALE)

HYBRIDS
Flavored ale
(spices, fruits, etc.)
Traditional
unhopped ale
Mead
spiced mead
Smoked beer
Cider and perry

Yeast and Fermentation
Lab yeast
Wheat, wit,
weizen, dunkelweizen,
hefeweizen
Flemish sour
browns
Cask-fermented

Wild yeasts
Lambic family
e.g., lambic
gueuze, faro
Some saisons

sible with those four basic ingredients. The American Homebrewers Association publishes a detailed list of beer styles (go to *www.beertown.org* to find this information and lots of other fascinating beer lore) that breaks down beer varieties far beyond their designations as ales and lagers. Later chapters in this book discuss the qualities and characteristics of many of these varieties of beer that come from different countries and regions, but here is a brief overview. It may take you a while to learn how to distinguish ales and lagers purely by taste, but here are some basics, to show you which varieties fall under which type:

Ale

◆ Pale ale
◆ India pale ale (IPA)
◆ Bitter and extra special bitter (ESB)
◆ Gold or blond ale
◆ Wheat beer (including hefeweizen, dunkelweizen, wit)
◆ Red ale
◆ Scotch ale
◆ Belgian ale, including dubbel, tripel, Trappist, and abbey ale)
◆ Brown ale
◆ Porter
◆ Stout (dry, sweet, oatmeal)
◆ Bière de garde

Lager

◆ Pilsner
◆ Anything labelled helles or dunkel
◆ Amber

- Märzen/Oktoberfest
- Bock (including Maibock, eisbock, and doppelbock)
- Schwarzbier
- Rauchbier (smoked beer)
- Light and low-carb beers
- Dry lager
- Malt liquor

Other types of beer combine ale yeasts with lager brewing techniques or vice versa to create a third "hybrid" category of beer that includes the German styles kölsch and altbier. Some use different strains of yeast, including lab-cultured yeast or the naturally fermenting wild yeasts often used in the fruity and sour lambic, gueuze, faro, and saison styles. Some add unusual flavorings. Some of these alternative choices include:

- Lambics, including fruit-flavored lambics like framboise (raspberry) and kriek (cherry)
- Cream ale
- Sake-yeast beer
- Ales and lagers brewed with grains other than barley, such as wheat, oats, or rye
- Fruit and vegetable beers (pumpkin, chili, berry, etc.)
- Flavored malt beverages
- Beers flavored with chocolate, cocoa, coffee, herbs, spices, honey, smoke, or other flavors
- Nonalcoholic beers or malt beverages (the alcohol is evaporated off after brewing)

As you can see, that simple term "beer" really does encompass a huge range of options, depending on the kind of grain, the way it was malted (sprouted then dried), the method by which the malted grain is turned into wort (beer prior to fermentation), the kind of yeast, the variety of hops, and the procedure for putting them all together. Beer can contain wheat, oatmeal, rye, or other grains in addition to the standard malted barley. Beer can be light or dark but also red, amber, almost white, or practically black. Beer can be sweet (malty) or bitter (hoppy), high or low in alcohol, fruity or spicy, herbaceous or yeasty, tangy or mellow, sharp or smooth. And the more you taste it, the more your palate will learn to distinguish among all these different, some-times subtle, sometimes obvious flavors and flavor nuances.

The brewery itself and the style of the brewer also in-fluence individual brands of beers within these many varieties. Beer may be crafted in a brand-new micro-brewery in America by highly trained certified master brewers or self-taught hobbyists-turned-professionals. Or it could come from a centuries-old brewery in Ger-many, Belgium, Ireland, England, Scotland, Czechoslo-vakia, or any other country. Whether you are brewing at home or in a large-scale commercial brewery, brew-ing beer involves multiple precise steps, and at each step, the flavor and quality of beer could potentially be enhanced or degraded.

Yet, despite its complexities, beer is, and always has been, a remarkably simple pleasure. Malt, hops, yeast, and water combine to make something very, very good. Let's take a closer look at how the brewer puts these four simple ingredients together.

Malt, Hops, Yeast, and Water

The very first beer might have happened purely by chance. Did someone mistakenly leave a bowl of grain outside? Maybe the grain, dampened by rainwater, sprouted, then slowly fermented with the help of wild indigenous airborne yeasts and a little more rain. Maybe somebody tasted that interesting bubbly liquid. Maybe he or she thought it tasted pretty good, and tried to repeat the happy accident.

Today, of course, brewing beer is a much more precise and complex process, not to mention more sanitary. However, the basic ingredients are essentially the same: grain, yeast, hops, and water. To get these ingredients, first the grain is usually turned into malt. Grain (usually barley) is malted by sprouting and drying it in a kiln under precisely controlled conditions. The brewer chooses the style of malt to use for the style of beer desired—this could be a light or dark malt, a grainy or a roasty malt, since malt comes in many different varieties, depending on the type of grain and how it is prepared.

Next, the brewer must choose the specific type of cultivated yeast, according to the style of beer. The brewer will also choose from a wide variety of hops—the flowers from the hop plants contribute the pleasing bitterness to beer and also serve as a natural preservative. And of course, good beer requires good, pure, palatable water. Brewers choose these ingredients based on quality and on certain characteristics that will influence the resulting beer in different ways. This is all part of the art of brewing.

WHAT ABOUT ORGANIC BEER?

Organic beer is still a relatively rare commodity, mostly because of the difficulty in finding good organic hops. Organic malt is easy to find because malt is a widely used product in the food industry. Hops, however—those delicate, bitter flowers used to give beer its characteristic flavor—are not only disease-prone but are used exclusively for brewing beer. Growing hops without chemicals is difficult and the demand is low, so growers haven't yet found a cost-effective way to make organic beer. Some do it, but it's a pricey endeavor. Of course, consumer demand has a big influence on what growers choose to produce, so if you care about organic beer, speak up and request that your local market carry some.

BREWING PROCESS IN A NUTSHELL

The primary brewing process, at its most basic, pivots around several critical steps:

1. Grain is malted (germinated or sprouted) and dried in a kiln.
2. The malted grain is cracked, then mixed with warm water.
3. Enzymes from the grain break down starch into fermentable sugars, contributing to the flavor of the beer and giving the yeast something to consume later in the brewing process.
4. The resulting sweet liquid, called wort, which formed from mixing the cracked malt with warm water, is drawn off from the now-spent grains.
5. The wort is boiled.

6. Hops will usually be added at this point, but can also be added anywhere further downstream in the brewing process.

7. The resulting beer is cooled quickly.

8. The appropriate yeast is added, and fermentation conducted as appropriate for the target style of beer.

9. The finished beer is transferred to containers appropriate for the consumer market, or sold straight to clients from the final fermentation vessel (the latter is how the brewpubs do it).

These basics result in beer, in its many forms. Each of these steps has the potential to go in many different directions, however, depending on a number of factors.

MALT: THE ESSENCE OF BEER

One of the first things the brewer must consider is what type of malt to use. Malt has a significant impact on the taste and color of the beer, so the type of malt the brewer chooses has to coincide with the type of beer planned. Typically, the brewer buys grain already malted. To make grain into malt, the grain is soaked in water until it germinates, sprouting tiny roots. This germination phase develops those enzymes used later in the brewing process to transform unfermentable starches into the fermentable sugars required by the yeast. This sprouted grain is then dried in a kiln. This entire process is called malting.

Malt can come from any kind of grain—wheat, oats, rye—but most beer is made, at least primarily, from malted barley. Barley is high in starch, so it produces lots of sugars. It is also low in protein, so it produces fewer clogging coagulated proteins during the brewing process. Compared to wheat, which is lower in starch and higher in protein, barley makes the ideal brewing grain. Wheat's soft hull and high protein suit it for baking bread, but barley's rock-hard hull makes it difficult to process and make into flour. However, when malted, the barley kernels soften. This is the first step in making beer. Chew on a kernel of raw barley and you might crack a tooth, but munch a handful of malted barley and you'll be wishing for a cereal bowl and a pitcher of milk. Malted barley tastes toasty and sweet.

MALT IN A CAN

Malted grain is one of beer's primary ingredients, but the process of malting grain, or even brewing from malted grain, is complex and takes time and space, not to mention the right equipment. To simplify the process, beginning home brewers may choose to use malt extracts, which come in liquid or powder form or neatly packaged in ready-to-boil cans. Some also combine malted grains with malt extracts for more complex flavor. Some ambitious home brewers choose all-grain brewing, a process with more steps and more chances for error but with potentially delicious results.

Brewers have many types of malts to choose from, each appropriate for different varieties of beer. A few brewers make beer from a single type of malt, but in the vast majority of cases, brewers use a combination of malts to get the desired effect.

To a brewer, malt is conceptually divided into two primary subcategories: enzymatic or "workhorse" malt, and specialty or flavoring malts. The so-called workhorse malts are kilned lightly, so they don't have a lot of dark, roasty flavor but they retain almost all their natural enzymes, which will turn starches into fermentable sugars. Specialty malts, on the other hand, are kilned at higher temperatures. Their enzymes may be cooked beyond functioning, but these malts contribute the bold, roasty flavors and deep, dark color of stouts, porters, and other dark, roasty beer styles. To add further character to different types of malts, the original grains can be processed in a variety of ways—soaked in water for a long or short time before drying, stewed or not stewed, dried at relatively cool or relatively hot temperature, dried slowly or quickly. Some examples of these different types of malts produced by various techniques include:

- ◆ Biscuit malt
- ◆ Black malt
- ◆ Caramel malt
- ◆ Chocolate malt
- ◆ Crystal malt
- ◆ Munich malt
- ◆ Pale ale malt
- ◆ Pilsner malt
- ◆ Vienna malt
- ◆ Wheat malt

Once the brewer selects the desired malt, the next step in the brewing process is to mash the malt. To do this, the brewer first cracks or grinds up the malted grains to release the powdery starch. This isn't a thorough grinding, but just enough to break open the hull and let the starch free so the enzymes formed during the malting process can have something to work on.

This milled grain then goes into a large tub called a mash tun, where it is combined with hot water to form a sort of malt stew. Warm water activates those enzymes within the grain, which work to transform that newly freed starch into fermentable sugars. These sugars are what the yeast will later convert to alcohol, CO_2, and other by-products to make beer.

As with every step in the brewing process, subtle differences in technique can affect the end result. The particular way the brewer heats the mash—to what temperature, and how quickly the temperature rises—affects the characteristics of the mash and the taste of the beer. Ale and lager mashing regimes, for example, are markedly different, reflecting the geographic and historical roots of these two divergent beer families.

After mashing long enough for starches to be converted to fermentable sugars, the malt has transformed from a bunch of wet, ground-up grain into a thick, dark, syrupy concoction. The next step is to strain this syrup through a device called a lauter tun, which has screens that act as sieves, straining out the barley husks and leaving only the clear, sweet, malty-tasting syrup, called wort (pronounced "wert"). Wort is, essentially, unfermented beer. The brewer then sprays the husk bed with water to rinse out more of the sugar. The initial syrup is the highest in sugar and is called the first runnings. While draining the wort and rinsing the malt bed, the brewer measures the wort's sugar percentage by weight until it is the desired level for the beer-to-be. The percentage of sugar is referred to as the "gravity" of the wort, and the higher the gravity, or sugar content, the higher the resulting alcohol content. High sugar means high alcohol because the more sugar the wort contains, the more food the yeast has to convert into alcohol.

Brewers run warm water through the lauter tun a second time, to extract sugar from the grain bed caught in the screens. These second runnings aren't as thick and sweet as the first, and will produce a less sweet brew, more moderate in alcohol. This second running is appropriate for certain kinds of beer, for example, classic Britsh mild table beers. Finally, the wort is poured into a kettle, ready to boil with the hops.

GET HOPPIN'

What would beer be without hops? It certainly wouldn't be inauthentic, if you'll pardon the double negative. Hops are a relatively recent addition to the brewer's repertoire, having been used for less than a millennium—a mere fraction of beer's long history. Yet, what we think of as beer today would hardly be recognizable without the addition of hops. It would be sweet and it would contain alcohol, but it wouldn't contain the pleasingly bitter taste we associate with beer. Hops are the perfect foil to malted grain, balancing the sweetness and adding a depth of flavor and aroma malt alone can't achieve.

Hops are vines (actually "bines" if you want to get technically botanical about it) with cone-shaped flowers that do a lot of great things to a batch of beer. Not only do hops flavor the beer, but they impart antimicrobial biochemicals that help to preserve the beer and minimize cloudiness. The more hops in a beer, the more bitter it tastes and the longer it will last. Some people love that bitter, hoppy taste, while others prefer a smoother, sweeter beer, but most beers contain at least some hops.

Like malt, hops come in numerous varieties, each with its own subtle characteristics, but most varieties of hops grow best in cool climates. The most popular locations for growing hops are northern Europe, England, the United States (primarily in the Pacific Northwest), and more recently New Zealand.

In general, hops come in two types: bittering hops and aroma hops. The brewer adds bittering hops to the boiling kettle of wort after mashing. The bittering hops don't contribute any aroma to the beer because any aromatic aspect is lost during the boiling process. If the brewer wants to impart hops as an aroma, aroma hops can be added toward the end of the boil, for an extra kick of flavor and that exhilarating hop aroma you experience when you take a big whiff from a freshly poured glass of beer. Brewers may also choose to add hops to the beer during fermentation, or during postfermentation aging. This process, called dry hopping, adds yet another flavor dimension to the finished product. Some brewpubs even serve beer by first running it through a long tube stuffed with hop flowers, for one final hop blast. Dogfish Head brewery in Delaware invented this gadget, which they call Randall the Enamel Animal, or an "organoleptic hop transducer module," but some pubs have since copied the idea using different names, such as "hop tower." Whole-leaf hops are packed into a three-foot cylinder attached to the beer line between the keg and the glass. The "randallized" beer tastes extra hoppy.

Different varieties, or combinations of varieties, will give individual characteristics to different beers, so once again, the brewer has choices to make that will ultimately influence the subtle and not-so-subtle aroma and taste of a batch of beer. Some of the available types of hops include the following:

- Cascade
- Centennial
- Challenger
- Chinook
- Fuggle
- Hallertau
- Kent Goldings
- Magnum
- Mt. Hood
- Northern Brewer
- Nugget
- Pacific Gem
- Perle
- Saaz
- Simcoe
- Spalt
- Sterling
- Tettnanger
- Warrior
- Williamette

Depending on the style of beer and the brewer's inclination, any variety of hops might be added to the wort—although there are certain hops varietals that are strongly associated with specific styles of beer. Classic American-style India pale ales (IPAs) are strongly associated with our native-grown Cascade hops, while a venerable Czechoslovakian pilsner often relies on the Saaz hops traditionally grown in the Pilzen region of the Czech Republic.

HOW DO YOU TAKE YOUR HOPS?

Beyond the many varieties of hops, hops are also available in different forms for brewing, from pellets to liquid to the whole dried flower. Each form will impart slightly different tastes to a batch of beer, so again, the choice is up to the brewer. Pellets and liquid keep longer in storage and can be easier to use, but some brewers prefer the natural dried flower form. Most people probably can't tell the difference in the final product between pellets, liquid hops, and dried flowers, although different brewers have their favorites and their own opinions about which hop forms are superior.

IT'S ALIVE! THE MIRACLE OF YEAST

So far, we have a big kettle of syrupy malt boiled with bitter hops. Sounds like beer . . . sort of. But it isn't beer yet. Beer's "magical" ingredient is yeast, and in days of yore, people really did believe that malty syrup turned to beer by some mystical process. Yeast, a living airborne microorganism (it's actually a fungus) that exists all around us, feeds on the malt and changes its sugars into alcohol and carbon dioxide, transforming a sweet, malty, hop-flavored syrup into a nutritious, bubbly, refreshing alcoholic beverage. Yeast does much more than make beer alcoholic, however. Chemical processes in the brew result in a wide variety of secondary flavor characteristics as the yeast works. Flavors from yeast can suggest fruit, spice, candy, vegetables, mushrooms, and many other flavors (see Chapter 2 for more on evaluating beer flavors). Yeast can also enhance the flavors already present in the malt, hops, and any other added enhancements such as additional sugars, fruit, or spices.

Just like malt and hops, yeast comes in many different varieties. Wild airborne yeasts were the first yeasts to ferment the first beers, but today, now that we understand how yeast works, we can control the process better and use particular yeasts that imbue the brew with just the right amount and type of flavor we want.

Certain yeasts have been purposefully cultivated for brewing beer, and these come mainly in two varieties: ale yeast and lager yeast. Each of these varieties has many subvarieties that will lend different flavors to the brew, but they differ in the way they ferment the malt sugars. Ale yeast works best at between 55 and 75 degrees Fahrenheit, fermenting at the top of the beer. Ales are more of an established tradition in England, France, and Belgium, and ales can be light or dark, or high or low in alcohol (gravity).

Lager yeast ferments best between 32 and 55 degrees Fahrenheit, and ferments at the bottom of the beer, generally for longer periods than the quicker-acting ale yeasts. Lagers are a German original that changed the face of beer on the planet. Just like ales, lagers can be light or dark, or high or low in alcohol. Both ale and lager yeasts can also be used in traditional or experimental ways, combining ale yeasts with lagering techniques, lager yeast with ale techniques, or even using less typical strains of yeast or natural wild yeasts. Each method will result in a different product.

But where does the yeast come into the brewing process? After the wort has been hopped, boiled for the right amount of time, and cooled, it is time for the yeast to do its job. It is time for fermentation.

The wort is strained to remove the hops and other sediment, including coagulated proteins that have accumulated from boiling and cooling. At this point, the brew is still "faceless" in that it can become an ale or a lager, depending on what kind of yeast the brewer chooses and how the brew is fermented.

The wort is cooled quickly to prevent contamination, then mixed with the appropriate kind of yeast in a large fermentation vessel. Then the magic begins. The beer ferments, a process that may take anywhere from a scant week to months, depending on style, fermentation temperature, and yeast strain.

YEAST APPRECIATION

Home brewers can buy beer yeast from home-brew supply shops in either dried or liquid culture form. Like all other brewing elements, the form and variety of yeast will affect the taste of the beer, and yeast can be the trickiest part of this complex equation. Keeping the yeast fermenting properly is a key step in successful brewing, and can make the difference between a flavorful beer with a pleasing fizziness and a weird-tasting batch of contaminated beer or, worse, a basement full of exploding bottles. If the beer gets contaminated with wild yeast, it can do some strange things—take on unusual tastes, get cloudy or murky or too fizzy. Remember, yeast is alive! It needs the right nutrition and conditions if you want it to behave. You have to *nurture* it.

Finishing the Beer

The final step in brewing is to age the beer for a while. Aging usually takes anywhere from ten days to a month, depending on the kind of beer and the desired flavor. Typically, ales age more quickly and lagers age more slowly because the latter ages in cooler temperatures. Some stronger beers like barley wines and Belgian strong abbey ales can benefit from years of aging, but this is usually done cellared in the bottle, like a fine wine. Cask aging is becoming increasingly popular with artisanal brewers in both the USA and Europe, who are discovering the amazing flavor marriages that can occur with this technique. Imagine a dense stout after aging in a cask previously used for aging port or whiskey, with all the subtle interesting flavors this cask wood could add to the beer. In general, however, after a brief period of aging, the beer is, at long last, ready to be put into kegs or bottles.

WATER INTO BEER

While the malt, hops, and yeast have a more obvious influence on the taste of beer, the quality of water that goes into the beer is also important. Some beers respond best to hard water and others taste more true-to-type brewed with softer water. Home brewers should use only high-quality pure water in their home brews. Most professional brewers use a reliable public water supply for the water in their beer, often coupled with some fairly basic water treatment, and the result is just fine. Current technologies such as reverse osmosis now allow a brewer anywhere on the planet to adjust the mineral content of brewing water to any desired specification. Some brewers claim their unique water supply adds an inimitable character to their beer, whether it is brewed from spring water straight from this or that mountain range, or tapped from a well with a source of water containing a unique mineral content.

The Evolution of the Beer Connoisseur

You can know a lot about how beer is made, but learning to taste and appreciate different varieties of beer from different countries and different regions within this country is an entirely different pursuit. Beer has become so popular, and good beer so widely available, that anyone interested in broadening his or her understanding about and appreciation of beer has ample opportunity to exercise this newfound hobby. You can gain lifelong friends and beer-brewing buddies when you dip your toe into the vast world of beer culture now bubbling away in America. Beer connoisseurs come in every possible guise these days—from the down-to-earth to the self-proclaimed "beer nerds" who can rival any wine connoisseur in the use of descriptive adjectives and the possession of a truly discerning palate. Most beer connoisseurs are interesting folks who really just want to enjoy the best beverage the human race has yet to invent, whether they log their thousands of tastings into a notebook or a website, or just stick to a few of their high-end favorites. Mostly, they are happy to find others interested in talking about, and drinking, beer. You could be one of them.

Drinking really good beer is to take a taste of human history and to sample the liquid fruits of one of the most basic human endeavors. Drinking really good beer is like a very tasty lesson in world cultures. Once you get more interested in the many types of beer available to you—and the types you may not be able to get in your state—you may even decide you would like to try to brew your own beer. Home brewing opens up an entirely new world of beer culture, as it awakens your creativity and places you in a long line of home brewers hearkening back to the dawn of civilization. Plus, you're going to be very popular when you've got a five-gallon bucket of home brew waiting to be tapped.

So what are you waiting for? Are you ready for that trip around the world, or down to your local brewpub with some serious knowledge under your belt? Are you ready to start swirling your glass, taking a whiff, and sipping what the beer world has to offer you? You don't even need to pack a suitcase—but you may want to have a bottle opener handy.

Let's go have a beer.

2

Beer and You

You love beer, and you know it tastes great with bar food, but when it comes to sampling the many types of beers and knowing what to expect, you may feel a little bit wary. You may like the sound of a Trappist ale, but will you like the taste? Will that coffee stout be too much for you, or will that pale ale bore you? Will the waiter laugh if you order a Guinness Extra Stout with your poached salmon? Will that delicate, fruity summer beer hold up to a big bowl of spicy jambalaya? And once you get that Oktoberfest lager or ESB ale in front of you, how will you know if it tastes the way it's supposed to taste?

More and more people are getting interested in learning about beer, but the subject can indeed seem overwhelming at times. Maybe you live near a local brewpub with a vast number of offerings and you want to get your name on a plaque on the bar for tasting one hundred beers. On the other hand, you don't want to barrel blindly through bottle after bottle of beer without getting anything from the experience, especially when some of those really good beers cost $5 to $10 per bottle or even more! You may not even have the first idea about what to order.

In this chapter, you'll find information on the nuts

and bolts of ordering beer, pouring it like a pro (or noticing whether the bartender is pouring it the right way), evaluating the beer, and even what beer to order with what food. You'll discover what beer tastes like, beyond the simple descriptions of "malty" or "hoppy"—for example, you might discern flavors of coffee or bubble gum, nutmeg or banana, prunes, peat, or even creamed corn in your beer—and you would be right! If you leave your mind open to what you smell, taste, and feel as you sample different kinds of beer, you will soon find that the realm of beer isn't nearly as mystical and intimidating as you may have thought.

First Things First

When it comes to tasting new beers, don't worry too much about rules. Instead, concentrate on what you are doing: *tasting new beers*. It's fun to taste some interesting beers, and even some not-so-interesting beers, in the service of educating your own beer palate. The trick is to pay attention to what you taste rather than swilling beer mindlessly. If you feel like trying a dark, rich porter, then order one! But really taste it when you drink it and think about what you taste. Take notes, even. If you are in the mood for a lighter, hoppier, refreshing pilsner, go for it! But notice how it tastes compared to that commercially brewed light lager you usually order. Can you describe some specific differences? If you are curious about what a coffee stout or a raspberry lambic might taste like, give them a try, but pay attention! Do you taste the coffee? Do you also taste chocolate or burnt toast or prunes? Does that raspberry lambic have a hint of wildflowers or a funky, sour taste underneath the obvious fruit? How carbonated is the beer? How does it feel on your tongue—rich, watery, viscous, sharp, oily?

But before you jump in with both feet and start working your way down the beer menu of your favorite beer-specialty pub, consider embarking on your journey with a group of interested friends, preferably some of whom are more experienced than you are in the world of beer tasting. This has numerous advantages, the most obvious being that you can split a single beer among four to six friends. Everybody gets a taste, and you can taste a lot more varieties over the course of an evening while still maintaining your appreciation for what you are tasting.

The more subtle advantage to tasting new beers with friends is that you get to learn how your palate sensitivities compare with those of the drinking public at large. Most people are hypersensitive to a few flavors—wheat or citrus, for example—and utterly palate-blind to a few others. If everyone at the table says, "Wow, taste that interesting nutmeg on the finish," and you just don't taste it, you might discover that these spicy notes aren't something your individual palate tends to recognize. Other flavors may be obvious, or not so obvious, to most people. For you, as a beer connoisseur, it's very important to cultivate your own knowledge of your personal sensitivities and palate "blind spots."

With this in mind, there is one cardinal rule to remember when tasting—and talking about—different kinds of beer. Try to avoid saying (or even thinking) nothing beyond "I like that beer," or, alternatively, "I don't like that beer." This does nothing for palate development. Try instead to think in terms of "I like that beer *because* . . ." This creates an analytical mindset that gradually will help you recognize specific attributes of beer flavor profiles as your palate develops the ability to recognize them. If you are doing your analytical drinking in a group of folks with a similar (or greater) level of interest and expertise, these specific evaluations will be helpful to you and everyone else, and give people something to compare their own experiences to. Practice being specific.

What to Drink

So what do you order first? If you plan to try several different kinds of beer in an evening, you will taste the beer better if you start with the lighter beers and work your way towards the darker beers. "Lighter" in this context refers to both the color of the beer and to the alcohol content or gravity (called %ABV). The subtle flavors and sparkling pleasures of lighter beers (such as pilsner, pale ale, and hefeweizen) can be trampled by the richer, heavier, sweeter, stronger tastes of brown ales, porters, stouts, and schwarzbier. Don't start with a walloping smoked beer or a syrupy mocha stout if you plan to drink a blond ale or a kölsch later. Not only will you lose the taste, but you might just be too full to enjoy anything else. Likewise, starting a tasting with a high-gravity Belgian is rarely a good idea, no matter how pale and innocuous it may look. At 10% ABV, that innocent-looking blond may run roughshod over your tastebuds.

The weather, the temperature outside, and the season can also influence what beers are appropriate to taste at any given time, and what beers will taste good to you. Light, citrusy wheat beers taste great as you lounge on the beach in the sun or take a break from all that yard work and need something to help you cool down. Deep, rich, dark beers and warming, higher-alcohol abbey beers taste more appropriate in the chilly winter months, perhaps enjoyed in front of a roaring fire or in a cozy brewpub after a satisfying dinner (maybe of Guinness beef stew or spicy chili flavored with smoked beer).

Many breweries, both large and small, make these distinctions even easier by releasing seasonal beers for limited times, to coincide with brewing traditions (or, quite frankly, as gimmicks). For example, Oktoberfest-Märzen, a lager traditionally brewed in Bavaria in the spring during cool weather then left to ferment in dark, chilly caves until fall to protect it from the summer heat, is released and marketed today in October, even though with refrigeration and modern technology, this seasonal brewing tradition is no longer a necessity.

WHAT ABOUT CARBS?

These days, many people counting their carbs wonder about drinking beer. Isn't it too high-carb for the low-carb lifestyle? Like most grain-based products and alcoholic drinks, beer does contain carbohydrates, but so-called low-carb beers are so low in flavor that you might as well drink club soda and stop fooling yourself that you are drinking beer! High-quality beer is a nutritious beverage that is worth every net carb, and really good beer needn't be consumed in quantity for full enjoyment because of its high flavor. If you are watching your waistline and saving your carbs for something special, consider passing the breadbasket in favor of a nice Belgian ale or substituting a heady chocolate stout for that slab of chocolate cake. Life is about choices, after all, and low-carb doesn't mean *no*-carb.

Depending on the season, you can usually find a wide variety of limited-edition beers, such as cinnamon or nutmeg-spiced or holiday red Christmas brews, spiced winter white (wheat) beers, crisp bright Maifest beers for spring, fruity and refreshing summer ales, and caramel-touched, malty autumn-themed beers. Ordering seasonal beers is fun and a great way to get into the holiday spirit, no matter what the holiday. You can't go wrong ordering a Bell's Oberon summer ale in July, an Ayinger Oktoberfest-Märzen in October, or a Belgian Bush de Noël on Christmas Eve.

Finally, consider your situation. Are you spending an evening with friends, or are you spending a quiet evening alone? Are you drinking beer with a meal, or as an enhancement to a social gathering? Here are some basic guidelines, although feel free to experiment with the beers you feel inspired to drink:

◆ Smooth beers with a lower alcohol content make a better choice for social evenings because they allow you to drink a few beers in succession without losing your ability to converse coherently. These are, appropriately, generally called session beers. Consider golden lagers, wheat beers such as hefeweizen and wit, English bitters, Scottish ales, or ambers to fuel your next gathering of friends.

◆ Richer, more complex, higher-alcohol beers are good for sipping and savoring in a quieter, more introspective context. Try one of the Belgian abbey ales, a richly layered mocha stout, a doppelbock, or a barley wine. You want to notice every sip of these jewels.

◆ Bubbly, sweet beers are good for celebrations. Consider a festive, bubbly, fruity beer such as framboise (raspberry flavored) or kriek (cherry flavored) lambic instead of champagne for your next celebratory toast or to welcome guests at the door.

◆ Pale golden beers with a high hop content can help to stimulate your appetite before a meal because of their bitter taste, which can really wake up your palate. Try serving India pale ale (IPA), extra special bitter (ESB), or a hoppy abbey beer such as Orval or Duvel as an aperitif.

◆ Dark, smoky, roasty beers make excellent after-dinner drinks. Try a smoked beer or a deep, dark, sweet barleywine or eisbock instead of cognac or Port to wind down after a meal. Some people like to enjoy a deep, roasty beer with a cigar in lieu of the typical dessert.

CAN'T GET THAT HERE: BEER REGULATIONS

You may not have to show your passport when you travel from Illinois to Michigan or Oregon to Washington, but if you want to get Bell's Sparkling Ale (brewed in Michigan) in Iowa or Millstream Schildbrau (brewed in Iowa) in Michigan, you're out of luck. Just try to order a Goose Island Honker's Ale (brewed in Chicago) in Los Angeles, or, for that matter, try to buy a six-pack of the same altbier you drank in Düsseldorf when you are back home in southern Georgia.

Many different beers appear in this book, but the truth is that you won't be able to find them all in your home state. While the major commercial brewers like Budweiser, Miller, and Coors sell their brews pretty much everywhere in the United States, smaller microbreweries don't have the resources to get their beers distributed in every state, and not every pub and market can get the legal approval necessary to sell every beer, especially those with a higher alcohol content. Different states make their own beer regulations regarding what alcohol content is allowed both for selling and for brewing, when beer can and can't be sold, and how much it will cost a vendor to sell beer. Even the definition of beer varies by state—some states insist, for example, on calling high-gravity beers "malt liquor," even if they aren't malt liquor.

If you love the beers that come from microbrews, you might have to do some traveling, but what better excuse to take a vacation? Look into any of the many beer tours popping up all over the United States and Europe (*www.beertrips.com* is a great resource), or create your own beer tour. Let beer be your next vacation's travel theme.

Glassware and How to Pour

Once you've settled on the brew of your choice, the bartender should pour it for you, either from the tap or from the bottle, into an appropriate glass. The beer should be at the right temperature for its style, and draft beers should come out of the right kind of tap. If you are drinking beer at home, or at someone else's house, you may have to do the pouring yourself, and you may find yourself suddenly taking an interest in the relative merits of different kinds of glassware. The basic geometry of the glassware—for instance, a tulip glass, chalice, snifter, pint glass, pilsner glass, or dimpled mug—can affect your perception of a beer. If you don't believe me, choose a high-flavor beer like a Belgian abbey ale and try sniffing and sipping it from a spacious wineglass, then from a pilsner glass. If you are paying attention, I bet you'll be able to tell the difference, both in how much aroma you get from the beer and even how it tastes when you first take a sip.

DO YOU REALLY NEED A GLASS? EVERY TIME?

If you've always enjoyed your beer from a bottle or a can, you may wonder why you should bother to dirty another glass that you'll just have to wash. Mass-market beers are meant to be enjoyed (dare I say tolerated?) right out of the bottle or can, but specialty beers best show off their color, aroma, flavor, and head when poured into a glass. (Traditionally, craft beer never comes in a can, but this is changing recently, with a few craft brewers giving cans a try. But you should still pour the beer into a glass!)

Different types of beers also have different types of glassware that best take advantage of that beer's qualities, although many people debate which beers work best in which glasses, so experiment to find your favorites. You can't really go wrong with a glass that has a spacious bowl and curves in slightly at the top for the best aromatic experience because this will trap the aroma, allowing you to stick your nose into the glass and take a good whiff. Bottle-conditioned beers also tend to have some yeasty dregs at the bottom, and pouring the beer carefully into a glass will keep the dregs in the bottle—although some people like to drink them, sometimes from a shot glass.

No matter what kind of glass you choose, drinking beer from a glass really does allow for maximum sensory appreciation, so do yourself a favor and make the most of your beer experience. If you are mowing the lawn, go ahead and lug that bottle or can with you, but if you are really focused on enjoying the taste experience, go ahead and dirty that glass.

How you pour can also influence your perception of a beer. A rough pour can result in too much foam (head), and you may have to sit and wait for the head to fizzle down a bit if it is consuming half the space in your glass. Some beers are supposed to be poured that way, however. A bartender who knows how to pour a Guinness, and pours it from the right kind of tap, will pour the beer vigorously and let it settle, a little at a time, so it can take a while to actually get your Guinness after ordering it. (If you get it right away, ice cold, feel free to raise your eyebrows—that's not how it is supposed to be served.) For most beers, however, a too-rough pour risks overflowing the glass and losing some of your beer. Too gentle a pour, however, can result in a beer with no head at all, especially with beers that tend to be lower in carbonation.

Different people and different cultures have different preferences for pouring and for the amount of head on a beer, so experiment with your pours and your preferences. Start with a moderate pour. Here's how:

◆ Tilt the glass at about a thirty-degree angle.
◆ Gently pour about half the beer into the glass.
◆ Hold the glass upright and pour the remaining beer into the glass slowly but at a more upright angle. If you aren't getting much of a head, pour a little faster.

Or, for a more vigorous head:

◆ Hold the glass upright.
◆ Quickly pour beer into the middle of the glass until the glass is about half full.

◆ Tilt the glass and slowly pour in the remaining beer, to control the head as it nears the top of the glass.

To amuse your friends at parties:

◆ Using a tall, narrow beer glass, like a pilsner glass, invert the glass over the top of the open beer bottle so the lip of the bottle is about half an inch from the inside bottom of the inverted beer glass.
◆ Quickly invert the glass and bottle so the beer is pouring right into the bottom of the glass from the bottle.
◆ Slowly lift the beer out of the bottle, just a little at a time, to control the head.
◆ Pray to the God of Beer that it works and the beer doesn't overflow everywhere. (It helps to use a generous glass. It also helps if you haven't already been drinking a lot of beer.)

Why bother with trying to create a nice head on your glass of beer? The purpose of a head on a glass of beer is threefold:

1. A nice head adds to an appreciation of the beer's color, giving you the opportunity to evaluate both the color of the beer and the color of the head, as well as the way the colors complement each other. Does the shade of the head match the color of the beer? You will usually find that pale beers have snowy white heads and dark beers have darker heads, ranging from light tan to brown sugar.

2. The head brings forth the beer's aroma. Aromatic compounds attach themselves to the foam and are released for your sniffing pleasure as the bubbles pop.

Take a good whiff of your beer right over the head and pay attention to what you can smell.

3. The head adds to the flavor of the beer when creamy foam mixes in your mouth with the beer itself. Different beers produce different heads with different tastes: a soft, maple-tinted head on a glass of Guinness draught will taste much different from a firm, frosty white puff of foam on a glass of hefeweizen. A lacy head with big bubbles has a different mouthfeel from a dense, rich foam with tiny bubbles.

How to Evaluate Beer

Once you've decided on a beer, you can swill it mindlessly, or you can decide to get the most out of the experience and really taste it. This is how you decide which beers, and styles of beers, you really prefer, but evaluating the taste of a beer can take you far beyond general impressions such as "This beer is good!" (Remember the "This beer is good *because*" mindset.) While pilsners will all share certain characteristics, for example, tuning in to the subtleties of taste will help you to distinguish which pilsners you prefer, and why. Bohemian pilseners, German pilsners, or American microbrewed varieties? Maybe you love stout, but find that one brand of oatmeal stout tastes creamy, rich, and smooth, while in comparison, another brand tastes harsher and more sour. (This could also be due to the fact that stout can be dry or sweet, and you might prefer one to the other.)

The taste of beer comes from different elements, as described in the first chapter: the types of malt, the types and amount of hops, the yeast, and the water quality/chemistry. Depending on the variety of malt and the way it was malted, malt can add flavors to beer such as caramel, coffee, espresso, and chocolate. The hops add aroma and bitterness, but this can be subtle or very pronounced, depending on how "hopped" the beer is, and whether hops were added after brewing for additional aroma. Hops are often responsible for adding floral or citrusy notes. Yeast can add the taste of yeast or bread, toast, biscuits, or cookies, but is probably most influential, in terms of taste, for the many secondary flavors it can produce in beer, such as cinnamon, clove, butterscotch, bubble gum, nutmeg, licorice, apple, pear, banana, citrus, and a vast variety of other subtle flavors.

Evaluating beer is a process that includes more than taste. The color of the beer, the color of the head, the effervescence, and the aroma all play key roles in the evaluation of beer, and that's before you even take a sip! The tasting of a product as complex as good beer is not a simple event, but rather an intricate choreography of sensory perceptions. Follow these steps to get the most out of your tasting experience:

1. After you pour the beer, look at it. What color is it? What color is the head? How foamy is the head, and how bubbly is the beer? Hold it up to the light. Is it transparent, translucent, opaque?

2. Now stick your nose over the foam and take a whiff. Swirl the beer in the glass to help release the aromatics. What do you smell? Orchard fruit? Citrus fruit? Dried fruit? Herbs? Spices? Chocolate? Coffee? Caramel? Toffee? Molasses? Honey? Flowers? Mushrooms? Peat? Tobacco?

3. Take a sip and pay attention to how the beer feels in your mouth. What sensations do you experience? Is the beer effervescent? Bubbly? Sharp? Creamy and

smooth? Sticky? Light and quick to disappear, or thick and mouth coating?

4. How does the beer taste, both in the front of your mouth and at the back of your tongue when you swallow? Do you taste the rich, sweet malt or the bitter hops first? What about last? Beers with high hop content tend to taste bitter and herbaceous, a taste that balances or even masks the rich malty taste. Beers with lower hop content tend to taste more of the malt. What other flavors do you detect? Licorice? Rhubarb? Berry? Espresso? Nutmeg?

5. What is the finish, or aftertaste? How long do you continue to taste the beer after you swallow it, and what tastes linger on your tongue? The aftertaste may be different from the initial taste of the beer. Do you taste a more bitter hoppiness on the finish? Does the sweet, malty, caramel flavor linger long after? Do you detect smokiness you didn't notice at first, or an herb flavor, or acidity? Is the finish long, or does the taste of the beer disappear almost immediately?

6. As you continue to drink the beer beyond those first sips, you can also pay attention to how the beer changes as it warms up and how the flavors intensify or fade as your palate becomes accustomed to the taste. Does the head quickly disappear, or does the beer retain a good layer of foam all the way to the end? Does it die down in rocky chunks or leave delicate lacing on the sides of the glass? Does the beer remain fizzy, or does it quickly lose its carbonation? All of these qualities add to the experience of evaluating a beer.

Don't worry about what you are "supposed" to see, smell, and taste. Just pay attention to what you actually *do* see, smell, and taste. Everyone is different, and your experience of a beer may vary from what others experience. Nothing wrong with that. The key is simply to be aware of the experience of the beer. That is how you will develop your beer palate.

FINDING THE RIGHT WORD

At a loss for words? Most beer lovers find that it greatly heightens the sensory experience if words can be attached to specific flavor notes. Here are some key terms to help you put words to your impressions.

To describe malt aromas and flavors (all of the following could be light to heavy, mild to harsh):

- Biscuit
- Burnt
- Caramel
- Cereal (Grape Nuts, Cream of Wheat, Oatmeal)
- Chocolate
- Coffee
- Cookie
- Espresso
- Hay
- Honey
- Molasses
- Nut (walnut, hazelnut)
- Roasted
- Toast
- Toffee

To describe hop aromas and flavors (all the following could be light to heavy, mild to harsh):

- Citrus (lemon, orange, grapefruit, lime)
- Flowers
- Fruit
- Grass
- Herbs
- Mint
- Perfume
- Pine
- Resin

To describe yeast and other secondary aromas and flavors (all the following could be light to heavy, mild to harsh):

- Apple
- Banana
- Black licorice
- Bread
- Brown sugar
- Bubble gum
- Butter
- Butterscotch
- Cassis (black currant)
- Chalk
- Charcoal
- Cherry
- Cinnamon
- Clove
- Cola
- Coriander
- Date
- Earth
- Ginger
- Grape
- Honey
- Lemon
- Maple syrup
- Mushroom
- Nutmeg
- Oak
- Orange
- Peach
- Pear
- Pepper
- Pineapple
- Plum
- Port
- Prune
- Raisin
- Raspberry
- Red licorice
- Sherry
- Smoke
- Soy sauce
- Tar
- Toffee
- Vanilla
- Vegetables (corn, green beans)
- Vinegar
- Wine
- Yeast

To describe beers that have been spoiled by sunlight, too much aging, contamination by spurious yeast, or for any other reason, you can use the following (by the way, in case you are worried, spoiled beer has never been shown to be dangerous to humans, it just tastes bad):

- Butterscotch
- Cardboard
- Chemical
- Medicine
- Skunk
- Sulfur

Beer might also have added ingredients like berries, chilies, coffee, or cocoa, which may import obvious or subtle nuances.

Beer Styles: What to Expect

You don't really need any instruction beyond paying attention when evaluating a beer's taste, but an idea of what certain styles of beer should taste like *in general,* can help you to feel more confident in your evaluation. The first thing to remember is that most beers can be classified as ales or lagers. Ales tend to be fruity and complex but they can be dark or light, low or high in alcohol, and very bitter or very malty, depending on the hop content and the type of malt used in brewing. They can also have a wide variety of aromas, depending on the type of ale. Lagers tend to be smoother and herbaceous or vegetal in character, but like ales, they can be dark or light, low or high in alcohol, and very bitter or very malty. Remember, the difference between lager and ale is in the yeast and fermentation method, not in the color or strength. Like ales, lager aromas can vary widely depending on many factors. At the beginning of your tasting practice, try tasting ales and lagers that look similar in color and see if you can distinguish the two. For instance, a pilsner (lager) versus a pale ale, or a porter (ale) versus a doppelbock (lager). With a friend, set up a "blind" taste test and you can both practice. (Even experienced tasters sometimes fail this test.)

The second thing to remember is that beers come in a range of colors, from light to dark, and the color influences the flavor, but not the alcohol content or bitterness. Third, although you can use many different adjectives to describe beer aromas and flavors, most beers tend to be on the "malty" side or on the "hoppy" side. You will see variations of these terms often in descriptions of beer. "Malty" means that the malt flavors predominate. These may be biscuity or bready, caramely or toasty, chocolaty or coffeelike. These are, of course, the flavors that come from the malt. "Hoppy" refers to beers with a high hop content, in which hop flavor and/or aroma predominates. No matter what malt the beer contains, a high hop content can tend to over-shadow the malt flavors in favor of an herbaceous or flowery bitterness in varying degrees. The ultimate high-hop beer is IPA (India pale ale), but many other beer varieties contain distinctive, even dramatic "hoppiness."

Beyond "ale" or "lager," "dark" or "red" or "light," and "malty" or "hoppy," beer substyles vary widely. The following guide isn't meant to bias your palate, and the tasting and aroma notes here are merely general guidelines and sometimes simply a matter of opinion, so don't take this as gospel but as guidance. You could also argue that many styles are left out of this chart, and I would agree. These are just some basics to orient you. When you are first learning about better beer and find-ing the many different options somewhat intimidating, you may find that this gives you a place to begin, to help you start understanding what to expect out of the dif-ferent styles of beer you choose to taste. For each style of beer (lagers, ales, and specialty beers), this chart is or-ganized roughly from lightest (in color and gravity) to darkest. Also keep in mind that if you try one pilsner or stout or wheat beer that you don't like, it doesn't mean you won't like other examples of that style.

LAGERS	ALES	SPECIALTY BEERS
		(ale/lager hybrids, specially ingredients, and unusual yeasts)
Pale lager: A light straw to golden lager with very little malt or hop character designed for mass appeal. Some are lightened (and cheapened) with adjunct grains like corn and rice.	Bitter and special bitter: British or British-style beers with a fair presence of hops, which impart their bitter flavors. Bitter beers are often fruity and low in carbonation. On the typical American palate, they often are surprisingly smooth—in contradiction to their name. ESB stands for Extra Special Bitter, a hoppy, strong, fruity beer with an amber color.	Wheat beers: Weisse, weissbier, and weizen all refer to wheat beers that are often cloudy and yeasty with the distinctive taste of wheat. Wheat beers may have a citrusy, fruity, or spicy aroma. Wit is a Belgian-style subclass of wheat beer with tangy citrus flavors and spices such as coriander and orange peel. Hefeweizen is a subclass of unfiltered German-style wheat beer, pale golden and cloudy with a yeasty flavor and secondary yeast flavors like banana, clove, or bubble gum.
Nonalcoholic beer: A basic pale lager with the alcohol removed via a vacuum-evaporation process at the end of brewing. So-called NA beer still contains trace amounts of alcohol.		

LAGERS	ALES	SPECIALTY BEERS (ale/lager hybrids, specialty ingredients, and unusual yeasts)
Pilsner: A golden lager with a dry flowery hop aroma. Take a deep whiff and see if you can detect a floral scent as well as hop bitterness. The style originated in Czechoslovakia, and Pilsner Urquell is the original and still the classic example.	Pale ale: A lightly colored ale with fruity aroma and high hop content. Comes in British and American styles, with American pale ales tending to be more citrusy and noticeably hoppy.	Kölsch (ale yeast with lager-style fermentation): A light golden beer style from Cologne, Germany; fruity, easy to drink, lightly hopped, and perfect for hot weather. Some American brewers imitate this style and call it kölsch, but real kölsch comes only from Cologne.
Vienna-style lager: Bronze to reddish with a malty caramel aroma and flavor. They don't make much of it in Vienna anymore, but it is a popular style in America and Germany.	India pale ale (IPA): High in hop bitterness because it was originally shipped to British occupying India, a high hop content helped to preserve the beer on its long trip overseas. This style remains popular because many people enjoy a very hoppy beer. You should be able to detect the hoppiness in the aroma, before you even take a taste. Golden to amber in color.	Alt (ale yeast with lager-style fermentation): A style born in the German city of Düsseldorf and characterized by a dark bronze color, hop bitterness and rich smooth mouth feel. Real altbier only comes from Düsseldorf, but some American microbrewers imitate this style and call it altbier.

Bock (helles and dunkel, or "light" and "dark"): A German term for a strong beer that may or may not be dark in color but is usually relatively high in alcohol, with a rich caramel aroma and malty taste. You can taste the hops, but they don't overwhelm the flavor.

Oktoberfest-Märzen: Seasonal autumn beers, typically amber to red in color, medium-weight in alcohol, and malty with caramel overtones.

Irish ale: This reddish ale is malty rather than hoppy and may contain a butterscotch or toffee flavor. It is a popular style in Ireland and in America, but some argue it is really just amber ale made in Ireland (or inspired by Ireland).

Amber ale: This category covers a wide range of American amber-colored ales of moderate strength. It is a catch-all category.

Mead (made with honey): Brewed from honey rather than grain, mead tastes like something between a beer and a wine. Sweet and rich but with the body and character of an ale, mead is in a class by itself (and tastes great with cheese!).

Fruit and spiced beers: These beers are brewed with added fruits, like citrus fruits, orchard fruits, and berries, and/or spices like cinnamon, nutmeg, and cloves. These are different from beers that suggest these flavors due to the yeast, and they vary widely according to the brewer's own creativity and recipe.

LAGERS	ALES	SPECIALTY BEERS (ale/lager hybrids, specialty ingredients, and unusual yeasts)
		Kriek: A Belgian style of beer brewed with cherries, ranging from very sweet to very sour.
Maibock: A light-colored seasonal spring bock beer with a pale color, high carbonation, and hoppy flavor, often relatively high in alcohol.	Scottish ale: Scotland's version of English bitter, this session ale is malty and sometimes lightly peaty.	Lambic: This Belgian style ale is naturally fermented with wild yeasts. Lambics can have an earthy, mushroomy aroma. When flavored with fruit, such as in the popular framboise variety flavored with raspberries, lambics are rich, complex, and sometimes sweet, particularly the popular Lindeman's Framboise. These make an excellent after-dinner drink or accompaniment to dessert. Other lambics can be quite unusual and are an acquired taste.
Doppelbock: Means "double bock" and is even stronger than a regular bock in alcohol content. Typically malty in aroma, and flavor, although some are high in hop flavor. Look for a dark color and aromas and flavors of toffee and espresso; perhaps almost port or sherry notes.	Scotch ale: Smooth, dark, and malty, this is a filling style of beer that often contains an earthy peatiness. It has higher alcohol than Scottish ale.	

Eisbock: The strongest bock, this is doppelbock made even more potent by freezing. When the ice is removed, the beer becomes more concentrated.

Schwarzbier: German for "black beer," this super-dark, practically opaque lager is less bitter than you might think. It has overtones of bittersweet chocolate and/or strong roasted coffee flavor and is brewed with very darkly roasted malt.

Dubbel/bruin: A medium-brown rich, malty, strong style of Belgian abbey ale sometimes made with candy sugar for a real alcohol punch and tangy sweetness that can smell and taste reminiscent of raisins. Some include the "classic Belgian" flavor note reminiscent of the more pleasant aspects of barnyard or wet horse blanket.

Old ale: A moderate to strong type of ale that is usually dark in color with a pleasant balance of caramely malt and mildly bitter hops. Some styles have no discernible hops.

Beers flavored with espresso, chocolate, vanilla, "milk" (lactose), and other flavor additions: These can vary widely in color, from a black espresso-flavored stout or smooth vanilla porter to light, easy-drinking ales flavored with fruits and vegetables like pumpkin, chili peppers; juniper berries, or spruce.

Rauchbier: Brewed with smoked malt, it has a characteristic smoky aroma and flavor that can be subtle or pronounced.

LAGERS	ALES	SPECIALTY BEERS
		(ale/lager hybrids, specialty ingredients, and unusual yeasts)
American malt liquor: A strong American style of cheap alcoholic beverage, often with added sugar. This is essentially a high-alcohol version of pale lager, often lightened with adjuncts like corn or rice. Short lagering time can make this style harsh.	Porter: A dark brown to black malty beer with moderate hoppiness. Common flavor notes include espresso, coffee, chocolate, and toffee.	Gueuze: Made with aged hops and unusual or wild yeasts, this pale, tart, complex-tasting beer isn't for everyone. This spontaneously fermented, traditional style of beer can vary widely in taste and often contains unusual, even strange aromas and flavors. How daring are you?
	Stout: A dark brown or black style of beer made with darkly roasted grains and ale yeast. Stouts vary widely in flavor and alcohol content. Typical aromas and flavors come from the dark roasted malt. Imperial stout, a strong, full-bodied stout with roasted coffee and chocolate flavors, may be almost black in color.	Bière de garde: Resembling an ale but meant to be stored for longer periods of time, this French style has a complex herbaceousness that may suggest licorice aromas and earthy flavors.

Trappist and strong golden abbey ales: Abbey beers, including Trappist beers and the Tripels, come from Belgium and are typically high in alcohol and complex in flavor and aroma. Look for different fruit and spice notes. Tripel is among the highest alcohol content among beer styles, typically above 9%.

Barley wine: A high-alcohol brew that can smell almost like sherry and is meant to be sipped and savored because of its rich and complex aroma and taste. It is typically very dark in color. Treat it like an after-dinner drink and use a small glass!

Cask-aged beer from casks formerly used for sherry, whiskey, etc: These specialty beers are aged for long periods and pick up subtle nuances from the liquors previously stored in the casks.

YOUR PERSONAL BEER RECORD

Many people who embark on tasting a large number of beers find that no matter how vivid the experience of tasting a beer was at the time, after months of trying lots of different beers, memory fades. Consider keeping a beer journal of all the beers you try, to help you remember what you tried, how it tasted, how you felt about it, even what food you had it with and who you were with at the time. Not only will this record be a valuable resource when you are trying to remember what you thought of a beer, but it can also be fun to read and remember your good beer times from the months and years past. You can also do this online at *www.ratebeer.com*. If you do this on your own, you might use a format similar to this:

Date	Occasion/Event/ Company/Food	Beer Name/ Style	Color	Head and Carbonation	Aroma	Taste	Notes/ Rating
1/19	Chilly winter evening, dinner with friends from my beer-tasting class	Three Floyd's Robert the Bruce Scottish-Style ale	Deep amber to mahogany	Caramel-colored head with light carbonation	Toffee, caramel, yeast, fruit (maybe orange?)	Creamy, malty, smooth, easy to drink	Tasted great with the pork roast! I would rate this beer 8/10.

Beer with Food

Further complicating an already complex picture, the food you eat with the beer you drink can impact and even dramatically alter the taste experience of a particular beer. Different beers naturally taste better with different kinds of food, although there are no exactly right or wrong pairings because much depends on individual preference. There are guidelines you can use to begin your experimentation pairing beer and food, however.

First, consider that food and beer can pair up in a variety of ways. You can have food and beer that match. For example, a salad dressing containing a spiced Belgian wit paired with that same beer could echo the flavors in the wit in two complementary contexts. Or consider the magnificent way a dark, rich, chocolaty stout complements a dark, rich, chocolaty torte. An earthy, peaty Scotch ale makes a great complement to the earthy flavors of mushrooms. Smoked beers (rauchbier) are a natural match for smoked foods—although you don't want so much matching going on that the pairing is completely redundant. A spicy, citrusy Belgian ale may be even more effective than rauchbier with that rack of ribs you just pulled off the grill.

This is where beer and food contrasts come into play. A cool, crisp, hoppy beer such as an ice-cold IPA makes a great contrast to super-spicy Mexican or Thai food. A rich, savory porter contrasts well with the briny flavors of shellfish. Pair a malty, dark bock beer with a plate of rich sausages and creamy cheeses. Instead of that chocolaty stout with your dark chocolate torte, you might try a tangy, fruity framboise lambic. A smooth, flowery pilsner adds excitement to a mild fish or delicate cream soup, and a dry, soft, pale ale makes the perfect foil for a medium-rare filet mignon—but try a richer, darker Scottish ale with that T-bone.

While there aren't really right or wrong answers when pairing beer with food, certain pairings really do bring out the best in both the beer and the food. Nobody says you can't experiment with different beer/food combinations you think sound promising, but you will probably get more out of the experience if you follow a few basic guidelines. Here are some tips to get you started:

◆ Match beers with certain specific flavors like caramel, smoke, or citrus with foods containing those same flavor elements. Citrusy wheat beers like hefeweizen taste good with chutney-topped or citrus-marinated pork, chicken, or fish, as well as with salad containing fruity elements (for example, lemon poppy-seed dressing, mandarin oranges).

◆ Light golden beers match light foods like salads and fish dishes. Try a kölsch, pilsner, or helles (light) bock beer.

◆ Medium-bodied red or amber beers go well with medium-bodied foods like chicken, turkey, lean beef, and whole-grain dishes, as well as saucy mild to moderately spiced foods like risotto, spaghetti, and rich fatty fish like salmon. Try Irish ale or an Oktoberfest brew.

◆ Pair spicy foods containing chilies, ginger, and curry with highly hopped beers. The bitter hops hold up to and complement the spicy flavors. Try an IPA, an ESB, or a hoppy pilsner.

◆ Pair rich, meaty foods, cheesy dishes, and creamy pastas with smooth, malty beers that don't have to cut through strong spices. Try an oatmeal stout, a doppel-bock, or a porter.

◆ Rich stouts with coffee and chocolate flavors match rich desserts with coffee and chocolate flavors. Try a schwarzbier or one of the richer, darker stouts such as an Imperial stout.

◆ Sweet, fruity beers and other sipping beers can stand alone as a fantastic dessert, or go well with rich custard-based, cream-based, or fruity desserts. Try framboise or a fruited specialty ale, maybe laced with pumpkin and cinnamon or wild mountain blueberries or a rich honey beer.

Evaluating beer is like learning about anything else. The more you practice, the more practiced you get. Keep trying different beers, be adventurous in your food/beer pairings, and always pay attention. Soon you'll be ordering beer with confidence and enjoying beer with the appreciation of a true connoisseur.

3

British Isles

In the British Isles, ales rule. Even though today lagers make up a greater percentage of the British beer market, the quality and history of British and Irish ales distinguish this region of the world as prime ale country. Whether golden, bronze, reddish, or black, British and Irish ales aren't typically high in alcohol (gravity) compared to ales in other countries, such as Belgium. The Brits enjoy pub culture immensely, and if the ale is too high in alcohol, sitting around for hours in the pub socializing with friends could become a real challenge.

JUST WHAT IS THE UK?

The United Kingdom, or UK, is a group of countries that have formed a jointly governed, united group. These include England, Wales, Scotland, and Northern Ireland. The Republic of Ireland, making up most of Ireland's land mass, is governed separately. However, the UK has long been rife with political struggle. All Ireland used to be part of the UK, but then much of Ireland broke away to become self-governing. Even so, social unrest in the Irish Republic has resulted in UK intervention. Meanwhile, groups within Wales and Scotland also struggle for independence, but are still, as of this writing, officially part of the UK.

Because the British Isles and Ireland contain so many internal barriers—not the least of which are large bodies of water and incendiary politics—ale evolved in many different ways all over the British Isles, spawning a great regional diversity in British and Irish ales that still exists today.

England

In the region surrounding London, most of England's brewing crops grow. Kent is home of Goldings hops, and one of the most famous hop-growing regions in the world. East of London in East Anglia, most of England's malting barley grows. London is home to two of England's most internationally renowned breweries: Fuller, Smith, & Turner and Young's. You may also encounter ales produced by Harvey's and Dark Star in Sussex, and Great Britain's oldest brewery, Shepherd Neame, in Kent. Perhaps due to nearby Kent, beers in and around London tend to be highly hopped, at least in comparison to others of the UK.

Heading north to Yorkshire, where the famous slate Yorkshire Square fermenters imbue the ales with a particular local character and an individual yeasty flavor, several smaller but famous breweries well known to U.S. beer aficionados steadily produce their wares: Theakston, its splinter brewery Black Sheep, and Samuel Smith.

Other notable British breweries whose ales are available to those not able to travel to England include Samlesbury, which produces Bass and Boddington's Pub Ale; Dunston, which makes Newcastle Brown Ale; Marstons; Wychwood; Moorhouses; Sarah Hughes; Ringwood, whose Old Thumper ale is exported, and also domestically brewed in Maine by Shipyard Brewing Company, under license; Greene King, which makes Morland Old Speckled Hen; and J.W. Lees.

Scotland

Just around the bend from England's northern border lies Scotland, a country that takes northern England's preference for rich, malty ales and runs with it. In Scotland's cold climate, warming ales do a body good. The principal ale styles in Scotland include—in order of increasing gravity and intensity—light, heavy, export, and wee heavy. In America, we tend to categorize Scottish beers as Scottish ale and Scotch ale. Scottish ale is typically sweet and strong with little sense of hops but an underlying earthy peatiness, while Scotch ale is deeper, bigger, and higher in alcohol, the most intense called "wee heavy."

The McEwan/Younger brewery is among Scotland's most famous in the United States. The brewery Traquair, located in a small castle that hosts a beer festival every spring, also exports several distinctive ales to the United States. Other notable Scottish brewers that export to the U.S.: Harviestoun, Belhaven, Orkney, Caledonian (they make McEwans), Williams Brothers (they make Heather Ales), and Broughton. Most Scottish beers come from Edinburgh or Glasgow.

Wales

Heading back down to Wales, just across the Irish Sea from Ireland, beer isn't particularly distinctive, although historians claim that in the Middle Ages, the classic Welsh ale was richly spiced and sweet with honey. Magor produces Murphy's Irish Ale but brews from Wales. The Brain's brewery doesn't export to the United States but its beers are common and popular in Wales. Wales also features breweries and beers with colorful names like the Bull Mastiff brewery's Son of a Bitch ale and Plassey's Dragon's Breath, but you probably can't find these in the U.S. You might be able to find Felinfoel's Double Dragon ale in the United States, and you can probably find their Thames Welsh ESB.

Ireland

Across that Irish Sea, in Ireland, Guinness is undoubtedly the most famous name, and this huge company has satellite breweries all over the world, manufacturing its famous Guinness Extra Stout, Guinness Draught, and Guinness Special Export in every corner of the globe. Check your bottle of Guinness to see where it was brewed. Guinness also makes Kilkenny, Smithwicks, and Harp, the latter a pale lager of no particular note, but better (some say), than some of the cheaper domestic lagers.

But Guinness isn't the only brewery in Ireland. People in other countries associate reddish ale with Ireland, although this style is more popular as an export than in Ireland proper. Stouts in Ireland tend to be drier and thicker than stouts in Wales or northern England, and they may contain hints of spice, peat, fruit, coffee, toffee, and nuts. Other Irish breweries of note for those in the U.S. include Beamish, Caffrey, and Carlow.

ICE-COLD BEER? THINK AGAIN . . .

You may crave an ice-cold beer, just because that is what you are used to drinking, but beer isn't actually meant to be served ice-cold. In fact, the ideal temperature for serving beer, although it varies somewhat from style to style, is significantly higher than the temperature of a beer fresh out of the refrigerator. Drinking low-quality, boring light lager ice-cold may keep you from noticing that the beer doesn't taste like much, but if you are drinking a really good beer—whether ale or lager—take it out of the refrigerator and let it sit for about twenty minutes at room temperature before drinking. Even pubs that should know better, both in Britain and in the USA, often serve beer too cold, so when you order that bitter, brown ale or stout, hold off. Wait. Let it warm up a little, allowing the volatile, aromatic gases to escape for your sniffing pleasure. A temperature of 50 to 55 degrees Fahrenheit is ideal for most ales. Then drink it . . . slowly. Now that's how beer is supposed to taste.

History

Long before the Brits knew anything about the hop plant, they knew all about ale. Throughout the Middle Ages, British ales were sweet, malty, and a primary food source, probably brewed primarily by "ale wives," whose job it was to cook food and brew beer. Around 1400, beer brewed with hops for bittering and preservation came to England from the Netherlands, and beer in England was changed forever . . . sort of. Hopped beer became the "new" beer, where it blossomed into different styles according to region. By 1500, ale and beer were considered separate: beer contained hops, ale did not. By 1600, the terms blurred as people brewed ale using hops.

In the 1700s, some beer historians claim that porter was, at the time, a combination of beer, ale, and another beverage called two-penny, and because it included all the main styles, it was called entire. Some people believe porter evolved because high malt prices forced brewers to use less malt. They would then kiln the malt more heavily to make up for the flavor loss, resulting in a deep, dark beer that had a strong flavor to hide any off flavors and a dark color to disguise any cloudiness. As porter became popular, so did the railway system, so porter became one of the first styles of beer to be distributed all over an entire country.

At first, porter was available in two strengths (gravities), the weaker marked with an X, and the stronger marked with an XX. Even more potent versions were shipped to other countries, including the Caribbean, and got to sport more X's. The Irish Guinness began brewing porter in the late 1700s.

In the 1820s, pale ale evolved as a style in Britain, and these two styles, the black and light, each had a wide fan base. Porter was also exported to Europe and even Asia. In Britain, it evolved into three styles: mild ales, the porter we know today (a style that disappeared from Britain decades before its recent reincarnation), and for the richer, deeper, fuller variety, stout. Stout evolved further with the development of drum roasting in the early nineteenth century. In 1820, the XX type of porter became Guinness Extra Stout Porter, and an XXX version became Foreign Extra Stout. By the 1970s, Guinness stopped brewing "regular" porter in favor of their now-famous stouts.

Meanwhile, the market for lager in Britain was gearing up. While lager existed in England before the turn of the twentieth century, it wasn't a popular style and was known mostly as the stuff the upper classes drank in the summer. But several large brewers thought lager had a future in Britain. One was Guinness, which built a brewery in Ireland specifically for brewing lager. Harp was the result and people drank it up.

By 1990, lager sales exceeded ale sales, and finally today, lagers have achieved a comfortable lead at more than half of all beer sales in Britain. And not everyone approves. UK-based CAMRA (Campaign for Real Ale) is an advocacy group fighting to restore ale as Britain's beer of choice. For more about CAMRA, visit their website: *www.camra.org.uk*.

Current Trends

Britain's love affair with lagers may interest some, but perhaps of greater note is Britain's influence on American microbrewers. A profusion of British styles is now produced in the United States, and if you taste them side by side—a British mild ale and a domestic mild ale, a British stout and a domestic stout—you'll notice the difference. British ales have subtle nuances, smoothness, and layers of flavor. American ales in the British style are distinctive—no mistaking their assertive flavor characteristics. Some people like to draw a comparison between the two countries' styles and the personalities of their inhabitants: reserved Brits versus out-there Americans. While exceptions certainly exist, it's worth a try to compare styles from both sides of the pond at any opportunity, and you'll see exactly what I'm talking about.

Beyond basic stylistic differences in these two countries, it also pays to take into account that a standard ale—best consumed as fresh as possible—may not endure the transatlantic voyage as well as the brewer would like. Hence, as in centuries past, the stronger beers still hold up to export conditions better than weaker ones.

As for the lager versus ale trend in Britain today, while megabrewed lagers have finally seized majority rule, Britain's microbrewers haven't given up the good fight. Many are producing excellent ales, exporting them all over the world, and gaining in reputation. Quality is paramount, and leaves many of the lagers in the dust. On the other hand, some microbrewers have also devoted part or all of their operation to the production of some interesting Bavarian-style lagers, with good result. As an example, Samuel Smith makes two: an organic lager and a pure brewed lager that both hold their own (both available in the United States). Stay tuned for what might happen next in the great ale/lager war of Britain.

Characteristic Types of Beer

While beers come in different styles in England, these styles are, to a great extent, really just names along a spectrum. Many of these types blur. Special bitters and ESBs (extra special bitters), for example, can be interchangeable, depending on whom you ask. Pale ale, a category some consider a specific type of ale, could also be considered an umbrella term that covers a wide range of bitters, ESBs, and pale mild ales. The same situation exists for darker ales, like the similar porters and

stouts. In other words, the individual beers listed in this
chapter might be listed under different styles in other
books or websites. The taster should consider the range
of UK and Irish beers to exist within a delicious spectrum from straw to black and delicate though dense
within each color range, rather than considering these
types to be strict divisions.

English Mild Ale

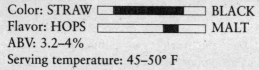

Color: STRAW   BLACK
Flavor: HOPS   MALT
ABV: 3.2–4%
Serving temperature: 45–50° F

Available in pale and dark versions, malty mild ale is
one of the more common styles of beer in England, but
virtually unheard of as an import in the United States.
Just a few breweries import their mild ales here, but
visit England and you can get a mild ale on tap in just
about any pub. On the other hand, some American microbrewers produce their own versions of mild ale such
as Pizza Port Dawn Patrol, available in California.
Compare the two if you have the chance, and you'll notice the difference: English mild ales tend to be more
subtle, whereas American versions make much more de-
fined flavor statements, but authentic English milds
should have virtually no sign of hops.
   English mild ales to try:

- ❏ *Gales Festival Mild (England)*
- ❏ *Moorhouse's Black Cat (England)*
- ❏ *Sarah Hughes Dark Ruby Mild (England)*

BITTERS

Color: STRAW ▭ BLACK
Flavor: HOPS ▭ MALT
ABV: 3–5%
Serving temperature: 50–55° F

This most popular of British ale styles is available everywhere, and often copied in the United States. Not particularly bitter (despite the name), bitter ale ranges in color from shimmery gold to light bronze and is a light, easy-drinking beer with a good, moderate balance of malt and hops. It differs from mild because of the discernible hops. Easy to drink, versatile, and low in alcohol, bitters are made for long evenings at the pub with friends. The bitter style can be subdivided into bitter, special bitter, and extra special bitter (ESB). Special bitter is fuller-bodied and sometimes higher in alcohol than bitter, and ESB has its own listing below.

British bitters to try:

❑ *Boddington's Pub Ale (England)*
❑ *Coniston Bluebird Bitter (England)*
❑ *Felinfoel Double Dragon (Wales)*
❑ *Samuel Smith's Organic Ale (England)*
❑ *Young's Dirty Dick's Ale (England)*

EXTRA SPECIAL/STRONG BITTER (ESB)

Color: STRAW ▭ BLACK
Flavor: HOPS ▭ MALT
ABV: 4.8–5.8%
Serving temperature: Minimum of 45° F

A stronger version of the classic English bitter, ESB (sometimes called premium bitter) has a higher gravity (alcohol) but not necessarily a higher bitterness, although hop bitterness can be strong. Sweet malt and a rich, full body balance the bitterness, and the amber color gives this style a further sense of balance.

British ESBs to try:

❑ *Adnams Suffolk Strong Bitter (England)*
❑ *Bass Pale Ale (England)*
❑ *Belhaven St. Andrews Ale (Scotland)*
❑ *Black Sheep Ale (England)*
❑ *Black Sheep Monty Python's Holy Grail (England)*
❑ *Fuller's ESB (England)*
❑ *Fuller's London Pride (England)*
❑ *Greene King Abbot Ale (England)*
❑ *Morland Old Speckled Hen (England)*
❑ *Orkney Red MacGregor (Scotland)*
❑ *Ringwood Old Thumper (England, but U.S. version may be brewed in Portland, Maine)*
❑ *Samuel Smith's Old Brewery Pale Ale (England)*
❑ *Shepherd Neame Bishop's Finger (England)*
❑ *Thames Welsh ESB (Wales)*
❑ *Wychwood Hobgoblin (England)*
❑ *Young's Ramrod (England)*

INDIA PALE ALE (IPA)

Color: STRAW ▭ BLACK
Flavor: HOPS ▭ MALT
ABV: 5–7.5% (some UK IPAs today are closer to 4%)
Serving temperature: Minimum of 45° F

This famous and unique style was exported to India during the days of British occupation and infused with intense amounts of hops in order to stay preserved through the long overseas journey. India pale ale, or IPA as it is affectionately known, is the beer of choice for people who love hops. Traditional IPAs were high in pleasant biting bitterness, fresh flowery aroma, and a crisp dry mineral character (due to the hard water used to brew them), with color ranging from pale gold to concentrated copper. IPA is another style that America took and ran with, and today's domestic IPAs are not only far more available than British IPAs in the United States, but many believe they taste more like the original IPAs due to the Americans' heavy-handed use of hops (this is controversial). American microbrewers have even invented a high alcohol "imperial pale ale" style. Modern British IPAs or "English IPAs" as they are sometimes called, tend to be lower in alcohol and hop bitterness than their American counterparts, resembling bitters or ESBs.

British IPAs to try:

❏ *Freeminer Trafalgar IPA (England)*
❏ *Fuller's India Pale Ale (England)*
❏ *McEwan's IPA (Scotland)*
❏ *Meantime India Pale Ale (England)*
❏ *Ridgeway IPA (England)*
❏ *Samuel Smith's IPA (England)*

IRISH (RED) ALE
Color: STRAW ☐■☐ BLACK
Flavor: HOPS ☐■☐ MALT
ABV: 4–4.5%
Serving temperature: 48–50° F

Medium-weight, with balanced hop-malt, this easy-drinking style has a moderate alcohol content and ranges from the shade of a shiny new copper penny to the shade of a very old copper penny. This style is probably more associated with Ireland as an export, and one could argue it is really an amber ale from Ireland, less popular than the ubiquitous stout. Many breweries in England also produce an Irish-style ale.

Irish ales to try:

- ❏ *Caffrey's Irish Ale (Ireland)*
- ❏ *Carlow O'Hara's Irish Red (Ireland)*
- ❏ *Kilkenny (Ireland)*
- ❏ *Murphy's Irish Red Beer (Wales)*
- ❏ *Smithwick's Ale (Ireland)*
- ❏ *Wexford Irish Cream Ale (England)*

BROWN ALE
Color: STRAW ☐▭▭▭▭ BLACK
Flavor: HOPS ☐▭▭▭▭ MALT
ABV: 4–5.5%
Serving temperature: 45–50° F

Brown ales have a reddish bronze to dark, toasty brown color, depending on the region (generally more red in the north, more brown in the south). This medium-weight beer has varying degrees of maltiness, but doesn't typically have noticeable hops. They may have a pleasant fruitiness or a rich nuttiness, the latter distinctive of "nut brown ales" and also of Newcastle's Brown Ale. Brown ales tend to have a low gravity (alcohol content), and this style is distinctive of England, whereas Ireland's mid-color ales tend to be more reddish in color and drier (less sweet). On the lighter side, brown ales grade into mild browns; on the heavier and darker side, they abut the gentler of the porters.

British brown ales to try:

- ☐ *Harvey's Tom Paine Original Brown Ale (England)*
- ☐ *Newcastle Brown Ale (England)*
- ☐ *Northumbrian Brown Ale (England)*
- ☐ *Samuel Smith's Nut Brown Ale (England)*

SCOTTISH-STYLE ALE

Color: STRAW ▭▭▭▭ BLACK
Flavor: HOPS ▭▭▭▭ MALT
ABV: 2.8–7%
Serving temperature: Minimum of 45° F

Scottish-style ale can vary immensely in color, flavor, and alcohol content, but the style in general is red to black with a strong maltiness, sometimes balanced by noticeable hops, sometimes not. Lighter Scottish ales are easy to drink but still malty, with a hint of caramel and butterscotch, and may be lighter in color, from amber to brown. A noticeable earthy peatiness contributes a distinctive regional flavor characteristic—to a greater or lesser degree—in many of these ales. Heavier Scottish ales might be low in alcohol but heavier in body, darker in color, and with a more pronounced malty sweetness. The style sometimes called Scotch ale or, in its native country, wee heavy, is the strongest of all, and has a separate section below.

Scottish-style ales to try:

- *Belhaven Scottish Ale (Scotland)*
- *Broughton Black Douglas Ale (Scotland)*
- *Inveralmond Lia Fail (Scotland)*
- *Orkney Dark Island (Scotland)*

SCOTCH ALE/WEE HEAVY

Color: STRAW ▭ BLACK
Flavor: HOPS ▭ MALT
ABV: 6.5–10%
Serving temperature: Minimum of 50° F

Scotch ale, or wee heavy, has a higher gravity (alcohol) than standard Scottish-style ale, with a deep, dark color, and thick, chewy maltiness—perfect for braving the chilling winter winds in the Scottish Highlands. Watch out for that ABV. These ales are so thick, rich, and warming that drinking one is almost like eating a meal.

Scotch ales to try:

☐ *Belhaven Wee Heavy (Scotland)*
☐ *Inveralmond Blackfriar Scottish Ale (Scotland)*
☐ *Isle of Skye Cuillin Beast (Scotland)*
☐ *MacAndrew's Stock Ale (England)*
☐ *McEwan's Scotch Ale (England)*
☐ *Orkney Skullsplitter (Scotland)*
☐ *Traquair Jacobite Flavored Ale (Scotland)*

PORTER

Color: STRAW ▭▬▭ BLACK
Flavor: HOPS ▭▬▭ MALT
ABV: 4.5–6.5% (darker, robust porters are on the higher side)
Serving temperature: 50–55° F

Deep brown (for brown porter) to ebony (for robust porter), often with garnet jewel tones around the edges when you hold them up to the light, porters have roasty, deeply toasted, even subtly burnt flavors, with an underlying rich malty-sweet fullness balanced by noticeable hop bitterness. Sometimes smoother or creamier than stouts and sometimes not, porters may be described as extra stout porters, just to confuse you. At the Great British Beer Festival competition, stouts and porters are linked together in a single category. Stouts evolved from porters, so the line is a blurry one. Complex with varying degrees of body and underlying flavors of coffee or espresso, black or dried fruits, and bittersweet chocolate, porters are filling and satisfying, standing in for dessert *and* a cigar, or complementing either.

British porters to try:

- [ ] *Flag Porter 1825 Original (England)*
- [ ] *Fuller's London Porter (England)*
- [ ] *Hambleton Nightmare (England)*
- [ ] *Harvey's Porter (England)*
- [ ] *J.W. Lees Manchester Star Porter (England)*
- [ ] *Nethergate Old Growler (England)*
- [ ] *RCH Old Slug Porter (England)*
- [ ] *Ridgeway Santas Butt Winter Porter (England)*
- [ ] *St. Peter's Old Style Porter (England)*
- [ ] *Salopian Entire Butt (England)*
- [ ] *Samuel Smith's Taddy Porter (England)*

STOUTS VERSUS PORTERS

In the traditional English thinking, the bitterness of stout should be derived more from the deeply roasted unmalted barley, whereas the bitterness of porters should be derived from ample use of bittering hops during the boil. In a true porter, the malt will hence contribute more to the sweet and caramelized tones of the beer. In contemporary brewing reality, however, the two styles tend to blend together.

STOUT

Color: STRAW ◀▭▭▭▭▭▭■■■▶ BLACK
Flavor: HOPS ▭▭■■■■■■▭ MALT
ABV: 3–6%; imperial stout: 7–12%
Serving temperature: Minimum of 50° F

The term "stout" encompasses an incredible range of products. If you haven't yet found one that you like, keep sampling! Stouts range from sweet milk or cream stouts (characteristic of England) with a caramely, malty flavor, all the way through dry stouts (characteristic of Ireland) with a hoppier balance and lingering dry finish. Specialty stouts are common, such as smooth, rich oatmeal stouts, or even stouts with the addition of chocolate or coffee. Imperial stout, a high-

gravity winter warmer, is among the densest and most intense beer styles on the planet. In the UK and Ireland, stouts cover a wide range, as this is a style of beer close to the hearts of beer lovers all over this part of the

world, whether smack in the middle of London, Edinburgh, Dublin or for that matter the United States. Scales above for flavor cover ranges for both sweet and dry stouts. Note that stout should be served at an even higher temperature than other British ale styles, around 55 degrees. Let your stout settle and warm up, or simply store them cellared instead of refrigerated. Watch the creamy froth barreling up from the bottom of the glass, then settling out into a rich, creamy, cinnamon-tinged head. Wait. Anticipation will make the experience all the more enjoyable.

British (sweet) and Irish (dry) stouts to try:

- ❑ *Beamish Irish Stout (Ireland)*
- ❑ *Broughton Scottish Oatmeal Stout (Scotland)*
- ❑ *Freeminer Deep Shaft Stout (England)*
- ❑ *Guinness Draught (check the label—not all are brewed in Ireland)*
- ❑ *Guinness Extra Stout (check the label—not all are brewed in Ireland)*
- ❑ *Hopback Entire Stout (England)*
- ❑ *Murphy's Irish Stout (Wales)*
- ❑ *Ridgeway Lump of Coal Dark Holiday Stout (England)*
- ❑ *Samuel Smith's Imperial Stout (England)*
- ❑ *Samuel Smith's Oatmeal Stout (England)*
- ❑ *Young's Double Chocolate Stout (England)*
- ❑ *Young's Oatmeal Stout (England)*

OLD ALE

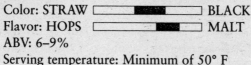

Color: STRAW ▭▬▭ BLACK
Flavor: HOPS ▭▬▭ MALT
ABV: 6–9%
Serving temperature: Minimum of 50° F

Rich, darkish, and warming, old ales are smooth, with varying degrees of bitterness. They get their name from the aging process. Whereas some beers can be ready in a week or might potentially age for a few months, old ales can age for years, which just makes them smoother and more complex. When old ales are aged in casks that once held port, whiskey, or other liquors, they can take on some of the flavor characteristics of the cask's previous tenants. Some old ales rival wine in alcohol content, and hence abut the strongest ale category of barley wine. Like stouts, old ales should be given a chance to come up in temperature before the pleasure of that first complex, soul-warming sip.

British old ales to try:

- *Broughton Old Jock Ale (Scotland)*
- *Burton Bridge Old Expensive Ale (England)*
- *George Gale Prize Old Ale (England)*
- *Greene King Strong Suffolk (England)*
- *Harviestoun Old Engine Oil (Scotland)*
- *Robinson's Old Tom (England)*
- *Theakston Old Peculiar (England)*

MEET MEAD AND ITS DESCENDANTS

Mead is an ancient and supposedly aphrodisiacal beverage made from fermented honey, without any grain at all. While its origin is probably in Egypt, mead has long been associated with England, as part of a bride's dowry, as a Christmas drink, and as a way to woo a lover. Not exactly a beer, not exactly a wine, mead exists in its own special category. Some meads are sweeter than others, but all taste distinctly of honey. Some meads are effervescent, others, "still," or without carbonation. The latter type makes an excellent holiday drink when warmed with spices, in the tradition of mulled wine. Try Lurgashall English Mead for a taste, to see why mead has endured for so long. (On a romantic date? For Valentine's Day?) Mead/beer hybrids like

Young's Waggledance, which contains large amounts of honey but is nevertheless a barley malt-brewed golden ale, can give you the best of both worlds: intoxicating honey sweetness with the reassuring anchor of hops and malt, along with a fanciful dash of sparkle.

ENGLISH STRONG ALE, BARLEY WINE, AND IMPERIAL STOUT

Color: STRAW ▭▭▭▭▭ BLACK
Flavor: HOPS ▭▭▭▭▭ MALT
ABV: 7–12%
Serving temperature: 50–55° F

These high-gravity ales tend to be sweet, malty, rich, and complex. They have their differences and some might not like grouping them all together, but they have a full-bodied, malty flavor and high alcohol in common. The high alcohol warms the body in the winter, and examples of this style are often given names including the word "winter." Amber to medium-brown, fruity with caramel or toffee sweetness, strong ale and barley wine usually have detectable but subtle hop bitterness. Imperial stout is the pitch-black cousin of strong ale, infused with generous quantities of deeply roasted grains. Some specialty ales in this category are cask-conditioned before leaving the brewery to impart nuances of port, sherry, or whiskey.

Their strength allows them to be cellared for further aging (this can be in years) to blend and mellow their flavors. Some winter or Christmas versions are a ruby red color, and Britain exports many brands of English strong ale to the United States. The cognacs of ales, these should be sipped from a snifter.

English strong ales, barley wines, and imperial stouts to try:

- ❏ *Adnams Broadside Strong Original (England)*
- ❏ *Black Sheep Riggwelter (England)*
- ❏ *Burton Bridge Empire Ale (England)*
- ❏ *Burton Bridge Old Expensive Ale (England)*
- ❏ *Fuller's 1845 (England)*
- ❏ *Fuller's Vintage Ale (England)*
- ❏ *Gales Christmas Ale (England)*
- ❏ *Harvey's a la Coq Imperial Extra Double Stout (England)*
- ❏ *Harvey's Christmas Ale (England)*
- ❏ *Harvey's Elizabethan Ale (England)*
- ❏ *Harvey's Imperial Stout (England)*
- ❏ *J.W. Lees Harvest Ale (England)*
- ❏ *Moorhouse's Pendle Witches Brew (England)*
- ❏ *Morland Hen's Tooth (England)*
- ❏ *RCH Ale Mary (England)*
- ❏ *Ridgeway Bad Elf Winters Ale (England)*
- ❏ *Samuel Smith's Imperial Stout (England)*
- ❏ *Samuel Smith's Winter Welcome Ale (England)*
- ❏ *Thomas Hardy's Ale (England)*
- ❏ *Traquair House Ale (Scotland)*
- ❏ *Young's Old Nick (England)*
- ❏ *Young's Special London Ale (England)*
- ❏ *Young's Winter Warmer (England)*

⑂ 4 ⑂
Germany, Austria, and Switzerland

In Germany, beer is more than a beverage. It is a way of life. Beer is so intrinsic to German culture that most Germans take it for granted. Beer is ubiquitous in Germany, although the variety of styles is more limited than in some other European countries like Belgium or Great Britain. In Germany, beer usually means one thing: pilsner. To the Germans, pilsner *is* beer, although other styles also exist, including some notable and popular styles of wheat beer, black beer, and bock.

In the United States, we consider pilsner a subcategory of lager—one that was invented in Czechoslovakia, no less, and not Germany. (In fact, Bohemian pilseners differ stylistically from German pilsners.) In Germany, however, "lager" is a pejorative term referring to an inferior pilsner. The difference can be confusing, partially because American brewers tend to divide beers by their biological differences, while German brewers tend to divide beers by style. In the United States, our "pilsners" may or may not qualify in the opinion of German brewers, but if we call a beer a "lager," the Germans will certainly agree (and it wouldn't be a compliment).

While the United States surpassed Germany in the

number of breweries as of 1997, and while many people murmur about how beer consumption in Germany is dropping, beer is still Germany's most important drink and a big part of German culture. Germany is home to the world-famous Oktoberfest and the world's most famous beer hall, the Hofbräuhaus. Both call Munich home. Bavaria, the state in which the great city of Munich lies, still gets to claim the highest per capita beer consumption of anywhere in the world. Beer halls, brewpubs, beer gardens, and restaurants offer many different brands in a few key styles: pilsner, helles (light), dunkel (dark), Märzen (the spring-brewed Oktoberfest beer), bock (including doppelbock, Maibock, and eisbock), schwarzbier (black beer), and weissbier or weizen (wheat beer).

In the United States, the mainstream perspective about German beer usually has something to do with Oktoberfest, giant beer steins, brass bands featuring tubas, and precision brewing methods. Most beer drinkers have heard of Beck's, Löwenbrau, St. Pauli Girl, all those beers we have long associated with Germany, but today, many smaller brewers exporting excellent beer from Germany to the United States have exposed Americans to a whole new side of beer in Germany. Later in this chapter, you may notice that many breweries are mentioned again and again in the lists of beers to try. Some of the names you'll see here and on the shelves of better beer stores include Warsteiner (Germany's largest brewery), Ayinger, Paulaner, Weihenstephaner, Spaten-Franziskaner, Weissbierbrauerei G. Schneider & Sohn, Mahrs Bräu, Schlenkerla, Jever, Erdinger Weissbräu, Köstritzer, Hacker-Pschorr, and of course Bremen-based Becks, which make both Becks and St. Pauli Girl, and Munich-based Löwenbrau. These breweries export their wares to give us all a taste of what the German beer industry has to offer, and make learning about German beer easier than ever before—you don't even have to leave your city limits.

Austria and Switzerland are less famous for their beers, but they are also lager-oriented (like Germany) and they too consider beer an important part of their culture. Very few Swiss and Austrian beers are exported to the United States, and the major brewers in these countries are owned by large conglomerates. Pilsners and bocks are probably the most popular. Austrian brewers of note include Castle Eggenberg, Gösser, Stiegl, Josef Sigl, and Hofbräu Kaltenhausen. For Swiss brewers, look for Hurlimann and Feld Schlösschen.

Not everybody likes German beer, and it's hardly blasphemy to say so. Many people prefer ales above lagers, and Germany is the birthplace of the lager style. But few can argue that Germany knows beer—especially the golden lager style, but also wheat beer, black beer, bock, and seasonal beers. The more you taste different beers from Germany, the more you will train your palate to recognize not only lagers, but lager subtypes like pilsner, Oktoberfest-Märzen, and doppelbock; not only wheat beers, but hefeweizen, Berliner weisse, and dunkelweizen.

History

Organized brewing probably began in the Middle East, but soon spread to northern Europe, particularly Bohemia and Bavaria. While the abbey style of beer is most often associated with Belgium, monks in Germany brewed beer too, and may have done so first. The former Benedictine monastery of Weihenstephan, just outside Munich, claims to be the world's oldest brewery, originating in 1040; they are still in operation, and you can buy their beer in America. Some breweries have been excavated that existed before this one, but they certainly can't claim that they are still in business. Abbeys still own several breweries in Bavaria, the center of brewing in Germany. Brewers in Bavaria probably discovered lagering by accident when they noticed that in cooler temperatures, beer took longer to ferment and the yeast dropped to the bottom of the fermenting vessel. Lager yeast wasn't isolated until the late nineteenth century, but the lagering *technique* dates from the 1500s. Back in those days, however, brewers didn't really understand yeast beyond the notion that the foam on the beer seemed to have transformative properties, and that this same foam could "seed" the next batch of beer.

Brewers began to age beer in caves and underground beer cellars, often cooled with ice from nearby rivers and lakes—the original method of lagering. To help these cellars stay cool during the summer, brewers sometimes planted groves of trees above the cellars, to help shade and insulate the fermenting beer. These shady areas made convenient and pleasant areas for drinking the beer when it was ready to be tapped, and hence the German beer garden was born.

In 1516, Bavaria passed a law called the Reinheitsgebot. This law stated that Bavarian brewers could use three and only three ingredients to brew beer: barley, hops, and water. This law didn't include yeast because brewers didn't yet understand that yeast was an essential part of fermentation. Supporters claimed that the law ensured the purity of beer, keeping cheaper or lesser grains out of the beer. This may also have encouraged people not to "waste" nutritionally significant grains like wheat and rye better used for baking. The Reinheitsgebot did prevent adulteration of beer with cheap light adjuncts such as corn and rice. Other countries, including the United States, have tried to make cheaper beer this way, something many beer lovers consider a mistake (or at least a pity). In Germany, the law was later amended to include yeast and a few other provisions, such as allowing the addition of wheat and added sugar in top-fermenting beers only (allowing for wheat beers such as hefeweizen, which are brewed with ale yeast).

Until the Industrial Revolution, breweries were limited primarily to homes and small farms, or on a larger scale in abbeys, and royal estates, with their adequate large space and resources. Once steam power became a ready resource, beer could be transported and the labor-intensive processes involved in brewing beer—from the initial delivery of barley to the malting, mashing, storing, and delivering beer—became much easier. The ability to travel also allowed brewers to go to other countries to study brewing. Gabriel Sedlmayr II, son of the brewmaster at the Spaten brewery in the early 1800s, traveled all over Europe and the British Isles, picking up techniques and samples. Later, Gabriel II took over the Spaten brewery and began to modernize the brewery's equipment and processes.

REINHEITSGEBOT: GOOD OR BAD?

Around the turn of the twentieth century, the power of the Reinheitsgebot was expanded to include all of Germany (not just Bavaria), to coincide with German unification. This meant that all German brewers had to adhere to its standards for brewing beer. In 1987, the Reinheitsgebot was repealed for brewers exporting their beer, and throughout the years several changes and exceptions have been enacted, but brewers in Germany must still follow its standards. Some people argue against the Reinheitsgebot, saying it limits brewer creativity, but many people still believe the Germany purity law is a good one, and many brewers in other countries, including the United States, also voluntarily choose to adhere to these guidelines. While the law doesn't dictate ingredient quality, many believe it does keep beer pure and encourages high standards of brewing.

Beer probably didn't turn golden in Germany until the late 1800s when Bavarians learned that brewers in the town of Pilzen in Bohemia were producing a clear, pale golden lager with a flowery aroma (pilsener), clarified by a high hop content and a variety of barley with a particularly low protein content (coagulated proteins can cloud beer). Different areas in Germany developed their own riffs on this style, but in general, southern Germany has for many years tended to produce maltier, darker beers, while northern Germans tend to focus more on lighter beers such as German pilsner and helles (lightly colored) versions of other styles like bock.

Other regions in Germany have their unique styles and are known for first producing certain types of beers:

◆ In Dortmund in Westphalia, the dry Dortmunder lager became popular, a style often called Dortmunder export today.

◆ In Cologne (Köln), the classic favorite is a light golden ale/lager hybrid called kölsch, a pilsner look-alike that uses ale yeasts but lagering techniques.

◆ In Düsseldorf, right across the river from Cologne, the malty, coppery altbier—another ale/lager hybrid— is the local favorite and the city's distinctive style. Both kölsch and altbier are brewed much in the way they were brewed for hundreds of years—using ale yeast, but lagering techniques (the reason they are considered hybrids).

◆ In Berlin, a cloudy, low-alcohol, sour-tinged wheat beer called Berliner weissbier remains a local favorite. Many German and Austrian breweries produce other varieties of wheat beer, particularly hefeweizen, another distinctive, citrusy wheat style cloudy with yeast, and a dark wheat brewed with ale yeast called dunkelweizen.

◆ Bamberg is famous for a smoked beer called rauchbier, a style many artisanal American brewers now imitate. This style uses smoked malt for a unique smoky taste.

◆ In what was once East Germany, an ancient style called schwarzbier ("black beer") has recently enjoyed an increase in popularity. Today's schwarzbiers are lagers brewed with darkly roasted malt. Japan was actually largely responsible for re-inventing this style.

Current Trends

While many Germans still drink in beer halls and beer gardens, brewpubs have become much more popular in recent years. These small, local establishments brew just enough beer to meet their own needs but don't ship out or sell their "house brew" beyond the doors of the brewpub. Often unfiltered, these kellerbiers or zwickelbiers have a style and character many people find more engaging than the standard pilsner.

Other styles are also gaining in popularity. The black schwarzbier characteristic of East Germany has enjoyed a recent surge in popularity. While traditionally southern Germany produced maltier beers and more wheat

---

MIX IT UP

A popular way to drink beer in Germany is to mix it with soda, such as Coke, 7-Up, or lemonade. Called radler, this soda-beer mixture is so popular that some German companies have bottled it. The low alcohol and thirst-quenching nature of radler make it popular with younger consumers in Germany, even if it may sound strange to people in the United States. To try radler at home, cut your dunkel beer with cola or your pilsner with lemon-lime soda at a proportion of approximately 1:1. This tradition is similar to shandy, a lemonade-beer concoction available in the U.K. and some tropical climates. Neither shandy nor radler have caught on in the U.S.

---

beers and northern Germany produced hoppier beers—
primarily pilsners—some of the southern styles have
been surging northward. Germans have also increased
their interest in organic beer (which they call bio or
öko) and lighter styles ("leichtbier") with lower alcohol
and fewer calories, probably both functions of Germany's obsession with natural health, environmentalism, and the organic food movement.

Characteristic Types of Beer

If it's a lager-style beer—including schwarzbiers, bocks,
doppelbocks, and a variety of seasonal beers, from
Oktoberfest-Märzen beers to Maibocks and Christmas-
themed Vienna-style lagers—you can probably find it in
Germany, but you can also find summery wheat beers in
a range of styles and colors, kölsches, and altbiers. Some
of the more popular types of beer available both in Germany and in America via German imports include the
following.

HEFEWEIZEN

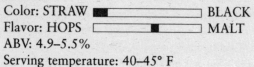

Color: STRAW ▮▭▭▭▭ BLACK
Flavor: HOPS ▭▭▮▭ MALT
ABV: 4.9–5.5%
Serving temperature: 40–45° F

This cloudy white style smells and tastes like yeast,
fruit from citrus to banana, and light, nutmeg-y clovey
spiciness. This unique top-fermenting style of wheat
beer gets its cloudiness from yeast sediment and the
wheat proteins. *Hefe* is German for yeast, and hence
anything with *hefe* in its name most assuredly should be

served with the yeast. It is customary to reserve the last inch or so in the bottle so that it can be swirled to suspend all yeast prior to adding it to the serving glass.

German hefeweizens to try:

- ❑ *Ayinger Brau Weisse (Germany)*
- ❑ *Edelweiss Hefetrüb Weissbier (Austria)*
- ❑ *Erdinger Weissbier (Germany)*
- ❑ *Franziskaner Hefe-Weissbier (Germany)*
- ❑ *Hacker-Pschorr Hefe Weisse (Germany)*
- ❑ *Hofbräu Münchner Kindl Hefeweizen (Germany)*
- ❑ *Maisels Weisse Original (Germany)*
- ❑ *Paulaner Hefeweissbier (Germany)*
- ❑ *Pinkus Hefe Weizen (Germany)*
- ❑ *Prinzregent Luitpold Weissbier Hell (Germany)*
- ❑ *Schneider Weisse Original (Germany)*
- ❑ *Schneider Wiesen Edel-Weisse (Germany)*
- ❑ *Tucher Helles Hefe Weizen (Germany)*
- ❑ *Weihenstephaner Hefe Weissbier (Germany)*

CLOUDY NO MORE

Another German wheat beer called Kristallweisen is just filtered hefeweizen—same taste, but crystal clear. Try:

- ❑ Erdinger Weissbier Kristallklar
- ❑ Franziskaner Club Weisse
- ❑ Weihenstephaner Kristallweissbier

BERLINER WEISSE
Color: STRAW ▆▆▆⬜⬜⬜⬜ BLACK
Flavor: HOPS ⬜⬜⬜■⬜⬜ MALT
ABV: 2.2–2.7%
Serving temperature: 40–45° F

Pale, almost white due to its cloudiness (a factor of suspended yeast), this is among the very lightest of German beers in both color and alcohol content. Surprisingly acidic and thirst-quenching, this beer contains lactic acid, and has lots of pleasingly fizzy carbonation and a refreshing fruitiness. It shouldn't taste hoppy or malty, but rather lightly refreshing. Traditionally served in large bowl-shaped glasses on stems, this is a summer beer, sometimes softened and sweetened with a dash of raspberry or herbaceous Woodruff syrup. This style is much more popular in Berlin (naturally) than in the U.S., but a few U.S. microbrewers have copied the style.

German Berliner weisse to try:

❑ *Berliner Kindl Weisse (in Germany, you can also purchase this beer with flavorings already added)*

PILSNER

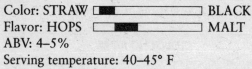

Color: STRAW ▭▬▭ BLACK
Flavor: HOPS ▭▬▭ MALT
ABV: 4–5%
Serving temperature: 40–45° F

Sometimes called "pilsener," the flowery, hoppy golden lager so ubiquitous in the United States is even more popular in Germany, but try a pilsner in Germany and you'll notice a big difference from the straw-colored lager in a can you might be used to drinking and calling "pilsner" at home. German pilsner, especially when straight from the tap, is usually fresher, fuller, hoppier, and more flavorful than mainstream commercial pale lager in America, and not the same style at all. German pilsner is also different from Bohemian-style pilsener from Czechoslovakia, where the style was born. German pilsners are lighter, less malty, and use different hop varieties. They may also be slightly higher in alcohol than their Czech cousins.

German pilsners to try:

- ☐ *Aktien Jubiläums Pils (Germany)*
- ☐ *Bitburger Premium Pils (Germany)*
- ☐ *DAB Pilsener (Germany)*
- ☐ *Jever Pilsener (Germany)*
- ☐ *Paulaner Premium Pils (Germany)*
- ☐ *Pinkus Organic Unfiltered Pilsner Beer (Germany)*
- ☐ *Pinkus Pils (Germany)*
- ☐ *St. Pauli Girl Lager (Germany)*
- ☐ *Spaten Pils (Germany)*
- ☐ *Stiegl Pils (Austria)*
- ☐ *Trumer Pils (Austria)*
- ☐ *Veltins Pilsener (Germany)*
- ☐ *Warsteiner Premium Verum (Germany)*
- ☐ *Weihenstephaner Pilsner (Germany)*
- ☐ *Weltenburger Kloster Pils (Germany)*

KÖLSCH

Color: STRAW ▭▬▭▭▭ BLACK
Flavor: HOPS ▭▭▭▬▭ MALT
ABV: 4.8–5.3%
Serving temperature: 45–48° F (or even a bit colder)

The pale, straw-colored beer, with its subtly flowery aromatics, originated in Cologne, and in Germany a beer may not be called kölsch unless it was brewed within Cologne or an allowed radius around the city. It is a beer fermented with ale yeast, but under fermentation conditions much more commonly associated with lager—slow and cool. Soft due to the local soft water in Cologne and subtly flavored with a hint of hops and a hint of malt but with neither dominating, this style should be clear, refreshing, and served cold, at about the same temperature as a pilsner. Few German kölsch beers are available in the United States, but visit Cologne and you can find them everywhere. Many American microbrewers imitate this style.

German kölsches to try:

☐ *Gaffel Kölsch (Germany)*
☐ *Reissdorf Kölsch (Germany)*

DÜSSELDORF-STYLE ALTBIER

Color: STRAW ▭▬▭ BLACK
Flavor: HOPS ▭▬▭ MALT
ABV: 4.3–5.0%
Serving temperature: 45–48° F

The copper-colored, malty style born in Düsseldorf, altbier uses ale yeasts with cold-conditioning lagering techniques. Popular not only in and around the brewpubs of Düsseldorf's Old Town, but elsewhere in Germany, and often imitated by American microbrewers, altbier is easy to drink. Generally made with darker malts and boasting a smooth, slightly fruity taste, altbier is traditionally served in short cylindrical glasses.

German Düsseldorf-style altbiers to try:

☐ *Diebels (Germany)*
☐ *Frankenheim Alt (Germany)*

❑ *Schwelmer Alt (Germany)*
❑ *Uerige Alt (Germany)*
❑ *Uerige Sticke (Germany)*

DORTMUNDER/EXPORT/HELLES:

Color: STRAW ▭ BLACK
Flavor: HOPS ▭ MALT
ABV: 5–6%
Serving temperature: 45–50° F

A light golden lager that is sweeter and fuller than pilsner, characteristic of the kind of beer brewed in Dortmund and often referred to as Dortmunder. The similar helles is lighter and has a dry, mineral character and can range from very pale to golden.

German Dortmunder/exports to try:

❑ *Augustiner Edelstaff (Germany)*
❑ *Ayinger Jahrhundert (Germany)*
❑ *Bürgerbräu Wolnzacher Hell (Germany)*
❑ *Gösser Export (Germany)*
❑ *Hacker-Pschorr Edelhell (Germany)*
❑ *Hofbräu München Original (Germany)*
❑ *Löwenbrau Original (Germany)*
❑ *Spaten Premium Lager (Germany)*
❑ *Weihen Stephaner Original Mild (Germany)*

OKTOBERFEST-MÄRZEN

Color: STRAW ▭ BLACK
Flavor: HOPS ▭ MALT
ABV: 4.5–5%
Serving temperature: 45–50° F

A medium-weight beer that can range from golden to a rich bronze with a slight suggestion of hoppiness but  with lightly caramelized or bready malt dominating the flavor. This brew, traditionally brewed in the springtime and aged over the summer months, is a popular seasonal offering in the fall, just in time for Oktoberfest (and a style Midwestern U.S. microbrewers in particular enjoy brewing). German Oktoberfest-Märzen beers to try:

- ☐ *Ayinger Oktober Fest-Märzen (Germany)*
- ☐ *Beck's Oktoberfest (Germany)*
- ☐ *Hacker-Pschorr Oktoberfest-Märzen (Germany)*
- ☐ *Hofbrau München Oktoberfestbier (Germany)*
- ☐ *Köstritzer Oktoberfest (Germany)*
- ☐ *Paulaner Oktoberfest (Germany)*
- ☐ *Spaten Oktoberfestbier (Germany)*
- ☐ *Spaten Oktoberfest Ur-Märzen (Germany)*
- ☐ *Weltenburger Kloster Winter-Traum (Germany)*

DUNKELWEISSEN

Color: STRAW ▭ BLACK
Flavor: HOPS ▭ MALT
ABV: 4.8–5.4%
Serving temperature: 50–55° F

Dunkelweissen (literally "dark wheat") incorporates more darkly roasted malts and hence has more of a darker, roasty flavor profile, but is othewise similar to a hefeweizen. Although it doesn't look like a typical wheat beer, dunkelweissen is lively, smooth, and thirst-quenching like other wheat beers, and less deep, dark, and roasty (and high-alcohol) than a weizenbock.

German dunkelweissen beers to try:

- [ ] *Andechser Dunkels Weissbier (Germany)*
- [ ] *Ayinger Ur-Weisse (Germany)*
- [ ] *Edelweiss Weissbier Dark (Austria)*
- [ ] *Erdinger Weissbier Dunkel (Germany)*
- [ ] *Franziskaner Hefe-Weissbier Dunkel (Germany)*
- [ ] *Hacker-Pschorr Dunkle Weisse (Germany)*
- [ ] *Julius Echter Hefe-Weiss Dunkel (Germany)*
- [ ] *Paulaner Hefeweissbier Dunkel (Germany)*
- [ ] *Tucher Dunkles Hefe Weizen (Germany)*
- [ ] *Weihenstephaner Hefe Weissbier Dunkel (Germany)*
- [ ] *Weltenburger Kloster Hefe-Weizen Dunkel (Germany)*

BOCK

Color: STRAW ▭ ▬ ▭ BLACK
Flavor: HOPS ▭ ▬ ▭ MALT
ABV: 6–7.5%
Serving temperature: 50–55° F

Typically a German brewery's most potent brew (except for a doppelbock, which is even stronger), bock has a high gravity (alcohol content), and is ideal for drinking in cold weather due to its warming properties. If the beer has helles or Maibock in the name, it will tend more toward the golden end of the color spectrum; traditional bock, more toward the brown. These are rich, full-bodied, strong, sweet, smooth lagers, no matter the color.

German bocks to try:

❑ *Einbecker Ur-Bock Dunkel (Germany)*
❑ *Einbecker Ur-Bock Hell (Germany)*
❑ *Mahrs Brau Bock-Bier (Germany)*
❑ *Mahrs Brau Christmas Bock (Germany)*
❑ *Spaten Premium Bock (Germany)*
❑ *Stieglbock (Austria)*

German Maibocks to try:

❑ *Einbecker Mai-Ur-Bock (Germany)*
❑ *Hofbräu München Maibock (Germany)*
❑ *Spaten Maibock (Germany)*

WEISSBOCK/WEIZENBOCK
Color: STRAW ▭ BLACK
Flavor: HOPS ▭ MALT
ABV: 6.9–9.3%
Serving temperature: 50–55° F

A malty, spicy, top-fermenting (ale yeast) wheat beer with low hops, high carbonation, and lots of fruity notes. Some are dark and some are lighter, but all contain enough yeast to make the beer cloudy. Weissbock is the strongest and maltiest of the German wheat beers.

German weissbocks/weizenbocks to try:

❑ *Erdinger Pikantus (Germany)*
❑ *Hacker-Pschorr Weiss Bock (Germany)*
❑ *Hopf Weisser Bock (Germany)*

❑ *Mahrs Bräu der Weisse Bock (Germany)*
❑ *Schneider Aventinus (Germany)*

DOPPELBOCKS AND EISBOCKS

Color: STRAW [▮▮▮▮] BLACK
Flavor: HOPS [▮▮▮▮] MALT
ABV: 6.5–10%
Serving temperature: Minimum of 50° F

An even more potent bock beer, Doppelbock (which means "double bock") is usually (but not always) dark in color, and most popular in southern Germany. Doppelbock names often end in *–ator*, after the very first doppelbock, Paulaner Salvator. Great for warming the body and soul on a chilly evening, doppelbocks pack a punch in both flavor and gravity, so a little goes a long way.

The potent eisbocks are frozen, and when the ice is removed, the remaining bock is extra strong because it is concentrated. A deep gold to dark bronze with noticeable malty flavor, eisbock is not for the faint-hearted. It is rich with deep, malty beer flavor and is, ironically for a beer made with ice, the most deeply warming and high-alcohol of the bock beers.

German doppelbocks to try:

❑ *Allgäuer Cambonator Doppelbock (Germany)*
❑ *Andechser Doppelbock Dunkel (Germany)*

❏ *Augustiner Maximator (Germany)*
❏ *Ayinger Celebrator Doppelbock (Germany)*
❏ *Castle Eggenberg Samichlaus Bier (Austria)*
❏ *Castle Eggenberg Urbock 23° (Austria)*
❏ *Höss Doppel-Hirsch (Germany)*
❏ *Hurlimann Samichlaus (Switzerland)*
❏ *Paulaner Salvator (Germany)*
❏ *Spaten Optimator (Germany)*
❏ *Tucher Bajuvator Doppelbock (Germany)*
❏ *Weihenstephaner Korbinian (Germany)*
❏ *Weltenburger Kloster Asam Bock (Germany)*

German eisbocks to try:

❏ *Castle Eggenberg Urbock Dunkel Eisbock (Austria)*
❏ *EKU 28 (Germany)*
❏ *Kulmbacher Eisbock (Germany)*
❏ *Schneider Aventinus Weizen-Eisbock (Germany)*
  (a wheat eisbock)

SCHWARZBIER

Color: STRAW ▭▭▭▭▭ BLACK
Flavor: HOPS ▭▭▭▭▭ MALT
ABV: 3.8–5%
Serving temperature: 48–53° F

If you haven't tried schwarzbier, you are simply not
allowed to say that you don't like dark beer. This one
breaks all the rules! A very dark, almost blackish or
even purplish beer, but not at all aggressively bittered,
possessing a delicate sweet and easy-drinking mouthfeel, this traditional beer from the former East Germany

is becoming more popular in Germany today, the most famous type coming from Köstritz, Germany.

German schwarzbiers to try:

- ☐ *Berliner Burgerbrau Bernauer Schwarzbier (Germany)*
- ☐ *Köstritzer Schwarzbier (Germany)*
- ☐ *Kulmbacher Mönchshof Schwarzbier (Germany)*
- ☐ *Neuzeller Kloster-Bräu Schwarzer Abt (Germany)*

THAT BEER IS SMOKIN'

Rauchbier is a unique style of beer made with smoked malt. While people probably brewed with smoked malts in many areas, this style gained fame in the city of Bamberg in Franconia. This lager should taste smoky and smooth, slightly sweet, toasty, and full of flavor, with perceptible hops to balance the malt and smoke, but primarily the smoke flavor dominates. Märzen, weizen, and bock styles also sometimes feature smoked malt, but any style could, theoretically, be made with smoked malt. Not everybody likes the unique flavor of smoked beer, but for those who do, rauchbier is a real treat. It also makes an excellent ingredient in soups, stews, and as part of a marinade or sauce for roasted meat. Some good examples of German smoked beer include:

- ☐ *Aecht Schlenkerla Rauchbier Märzen*
- ☐ *Aecht Schlenkerla Rauchbier Weizen*
- ☐ *Altenmünster Rauchenfelser Steinbier*
- ☐ *Spezial Rauchbier Lager*

5

Belgium and
the Netherlands

Belgium may be trendy among beer connoisseurs these days, but in my opinion, no country deserves the attention more than this tiny corner of Europe with the most vastly varied and interesting selection of beers in the world. Although monks in monasteries have been brewing beer for centuries in other countries (like Germany), Belgium is most known for this combined venture of faith, brewing, innovation, and marketing. Belgian abbey beers are ales, made with top-fermenting yeasts, but they aren't Belgium's only style, by any means. Belgium is also famous for its unusual lambics, its sour Flemish ales, its spiced wheat beers, and its spectrum of potent pale and amber ales.

Belgian beers are mostly bottle-conditioned (meaning they are "alive" with yeast carried from the fermentation into the bottle, so they continue to ferment after bottling) and boast a huge flavor range and some truly unique tastes. Some Belgian beers challenge even the most experienced beer critic to describe them. Many people contrast Belgium with Germany to argue against German's purity law, because creative Belgian brewers are able to achieve such interesting results with added ingredients that fall far outside traditional German brewing regulations. Herbs and spices are more common here than in any other brewing region, but are used with a quintessentially European restraint, so they complement, rather than overwhelm, the palate. (Spicing in an American microbrew is likely to taste much more obvious than spicing in a Belgian beer.) Then again, Belgian beers have enough about them to overwhelm novice beer palates, from pucker-inducing gueuze lambics to innocent-looking pale tripel ales that clock in at a stunning 10% alcohol plus.

BOTTLE CONDITIONING

Bottle-conditioned beers contain living yeast and continue to age and mature in the bottle. This provides an additional opportunity for the yeast's metabolic processes to create deeper and more intricate flavor nuances. Brews with 8% alcohol by volume or higher can benefit from cellaring, just as a fine wine does. Cellaring duration could run from a few years up to twenty. In comparison, strong British barley wines have been known to reach their peak at around forty years of cellaring. Maybe Belgian beers could also benefit from a longer cellaring, but perhaps the monks simply couldn't wait any longer.

All over Belgium, people cook with beer, using it in food perhaps more than anywhere else in the world. Belgians like to say that what wine is to France, beer is to Belgium, boasting that their many styles of beer rival France's wine culture in history, quality, and variety. Belgium is also known for its world-class chocolate and its seafood. While pilsner and other straightforward lagers are popular for mass consumption in Belgium, it couldn't be easier to find really interesting and different styles. Many Belgian drinking establishments boast a beer menu featuring hundreds of beers in every representative style. These classic styles include spontaneously fermented lambic beers, white wheat beer, Flemish red or brown beer, special amber ale, high-gravity (alcohol) golden ale, and monastery or abbey ale that is typically fruity, malty, and strong but can be as pale as an angel's halo or as dark as the devil himself. Belgian brewers may also imitate styles of British ale or German lager, or even American microbrew, such as Urthel Hop-It, a Belgian interpretation of a Pacific Northwest IPA!

In the north, West Flanders is known for a sour, dark red beer and the beer-producing Trappist monastery Westvleteren, Belgian's smallest Trappist brewery. In East Flanders, a sour brown ale is the characteristic style. In Antwerp is the Trappist monastery Westmalle, perhaps Belgian's least tourist-friendly brewery, known for its potent triple (or tripel) style of abbey beer. Also in Flanders, the Achel Trappist monastery began producing beer again only in 1998, after closing down their brewing operations for almost one hundred years (the brewery was destroyed in World War I). Achel has an on-site pub and claims to be the world's only Trappist brewpub. Other popular breweries in this region include Corsendonk, Duvel, and Rodenbach, to name just a few of the many Flanders-based breweries.

In Brussels and Brabant, lambic is the regional style. Most beer connoisseurs agree that lambic is one of the world's most curious and bewildering beer styles. True lambic is brewed along Brussels' Senne River. Made with unmalted wheat and barley malt, and a heavy dose of aged hop flowers, lambic is then allowed to ferment via the natural airborne yeasts of the area, which imbue these beers with their enigmatic flavors. Lambic is then often aged in wine barrels. Lambics can be sweet and fruity (typical of aged lambics), dark and intensely sour (characteristic of young lambics), or a multitude of manifestations in between. Lambics are often blended with cherries, to make kriek, or raspberries, to make framboise or frambozen. When old and young lambics are blended and aged, the result is called gueuze. Faro is a dark, sweet version of lambic with added candy sugar. Lambics are sometimes served with sugar and a muddler. A few of the better-known breweries in the Brussels area include Artois (their popular pilsner, Stella Artois, is universally available), Hoegaarden (famous for its white wheat beers), Cantillon (an esteemed traditional lambic producer, as well as functional museum), and Lindemans (famous for its widely distributed framboise, kriek, and other lambics).

In Walloonia (French-speaking southeastern Belgium), the country's largest Trappist monastery brewery, Chimay, as well as the Trappist monasteries of Rochefort and Orval in Luxembourg (Luxembourg is actually a Belgian province) characterize the region. Numerous pivotal smaller private artisanal breweries pepper the region as well, such as the highly acclaimed Auchouffe, Binchoise, and Caracole breweries.

The Netherlands, to the north of Belgium, produces three beers most beer-drinking Americans know: Heineken, Amstel, and Grolsch. The craft beer scene in the Netherlands is woefully underrepresented in USA markets, as this tiny country produces more than seven hundred specialty products. Lagers characterize the most popular Netherlands beers, particularly the ubiquitous pilsner and bock beers (or bok, as they spell it), often seasonal. Excellent Bokbierfeesten (bock beer fests) are thrown annually in both Amsterdam and Utrecht, and would be the finest opportunity for an American traveler to get to know the specialty Dutch brews that are increasingly produced by more and more Netherland-based microbrewers.

WHAT ARE THE NETHERLANDS?

A tiny country nestled in the crook of Belgium and Germany, bordered to the west by the North Sea, the Netherlands is often inaccurately called Holland. Holland actually consists of two provinces: Noord Holland and Zuid Holland. This is just a small fraction of the country that, in its entirety, is the Netherlands.

History

A Celtic tribe originally inhabited Belgium, and for centuries, this has been a land of beer—brewing, beer cuisine, beer lore, and a dominant link between beer and the Almighty. When Julius Caesar first invaded Belgium in 57 B.C., the Romans noted the curiously strong Belgian brand of beer. Saint Arnoldus, patron saint of brewers, convinced Belgians to drink beer, instead of water, during the time of the plague.

Some of Belgium's most notable beers come out of its Trappist monasteries. In medieval Normandy, Cistercian monks who believed that other monasteries were becoming too lax in their observances formed the abbey of La Trappe. This strict order was called the Cistercian Order of the Strict Observance, and they were known for their silence and austere vegetarian diet, although silence was not a requirement. Later, they were called the Trappists. The French Revolution forced the order to flee and go into hiding. Many of these monasteries still exist today all over Europe and in other countries around the world, but just a few of them brew beer.

Long ago, monks brewed beer for their own consumption because this nutrient-rich beverage helped to sustain them at a low cost. However, with the advent of World War II, many monasteries were left without resources. Selling beer allowed them to survive and support themselves. Today, local water, isolation, and great care and precision in brewing methods make abbey beers among the best beers in the world. (Perhaps divine influence also plays a role?) The six Trappist breweries in Belgium have all revamped and modernized their facilities since most of them were destroyed during one war or another. For more on the individual history of the Trappist monastery breweries, see individual sections below.

Current Trends

Belgium may be a tiny country but it has a lot of culture happening within its borders. In the northwest, the population speaks Flemish. In the southeast, French. In the east, in small pockets, people speak German. Perhaps because Belgium has been so often conquered and subjugated by other cultures, each tiny region tends to hang on for dear life to its traditions, including its individual local beer style, and some of these are so unusual and surprising to the American palate that they could certainly qualify as "acquired tastes."

But some of Belgium's most interesting brewing traditions have been lost as industry giants like InBev and
Alken-Maes buy up medium-sized brewers and seem to
be encouraging more mass-consumption-oriented beers.
Light lagers, only infinitesimally better than their U.S.
counterparts (if at all) are becoming more and more
ubiquitous in Belgium and are the already-established
favorite in the Netherlands. Be sure to have one of
these—Heineken, Amstel, Maes, Jupiler, or Stella Artois—so that you can understand the difference between
for-the-masses megabrewed lagers and the really unusual Belgian ales coming out of this region.

Yet, in the face of this "dumbing down" of beer in a
country where beer has traditionally been at its most
inimitable and unique, a hearty band of artisanal brewers stands determined not to let Western Europe's spec-
tacularly diverse beer culture disappear. These smaller
brewers consist of two primary subgroups: those who
manage ancient breweries and have fortified themselves
against the onslaught, and tiny, bold new artisanal
breweries that operate under the radar of the giant corporations. The smallest of these has a staff of precisely
one person (Fantôme). Consumer groups have also
formed to support craft brewers in the region, and Belgian beer continues to rise in popularity in the United
States, as more and more people gain an appreciation
for beer that is not only beyond the scope of commercially produced light lagers, but pushing the envelope.
Additionally, the Belgian government stands firmly behind traditional brewing; brewers are taxed on a sliding
fee schedule that gives small artisanal enterprises significant tax breaks—a privilege small brewers in several
other Western European countries *don't* receive.

TIMELY TRAPPISTS

Trappist brewing conjures up visions of robed monks lovingly tending the brew kettle over an open fire. In today's world, the brewer-monk is far more likely to sit in front of a computer console, digitally conveying his product through the brewing process. If you want wood fires and open kettles, you'll have to look to the smaller, younger breweries such as Caracole, where the large bottles are also still lovingly filled and corked by hand, one at a time.

In the Netherlands, lager production is much more common. This isn't really surprising, since the Dutch language is more like German than French, and lager is the style characteristic of Germany. Netherlands specialty beers tend to stick around the city in which they're produced, making it more difficult to walk into a Nederlandse Bierkroeg Speciaal (a Dutch specialty beer pub) to get an idea of the entire country's beer. This also makes it very difficult to get an idea of the Dutch artisanal brewing scene without actually visiting the country—the Dutch brewing industry simply hasn't seen the international acclaim that the Belgians have won.

The specialty beer scene in the Netherlands seems to revolve mostly around Belgian beers, or imitations of Belgian beers, at least to a rather disproportionate extent in a country that produces more than seven hundred different beers under its own flag. This has not always been the case; during the heyday of the Dutch imperial period, beer was a very common export from the Netherlands, and even played a part in helping the Netherlands to acquire Friesland.

DON'T ORDER A BEER!

When in Belgium, avoid ordering "a beer, please." You are likely to get a basic, run-of-the-mill lager. Ask, instead, to see the beer list, and be specific in your order. This will provide you with the key to unlock the hundreds of beer choices many Belgian drinking establishments have to offer.

Trappist Ales

In Belgium, the Trappist beers are certainly the most famous. Because "Trappist" isn't a style, but rather refers to who actually brews the beer, each of the six Trappist monasteries in Belgium gets an individual category below, but check in the next section, "Characteristic Types of Beers," for specific statistics about the individual styles. For instance, Westmalle abbey makes a dubbel and a tripel, described further on as styles that can be made by Trappist monks or by secular brewers. The same goes for Chimay's pale blond ale and red (amber) ales, or Achel's blond and bruin ales, for example. In many cases, the Trappist ales are simply individual variations on the Belgian styles of pale/blond strong ale (sometimes called tripel), amber ale, or the potent high-alcohol amber ale called quadruple.

The most famous of Belgium's abbey beers come out of the six officially designated Belgian Trappist monasteries: Achel, Orval, Westmalle, Westvleteren, Chimay, and Rochefort. While many other breweries, in or associated with abbeys in Belgium and elsewhere, including in the United States, produce "abbey beers" or "abbey-style" beers, the word "Trappist" cannot be on the label without the official designation as a Trappist monastery, marked by the "Authentic Trappist Product" seal. This was a fairly recent development, in the grand scheme of Belgian beer brewing. In 1946, Westvleteren's St. Sixtus abbey decided to license the Sixtus name to the St. Bernardus commercial brewery. When other breweries tried to follow suit and claim links to other Trappist monasteries, the International Trappist Association formed in the mid-1990s and put their system in place to clearly define what was and was not a Trappist beer. The following six monasteries are the only ones allowed to use the term "Trappist" (although a few American microbrewers have lifted the name and use it on their own products—if they are lucky, they will not be struck down by any lightening bolts).

ORVAL

Founded by Benedictine monks from Italy in 1071, the Orval abbey, in a valley in Ardennes, was rebuilt in the twelfth century by Cistercian monks from France. In 1793, the abbey was attacked by French revolutionaries who thought the monks were hiding Louis XVI within the monastery's confines, and the abbey was heavily damaged. Not until the twentieth century did Trappist monks decide to rebuild. The construction began in 1926 and took more than twenty years, but the new structure is a masterpiece of architectural eclecticism, with elements of Romanesque, Burgundian, and Art Deco styles.

In 1931, a brew house was added, and the beer brewed at Orval was influenced by German brewer Pappenheimer, who advised the monks on technique in the 1930s and helped them to create a recipe that incorporated dry-hopping (adding hops to the fermented beer, primarily for the aroma). Unlike some monastery breweries, Orval makes only one beer: Orval, a peach-colored ale brewed with crystal malt, German

Hallertauer and Styrian Goldings hops, and the well water of the region. The monks ferment Orval three times. The dry-hopping also adds a long, bitter finish. The combination of bitter and sour are perfect for stimulating the palate, so try Orval as a before-dinner drink. This beer is widely available in the United States.

WESTVLETEREN

The tiny Westvleteren abbey of St. Sixtus in Flanders added a brewery in 1838 to brew beer for internal consumption, but the monastery began to sell their beer in the 1920s. Monks from this abbey left to form the Chimay monastery in 1850, and that brewery is now the most well-known and largest Trappist brewery, but the abbey at Westvleteren remains purposefully small and secluded, and produces only a small amount of commercial beer each year.

Across the street from the abbey, the Café de Vrede serves the abbey's brews, which have no labels on the bottles and are distinguished only by the different colors on their caps: green, blue, and yellow. These beers, brewed with pale malt, northern brewer hops, and added candy sugar, are all unfiltered and bottle-conditioned. The Green Cap beer is a pale ale, sometimes called blond, and weighs in at 5.6% ABV. The Blue Cap is a strong Belgian amber ale, stronger and darker than the blond at 8.4% ABV, and the Yellow Cap, also called Abbot, is a dark, strong ale at a potent 10.6% ABV and aggressive fruity malt and hop flavors.

CHIMAY

When the Prince of Chimay donated land to the Westvleteren abbey in the mid-nineteenth century, seventeen

---

CIRCA . . .

While many sources provide exact dates that various Trappist monasteries (and other breweries in Europe, for that matter) were built, destroyed, and rebuilt, or when exactly they started selling beer to the general public, the fact is that disruptions of war and conquest can sometimes make it difficult to pin down exact dates for brewery operation. Additionally, abbeys often began brewing for house consumption and only later offered their products for public sale, so exact dates may not be so exact when it comes to these historical events.

Trappist monks were allowed to open a new abbey, called the Abbaye de Notre-Dame de Scourmont. In 1862, a brewery was built into the abbey, although the abbey itself wasn't completed until 1864. The monks used the pure, soft well water to brew beer for their own consumption and to finance the abbey. (Today, Chimay is still brewed with this same soft water, giving it a unique taste.) At first, beer sales were limited, but in 1925, the abbey began to distribute their beer to a wider audience, and they were the first Trappist brewers to export beer on such a scale.

During World War II, the Nazis removed much of the brewing equipment, but after the war, the monks stepped up production to raise funds to rebuild. To improve their operation, Chimay hired the seminal brewing scientist Jean De Clerck from the brewing faculty at Leuven University to advise them. They designed new brewing tanks and isolated a pure yeast culture that gives Chimay its unique fruity taste. Chimay comes in three types: Red or Premier, 7% ABV, a coppery color with black currant and nutmeg notes; White or Cinq Cents, 8% ABV, a peach-colored citrusy beer; and Blue or Grande Cru, 9% ABV, a darker copper with big fruit, spice, and hops.

WESTMALLE

The Westmalle abbey was built in 1804 by Trappist monks fleeing the French Revolution. Just outside Antwerp, this brewery began to sell beer commercially in the mid-1800s, but only to the locals. In the 1920s, they expanded sales to other regions, and in 1934 an architect redesigned and enlarged the brew house, installing copper brewing vessels and a direct-flame-fired brew kettle. The caramelizing effect the direct flame has on the malt instills Westmalle's ales with their own toasty toffee flavors.

According to some sources, Westmalle was the first abbey to coin the term "tripel," and also possibly the term "dubbel" (not everyone agrees). The abbey's dubbel, or double, is a darker, fruity, almost chocolaty malt-infused brew made with dark malts that suggest sweet tropical fruits and chocolate on the finish, balanced with hops that add a complex dryness. The tripel, or triple, is a golden, fruity, hoppy brew intensely warming, with a high alcohol content of 9.5% ABV. With hints of citrus and pleasant hop bitterness and aroma, tripels may look thirst-quenching but are made for appreciative sipping. While both styles are generally high in alcohol, and while tripels usually exceed dubbels in alcohol content, the terms also designate the differences in color, flavor, and aroma.

ROCHEFORT

The abbey of St. Remy, just outside the town of Rochefort, was built in 1230. At the turn of the seventeenth century, the monks added a brewery for brewing their home-grown barley and hops into ale for internal consumption. As was the case with many abbey breweries, this brewery was wrecked during the French Revolution during the last decade of the 1700s, but Trappist monks from the Achel area helped to rebuild the abbey in 1887, and the brewery in 1889. In the 1960s, the brewery was modernized, but the brewing philosophy of the monks remains the same as it always was: to brew a dark, rich, highly nutritious beer to sustain the monks.

All three varieties of Rochefort Trappist Ale have a darkish, malty-sweet quality with varying strengths and slight color differences. The reddish Six has a 7.5% ABV, subtly hopped and sweetly malted. The Eight has an ABV of 9.2%. This copper-hued ale suggests dried fruit, roasted barley, and yeast. The red-brown Ten, at 11.3% ABV, is intensely warming, with dramatic aromas and flavors of chocolate and rich fruit.

ACHEL

The Trappist abbey at Achel, just across the border from the Netherlands, was founded in 1845, but was destroyed during the First World War. Rather than rebuilding the abbey immediately after the war, the monks made their living by farming, but in 1998 the brewery was restored to raise money for the abbey as well as to supply the monks with better beer than they could buy elsewhere. Achel recruited the Westmalle abbey's brewer, Father Thomas, to help them with their brewing efforts. While many abbey breweries sell their ales to local brewpubs, Achel has its own onsite brewpub, something that makes this Trappist abbey truly unique.

Achel makes six varieties of ale, with both a blond and a brown at each of the 5% and 8% ABV, plus the Achel Extra Bruin—at a more traditional abbey ABV of 9.5%—and a Zommer (summer) Extra Blond. The delicate 5% bruin borders on an amber or copper ale, and it is yet unclear if the Zommer will remain a one-off brew commemorating the seventy-fifth birthday of Abt Marc Gallant, or whether it might go into further production as a seasonal product. Their thirst-quenching blond beers are dry, floral, and fresh. The browns have a darker, bronzer color with a more aggressive malt taste and roasty flavors balanced by pungent, peppery hop aroma and a long dry finish, in which the 8 is naturally more robust than the 5. The Achel Extra Bruin is a winter brew, a warming and potent 9.5%.

Characteristic Types of Beer

Encompassing its famous Trappist ales and the efforts of hundreds of other abbey and secular brewers, Belgium has some unique characteristic styles: pale ale and strong pale ale (often called blond), amber and strong amber, the dark malty dubbel, the strong golden tripel, and the even more dramatically potent quadruple. Flemish sour brown, a wide variety of lambics, some interesting seasonals, even a few stouts round out the complex picture. In the Netherlands, light lagers may dominate but a few independent breweries are experimenting with the styles of other countries, such as Gulpen's Gulpener Dort (the Dutch take on German Dortmunder), and some experimental blends that combine different styles.

Unless otherwise indicated, the beers listed below are from Belgium.

BELGIAN-STYLE WHITE OR WITBIER/WHEAT BEER

Color: STRAW ▉▉▉▢▢▢▢ BLACK
Flavor: HOPS ▢▢▢▢▉▢▢ MALT
ABV: 4.8–5.2%
Serving temperature: 40–45° F

Belgian white ales, called tarwebier in Flemish or, in French, bière blanche, are made with unmalted wheat, malted barley, and are typically flavored with coriander and orange peel (a spicing tradition many American microbrewers imitate). Usually served cloudy with yeast and bottle-conditioned in the tradition of many Belgian beers, Belgian-style wheat or white beers typically have a modest but discernible hop bitterness, fruity/citrusy flavor, a satisfying yeastiness, and a clean, fresh taste. The moderate alcohol content makes these beers a good option for summer thirst-quenching, complemented by the clove and nutmeg flavor notes often derived from the specialty yeasts that create these brews. Coors-brewed Blue Moon is a popular American interpretation of this style. Ease in by trying Hoegaaden—you may never look back.

Belgian witbiers to try:

❑ *Abbey des Rocs Blanche des Honnelles (Belgium)*
❑ *Hoegaarden White (Belgium)*
❑ *La Caracole Troublette (Belgium)*
❑ *St. Bernardus Blanche (Belgium)*
❑ *Scheldebrouwerij Hansje Drinker (Netherlands)*
❑ *Vuuve (Belgium)*
❑ *Wittekerke (Belgium)*

BELGIAN PALE/BLOND ALE

Color: STRAW [▮▮▮▮▮] BLACK
Flavor: HOPS [▮▮▮▮▮] MALT
ABV: 4–8%
Serving temperature: Minimum of 45° F

Light to deep gold in color, lightly hopped and delicately malty, Belgian blond or pale ales may look like pilsners but they have a rich, fruity taste wrapped in crisp hops. Pale/blond ales tend to be strong in Belgium, many hovering around 6–8% in alcohol and a few much higher. (See below for a separate category on strong blond ales/tripels over 8% ABV.) All the lighter-colored ales in Belgium really fall on a spectrum, but will be divided here in general by strength.

Belgian pale/blond ales to try:

❑ *Achel 8 Blond (Belgium)*
❑ *Affligem Blonde (Belgium)*
❑ *Corsendonk Agnus (Belgium)*
❑ *De Ranke XX*
   Bitter (Belgium)
❑ *La Binchoise*
   Blonde (Belgium)
❑ *La Caracole Saxo*
   (Belgium)
❑ *La Chouffe*
   (Belgium)

❑ *La Trappe Blond (Netherlands)*
❑ *Leffe Blond (Belgium)*
❑ *Lucifer (Belgium)*
❑ *Orval (Belgium)*
❑ *Westvleteren Blond (Green Cap)*

LAGER, ANYONE?

Belgium and the Netherlands don't make lager the focus of their specialty beer scene, but here are a few notables to try:

- ❑ *Amstel (Netherlands)*
- ❑ *Bavaria Pilsener (Netherlands)*
- ❑ *Christoffel Blonde (Netherlands)*
- ❑ *Grolsch Premium Pilsener (Netherlands)*
- ❑ *Heineken (Netherlands)*
- ❑ *Jupiter (Belgium)*
- ❑ *Maes Pilsener (Belgium)*
- ❑ *Stella Artois (Belgium)*

STRONG PALE/BLOND AND TRIPEL ALES

Color: STRAW ▭▭▭▭▭▭ BLACK
Flavor: HOPS ▭▭▭▭▭▭ MALT
ABV: 8–12%
Serving temperature: Minimum of 45° F

Strong pale/blond/tripel ales are a light brilliant gold in color, richly hopped and richly malted. To achieve a light color but a depth of complex flavor and a higher ultimate ABV, these strong ales are often brewed with Belgian candy sugar, softening any sense of hop bitterness and accentuating this ale's natural fruity and caramelized characters. "Tripel" is a term originally coined by the Trappists, but other brewers use it, too. A tripel is really just one

Westmalle TRIPEL Ⓐ TRIPEL trappist ale

BREWED & BOTTLED BY THE TRAPPIST MONASTERY OF WESTMALLE
PRODUCT OF BELGIUM   330ml

way of labeling a stronger Belgian pale ale. In a few cases, you will see a beer labeled as a tripel or triple with an ABV of less than 7–8%, but in these cases it is much more of a marketing ploy than an authentic tripel, or even a genuine effort to imitate an authentic tripel.

Belgian strong pale/blonds and tripels to try:

- ☐ *Affligem Triple (Belgium)*
- ☐ *Augustijn (Belgium)*
- ☐ *Bornem Triple (Belgium)*
- ☐ *Chimay Cinq Cents (Belgium)*
- ☐ *De Dolle Dulle Teve 10 (Belgium)*
- ☐ *Delirium Tremens (Belgium)*
- ☐ *Duvel (Belgium)*
- ☐ *Gouden Carolus Triple (Belgium)*
- ☐ *La Bière du Boucanier Blonde (Belgium)*
- ☐ *La Trappe Tripel (Netherlands)*
- ☐ *Maredsous 10 (Belgium)*
- ☐ *Moinette Blonde (Belgium)*
- ☐ *Petrus Triple (Belgium)*
- ☐ *Piraat (Belgium)*
- ☐ *Rochefort Trappistes 8 (Belgium)*
- ☐ *St. Bernardus Tripel (Belgium)*
- ☐ *St. Feuillien Triple (Belgium)*
- ☐ *Satan Gold (Belgium)*
- ☐ *TIJ Natte (Netherlands)*
- ☐ *Tripel Karmeliet (Belgium)*
- ☐ *Urthel Hibernus Quentum (Belgium)*
- ☐ *Westmalle Tripel (Belgium)*

DUBBEL

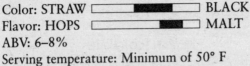

Color: STRAW ☐━━━━━━━☐ BLACK
Flavor: HOPS ☐━━━━━━━☐ MALT
ABV: 6–8%
Serving temperature: Minimum of 50° F

Belgian dubbel, or double, is a full, rich, dark brown ale with roasty, even faintly burnt malt flavors and suggestions of caramel, nuts, and chocolate. Darker than ambers due to the more deeply roasted malts, dubbels aren't typically as high in alcohol as some of the more intense and higher-gravity blond/tripel or dark amber ales. You might be able to detect a hop aroma, but it won't be dominant in this rich, flavorful beer. Dubbels often have a dense, thick, fluffy head.

Belgian dubbels to try:

- ☐ *Affligem Dubbel (Belgium)*
- ☐ *Bornem Double (Belgium)*
- ☐ *Chimay Premiere Red (Belgium)*
- ☐ *Corsendonk Pater (Belgium)*
- ☐ *Duinen Dubbel (Belgium)*
- ☐ *Grimbergen Double (Belgium)*
- ☐ *Grottenbier Bruin (Belgium)*
- ☐ *La Trappe Dubbel (Netherlands)*
- ☐ *Leffe Brune (Belgium)*
- ☐ *Moinette Brune (Belgium)*
- ☐ *Rochefort Trappistes 6 (Belgium)*
- ☐ *St. Bernardus Pater 6 (Belgium)*
- ☐ *St. Bernardus Prior 8 (Belgium)*
- ☐ *St. Feuillien Brune (Belgium)*
- ☐ *TIJ Natte (Netherlands)*
- ☐ *Val-Dieu Brune (Belgium)*

☐ *Westmalle Dubbel (Belgium)*
☐ *Westvleteren Extra 8 (Trappist)*

BELGIAN SCOTCH ALE

Belgian-brewed Scotch-style ales are related to dubbels by virtue of both strength and color. Theses ales represent an interesting twist on a style typical of the British Isles. The most likely candidates here are:

☐ *Brasserie Achouffe's McChouffe*
☐ *Scotch Silly from Brasserie de Silly*

BELGIAN STRONG AMBER ALE

Color: STRAW [▭▬▭] BLACK
Flavor: HOPS [▭▬▬▭] MALT
ABV: 5–10%
Serving temperature: Minimum of 50° F

Coppery to deep bronze amber or sometimes a deep red, medium in body and dark, but not as dark as the dubbels with their deeply roasted malts, Belgian amber ale is strong with generally modest hop flavor and aroma and layers of interesting soft fruit flavors. The malt flavor can be subtle or more forward, and sometimes Belgian brewers add herbs or spices to their amber ales. Amber ales are also often higher in alcohol than dubbels, although they may not taste as if they are. When it comes to Belgium's darker beers, just as with other categories, you will find a spectrum. Dubbels are the browner, roastier, lower-gravity ales, while ambers can be lighter to deeper and higher in alcohol. Quadruples are the most potent of the amber ales, and, because of this, the line between amber ales and quadruples is, by nature, a bit blurry. In this book, ambers include those deeper-colored ales up to about 10% ABV. Beyond 10%, amber ales are considered in the quadruple section below.

Belgian strong amber ales to try:

❏ *Bruegel Amber (Belgium)*
❏ *De Dolle Bos Keun (Belgium)*
❏ *La Binchoise Reserve Speciale (Belgium)*
❏ *La Caracole Ambrée (Belgium)*
❏ *Pauwel Kwak (Belgium)*
❏ *Satan Red (Belgium)*

BELGIAN STOUT?

While stout is normally associated with the United Kingdom and Ireland, a few Belgian brewers make stouts. This rare and wonderful category of Belgian beers isn't easy to find, but look for:

❏ De Dolle Extra Export Stout
❏ Ellezelloise (a.k.a. Quintine) Hercule Stout
❏ Troubadour Obscura

QUADRUPLE ALE

Color: STRAW ⬛⬛⬛⬜⬜ BLACK
Flavor: HOPS ⬛⬛⬜⬜⬜ MALT
ABV: 10–12%
Serving temperature: Minimum of 50° F

This high-gravity brother of amber ales encompasses those that exceed 10% ABV. Quadruples are typically deep and warming with rich layers of dried fruits, chocolate or coffee tones, and, frequently, the addition of Belgian candy sugar prior to fermentation to amp up the alcohol level as well as the rich sweetness of the roasted malt. This is a serious ale for savoring slowly.

Belgian quadruples to try:

- ❏ *Achel Extra Bruin (Belgium)*
- ❏ *Bush Ambrée (Belgium)*
- ❏ *Gulden Draak (Belgium)*
- ❏ *Het Kapittel Abt (Belgium)*
- ❏ *La Trappe Quadruple (Netherlands)*
- ❏ *Rochefort Trappistes 10 (Belgium)*
- ❏ *St. Bernardus Abt 12 (Belgium)*
- ❏ *Westvleteren Abt 12 (Belgium)*

SEASONALS

Belgian brewers love holidays. What a great excuse to brew something special for spring, summer, and certainly Christmas. With the recent introduction of the more American-style celebration of Halloween, the Belgian brewers have discovered that they have yet *another* holiday excuse to go experiment in the brewpot, and Halloween beers are becoming increasingly popular, especially from the smaller brewers. Expect seasonals to have a little bit more to do with marketing and a bit less to do with brew house experimentation than the true Saisons listed in the next section, although some people lump these two categories together. (This is not meant as a pejorative, nor to imply a complete absence of experimentation in the seasonals.) The seasonals listed opposite are all cold-weather seasonals, and all strong amber ales with spice notes ranging from about 9 to 12% ABV. This is typical for seasonals, which are frequently spiced and higher in alcohol than their nonseasonal counterparts.

Belgian seasonals to try:

- ☐ *Corsendonk Christmas Ale*
- ☐ *De Dolle Stille Nacht*
- ☐ *Delirium Noël*
- ☐ *Fantôme Black Ghost (a Halloween ale)*
- ☐ *Fantôme de Noël*
- ☐ *Fantôme Hiver (Winter)*
- ☐ *Le Moneuse Speciale Noël*

SAISONS

Color: STRAW ▭ BLACK
Flavor: HOPS ▭ MALT
ABV: 4.5–9%
Serving temperature: 50° F, but this can vary greatly depending on the beer

Saison is French for "season," and this term originally indicated that these beers were made from seasonally available materials. Modern transportation and refrigeration have blurred our ancient ideas of seasonality, so the term has come to be associated with locally produced "farmhouse" or "country" ales, often with interesting, even experimental ingredients. Those frugal Belgians will make every effort to use any glut of seasonal produce that would otherwise be wasted, stopping just short perhaps of parsnips. Saisons tend to be produced by really small, often quirky family-run breweries, whereas the seasonals are more likely to be products of small breweries. Occasionally now they are being produced by the mid-range player as well. Saisons are typically gold to amber in color and can have some truly unusual aromas and tastes reminiscent of earth, mold, horse blanket, or that *je ne sais quois*. Sometimes they are dry-hopped, spicing is the rule rather than the exception, and anything remotely genuine will be bottle-conditioned, but really, anything goes.

Belgian saisons to try:

- ☐ *DuPont Avec Les Bons Voeux (Belgium)*
- ☐ *DuPont Biere de Miel (Belgium)*
- ☐ *Fantôme Pissenlit (Belgium)*
- ☐ *Fantôme Saison (Belgium)*
- ☐ *Foret (also called Moinette Biologique, this is an organic ale, Belgium)*
- ☐ *Saison de Pipaix (Belgium)*
- ☐ *Saison Dupont (Belgium)*
- ☐ *Silly Saison (Belgium)*
- ☐ *Troubadour Blond (Belgium)*
- ☐ *Any Vapeur de Papaix product (the batches vary so much they are each unique, Belgium)*

GRUIT

Pronounced "grout," this ancient style of unhopped beer is based on usual grains, plus herbs and spices. Gruits are still produced in the Netherlands from at least one brewery in Haarlem, but they are hard to find in their homelands and harder still to find in the USA (although a few U.S. microbreweries do produce a similar style). The term "gruit" is disappearing from the vernacular, being replaced by the broader term "herbed/spiced beers," indicating that these beers may also be hopped—a dramatic deviation from traditional gruit production.

FLEMISH SOUR BROWN/FLEMISH BURGUNDY/ "OUD BRUIN" ALE

Color: STRAW ⬜ BLACK
Flavor: HOPS ⬜ MALT
ABV: 4.8–5.2%
Serving temperature: 50–55° F

This sour brown ale gets its twang from lactic acid produced during a complex fermentation process. It has a puckery, tart taste with very little bitterness and no hop aroma. The color comes from roasted malt, and this style often has an oaky flavor beneath the pucker. Some are cloudy and some are quite fizzy. Precise distinctions between these three categories will probably remain forever lost in the mists of time, but they all share the quality of being fermented by organisms in addition to the usual yeasts. In this, these beers share a kinship with the lambics. For many American beer drinkers, this is an acquired taste. Try these as you work your way toward an appreciation of some of the equally unusual lambics (see below), which can be even more intense and "unbeerlike," if one is to maintain a traditional mindset. Some of these ales include cherries, and are labelled "kriek," further blurring the line between Flemish sour ales and fruit-infused lambics.

Flemish sour ales/"oud bruins" to try:

❑ *Liefmans Goudenband (Belgium)*
❑ *Liefmans Kriekbier (Belgium)*
❑ *Mestreechs Aajt (Netherlands)*
❑ *Monks Café Flemish Sour Red Ale (Belgium)*
❑ *Petrus Aged Pale (Belgium)*
❑ *Petrus Oud Bruin (Belgium)*

❑ *Reinaert Flemish Wild Ale (Belgium)*
❑ *Rodenbach Classic (Belgium)*
❑ *Rodenbach Grand Cru (Belgium)*
❑ *Verhaeghe Duchesse de Bourgogne (Belgium)*
❑ *Verhaeghe Echt Kriek (Belgium)*
❑ *Verhaeghe Vichtenaar (Belgium)*

SPONTANEOUS FERMENTATIONS: LAMBICS AND GUEUZES

Color: STRAW ▢▮▮▮▮▮▯▯▯ BLACK
Flavor: HOPS ▢▯▯▯▯▯▮▮▮ MALT
ABV: 5–6%
Serving temperature: Minimum of 45° F but varies greatly depending on the beer

This family of spontaneously fermented ales is loosely regarded as the lambic family because all products here are initially derived from lambics. In its pure form, lambic is spontaneously fermented with wild yeasts rather than cultured ale or lager yeasts. Up to two dozen different microorganisms have been found contributing to the fermentation process of a single lambic. Lambic is typically hazy, low in carbonation, and has an intensely sourish, startling (to the uninitiated) taste. It is usually aged for several years.

Experimental as lambic may seem, brewers tend to do a lot with this category, mixing in fruit, combining the more sour young lambics with more complex aged lambics to create gueuze, or muddling the lambic with sugar to make it more palatable (although some people like it just fine the way it is). Current Belgian regulation of the use of the word "lambic" in labeling is so lax as to be practically nonexistent, but all authentic lambics have three things in common: spontaneous fermentation with wild yeast, at least 30% wheat in the grist (in other words, not all barley), and the use of aged hops to contribute flavor but no hop aroma (aged hops lose their aroma). Each subcategory of lambics, below, has its own listing of beers to try. In Flemish, lambic is lambiek.

Unblended lambics to try:

❑ *Cantillon Bruocsella 1900 Grand Cru (Belgium)*
❑ *Cantillon Iris (Belgium)*

Fruit Lambic

The result of the initial fermentation from the process outlined above, which typically takes two to three years, fruit lambics combine fruit with the basic lambic after aging. The fruit is then steeped for an additional period of six weeks to six months to create the fruit flavor, and the lambic takes on the color of the fruit. Cherry (kriek), raspberry (framboise or frambozen), peach (peche), and currant (cassis) flavors are all available stateside.

Fruit lambics are usually sweeter and more palatable to those new to lambic than the pure, unblended type of lambic. Some can be quite surprising in their own right, however. Certain cherry-flavored krieks can be

intensely sour, and black currant–flavored lambics can taste pretty unusual. Lindemans is certainly the most famous exporter of lambics in the United States. While not the most classic lambic, the

Lindemans raspberry, peach, and cherry lambics are sweet, fruity, fizzy, and irresistible to people who don't mind a sweeter, fruity flavor in their beer. Some people claim these are the beers for people who don't like beer. They make for a heavenly celebratory beverage (you'll never miss the champagne). If you find yourself enjoying them, look also for kindred fruity selections in the chapter on French beers. Also, lambic—because of its low pH—lends itself to cooking and marinating applications. If you don't enjoy it from a glass, try it as a substitute for vinegar the next time you make a vinaigrette dressing.

Fruit lambics to try:

- ❑ *Boon Framboise (Belgium)*
- ❑ *Boon Kriek (Belgium)*
- ❑ *Cantillon Kriek (Belgium)*
- ❑ *Cantillon Lou Pepe Framboise (Belgium)*
- ❑ *Cantillon Rose de Gambrinus (Belgium)*
- ❑ *Liefmans Frambozenbier (Belgium)*
- ❑ *Liefmans Kriekbier (Belgium)*
- ❑ *Lindemans Cassis Lambic (Belgium)*
- ❑ *Lindemans Framboise (Belgium)*
- ❑ *Lindemans Pêche Lambic (Belgium)*
- ❑ *Lindemans Kriek (Belgium)*

Gueuze

This lambic variation is a blend of relatively younger, more aggressively sour lambics and older, more complexly flavored lambics. It is not fruited. One traditional serving of gueuze is in a stout, narrow-sided tumbler with sugar cubes and a "stomper," so that you can sweeten your gueuze if you desire.

Gueuzes to try:

- ☐ *Cantillon Gueuze (Belgium)*
- ☐ *Drie Fonteinen Oude Gueuze (Belgium)*
- ☐ *Girardin Gueuze Black Label (Belgium)*
- ☐ *Hanssens Oude Gueuze (Belgium)*
- ☐ *Lindemans Gueuze Curvée René (Belgium)*

Faro

This final lambic category is actually gueuze with the addition of brown sugar or darkly caramelized candy sugar already added in. This style is hard to find in the United States, but you might be able to find them occasionally by some of Belgium's better-known breweries. Keep your eyes open for them.

Faros to try:

- ☐ *Boon Faro Pertotale (Belgium)*
- ☐ *Cantillon Faro (Belgium)*
- ☐ *Chapeau Faro (Belgium)*
- ☐ *Lindemans Faro (Belgium)*

🍺 6 🍺
The Rest of Western Europe

People associate Western Europe with wine, to a large extent, but beer is much beloved in this part of the world, even if it isn't as widely produced or commonly exported to the United States as its grape-based cousin. Beer is enjoying a vibrant renaissance even in some pretty obscure corners of Western Europe, with increasing numbers of microbrewers producing beer in the styles of the UK, Germany, and some of their own, such as France's bière de garde.

As in most European countries, if you order a beer, you are likely to get a pale lager, but as people continue to press for more interesting beers—better pilsners, bocks, and Vienna styles out of Germany, spiced ales in the Belgian tradition, porters and stouts in the tradition of the UK—these intriguing, even experimental, beers are becoming more and more widely available. While Europe's microbrewing scene has enjoyed new energy and experimentation in the past decade, however, the other countries in Europe beyond Germany and Belgium and across the sea from the UK continue to learn from and derive their brews from these beer-centric areas. The good news is that if you would rather drink beyond the confines of pale lager, you have more options from Europe than ever before.

History and Current Trends

Throughout much of Europe, beer has long been considered part of a basic diet, and at some stages, the drink for the masses (as opposed to wine, the deities' preferred beverage). In countries like France and Italy where food and drink have always enjoyed the highest status and quality, people can't help but appreciate good beer. If Europeans put their hearts and souls into making and enjoying wine, why wouldn't they do the same in their breweries? Fortunately for the rest of the world, they always have—at least on the local level.

Beer changed in several important ways all over Europe at the beginning of the nineteenth century, when the Industrial Revolution facilitated the shipping of beer beyond the local brewing scene, and the invention of refrigeration allowed brewers to brew whenever they wanted, without regard to the weather and seasons. But while people tend to think that all the really important brewing innovations have happened in Germany and within the confines of Belgian monasteries, two of the most significant happened elsewhere in Western Europe.

When the French microbiologist Louis Pasteur penned his "Études sur la Bière" ("Studies Concerning Beer") in 1876, people finally began to understand the important role yeast plays in fermentation. Before this time, people thought beer and wine fermented spontaneously from within, but Pasteur proved that fermentation happened due to the "contamination" by yeast spores from outside. He thereby gave credence to germ theory, then proceeded to develop the pasteurization process, to prevent beverage contamination by undesirable organisms. These discoveries changed both the beer and the wine industries forever.

Another beer-significant scientist, Christian Hansen of Denmark, discovered that he could artificially culture yeast. He isolated a single yeast cell and induced reproduction. This led to the development of pure yeast strains, a technology that allowed brewers to produce more consistent beer, unadulterated by ambient wild yeasts.

In the 1960s and 1970s, many European countries became interested in beer again (after the furor and destruction from all those world wars had finally subsided, for the most part), and craft brewers continue to emerge in every European country. Today, it's hardly surprising that large brewing conglomerates control many of the breweries in Western Europe, and that the result is that good ol' pale lager everyone seems to crave. This is happening all over the developed world—in Belgium, in Germany, in the UK, and obviously in the United States. But each individual country in Europe is doing its own thing to fight the trend to drag all beer down to the level of the mediocre. The tightening of the European Union into a unified trade group is having the effect of introducing the entire area to beers that were previously unavailable, and this is broadening the brewing scene as a whole across "nonbeer" Western Europe.

Here's a closer look by region.

FRANCE

In 1970s France, the breweries Castelain and La Choulette were the first to experiment with brewing ales in a world rife with mega-popular lagers. This started a trend that encouraged others to follow suit. Small breweries and brewpubs in Brittany and Lille began to pick up speed, and today, while the number of breweries in France can't rival the number of its wineries, a respectable group produces some interesting beers inspired by UK ales, German wheat beers, and Belgian spiced ales, as well as the traditional style of France—bière de garde. The organic trend in Germany has also influenced France, and many small breweries produce organic beer.

Kronenbourg and Heineken control many of the larger breweries in France, but in two brewing-intensive areas, large-scale brewers aren't the only game in town. In French Flanders, many microbrewers specialize in bière de garde. This style is so-named because of a secondary fermentation—the verb *garder* in French means "to store"—and is characterized by fruity malt, low hops, the possibility of some spicing, and a moderate alcohol content.

The other important brewing area is in eastern France, near Strasbourg, where brewers are producing both German and UK styles: porters, Scotch ales, and a variety of localized German-inspired lagers. Another unique style of this region is a beer made with smoked malt called bière au malt de whisky, but you will probably have to go to France to find any. The French also enjoy producing seasonal beers, particularly spring beers, called bières de mars, and beers for the winter holidays, often with the word "Noël" in the name.

ITALY

While southern Italy produces wine, northern Italy feels the influence of Germany to the north, and northern Italian brewers have been brewing beer for centuries, on a small scale. Today the artisanal brewing scene in Italy is nearing the explosion point, as beer just keeps getting bigger—and trendier—in Italy. The German influence is still discernible today in seasonal bocks and Dortmunder-inspired brews. In Italy as elsewhere, large conglomerates govern the mass-market beer scene, producing mostly light pale lagers, but in the last few decades, microbrewers and brewpubs keep sprouting, inspired by the long-standing beer tradition in this region. Heineken and Denmark-based Carlsberg have a strong presence in Italy, having taken over smaller breweries like Poretti, Moretti, and Von Wunster. Italian-based Peroni is the largest native brewery. Other breweries include Birra Dreher, Castello di Udine Spa, and Menabrea/Forst, whose beers you may be able to find in the U.S. Interesting small craft brewers of ale in Italy that export include Baladin and Panil.

SPAIN, PORTUGAL, AND GREECE

Elsewhere along the southern coastal regions, where the climate is just right for wine, beer is a small enterprise but brewers are nevertheless doing some interesting things. In this sunny, warm region, fizzy thirst-quenching pilsners and pale lagers dominate, but you can also find a few examples of darker German styles like bock and other dark lagers, and the occasional experiment with unusual local ingredients. Again, however, you will have to travel to this region to get a sense of what is really going on with the native beer, as few examples are exported to the United States.

SCANDINAVIA

In the chilly northern countries of Denmark, Norway, Finland, and Sweden, the German lager influence

---

FINNISH YOUR BEER

An ancient traditional style in Finland, called sahti, is brewed with juniper berries and typically has some rye in the grain mash. An unusually sweet beer, sahti is often produced locally or home brewed by the Fins, and it is easy to find when in Finland, but not so easy to find in the United States. The Lammin brewery exports their brand of sahti, and you might be able to find it in the United States, but it won't be easy. The best place to try sahti is in Finland.

---

is strong. The Carlsberg brewery in Denmark perfected lagering in 1883 and was the first country in northern Europe to produce lagers as an official style. Christian Hansen's yeast discoveries came out of a Carlsberg laboratory, and lager yeasts were actually called carlsbergensis in honor of that brewery for roughly a century. Today Scandinavia is enjoying a craft-brew renaissance, with Denmark at its center. Denmark's mild lagers get more interesting around the holidays, including Christmas and Easter. A local style called hvidtøl is a low-alcohol sweet beer, and some breweries produce porters and stouts using lager yeasts, an interesting way to combine German technology with UK flavor. Carlsberg and its affiliates remain a significant force on the Northern European scene.

Norway has a beer purity law inspired by Germany's, and its largest brewer, Ringnes, owns many of the smaller breweries in this country. As elsewhere in Scandinavia, pilsners, dark lagers, and seasonal brews dominate. In Finland, an ancient type of beer called sahti has always been a local favorite. The Finns have a long-standing love of beer, and a German as well as a Czechoslovakian influence is obvious in the Finnish-brewed beers. The largest Finnish brewer is Hartwall, and the Lammin brewery produces sahti for export. Helsinki holds an annual beer festival every spring, but if you miss it, you might catch the Stockholm Beer Festival in Sweden in the fall.

Characteristic Types of Beer

EUROPEAN-STYLE PILSNERS, PREMIUM LAGERS, AND PALE LAGERS

Color: STRAW ▰▰▱▱▱▱▱ BLACK
Flavor: HOPS ▱▱▱▰▱▱▱ MALT
ABV: 4–6%
Serving temperature: 40–45 ° F

European-style pilsner and its related premium lagers are straw to gold with a medium body and may be brewed with any grain, including rice, corn, or wheat, in these countries beyond the reach, or influence, of the German purity law. Low to moderate hops balanced by low malt and relatively low alcohol give these beers a thirst-quenching light body.

European-style pilsners and premium lagers to try:

❑ *Aass Pilsner (Norway)*
❑ *Athenian (Greece)*
❑ *Birra Moretti (Italy)*
❑ *Carlsberg Lager (Denmark)*
❑ *Cruzcampo Premium Lager (Spain)*
❑ *Fischer Bitter (France)*
❑ *Fischer Tradition (France)*
❑ *Hijos de Rivera Estrella Galicia (Spain)*
❑ *Kronenbourg 1664 (France)*

☐ *Mythos (Greece)*
☐ *Peroni Premium Lager (Italy)*
☐ *Tuborg Gold Premium Lager (Denmark)*

BIÈRE DE GARDE

Color: STRAW ▭▬▭ BLACK
Flavor: HOPS ▭▬▭ MALT
ABV: 4.5–8%
Serving temperature: 50–55° F

This French style ranges from gold to deep bronze. Malty, sweet, and fruity with subdued hops, some of these beers have an earthy aroma reminiscent of Belgian abbey ales. True bière de garde is bottle-conditioned and is hence fermented twice, a characteristic of this style. All beers listed below are from France; not all are bottle-conditioned. If you want the most authentic thing, be sure to ask your local bottle shop for a bottle-conditioned product.

Bière de gardes to try (all come from France):

☐ *Castelain Blond Bier*
☐ *Castelain Jade (an organic version)*
☐ *Choulette Sans Culottes*
☐ *Jenlain Ambrée*
☐ *Jenlain Blonde*
☐ *La Bavaisienne*
☐ *La Choulette Ambrée*
☐ *La Choulette Framboise (a raspberry-infused version)*
☐ *3 Monts*

BELGIAN-STYLE STRONG ALE

Belgium has an undeniable influence on the rest of Europe when it comes to beer, and many breweries in France, Italy, and Scandinavia imitate Belgian styles, from abbey ales to strong blonds to potent ambers rivaling Belgium's quadruple style. I am not including a rating chart here because in Europe these range dramatically, from pale to dark, sweet to hoppy. This style is typically relatively high in alcohol, usually over 6% and some over 10%. Some of the higher-gravity styles are seasonal, brewed for the winter holidays when those warming qualities are most desirable. Serving temperature also varies greatly depending on the beer. Just a few are listed here, as these can be difficult to find in the United States.

European Belgian-style strong ales to try:

❑ *Belzebuth (France)*
❑ *Fischer Amber (France)*
❑ *Super Baladin (Italy)*

SEASONAL EUROPE

Just as in Belgium, other Europeans enjoy making seasonal beers. These are often bocks, Vienna-style lagers, or Belgian-style strong ales. Many of these are locally produced and locally or regionally consumed. Again, these examples vary quite a bit all over Europe. Besides, you may be able to find only one or two of these in the United States. Look for:

❑ *La Choulette de Noël (France)*
❑ *Noel Baladin (Italy)*

Bock and Other German Styles

Many countries in Western Europe are influenced by Germany's skill with the lager style, imitating bocks and doppelbocks as well as Vienna-style lagers, dunkel (dark) lagers, and wheat beers in the German tradition. Many of Europe's bock and Vienna styles are seasonal offerings, in their strongest incarnations. As in Germany, bock and doppelbock are malty, full-flavored lagers with flavors of toffee, caramel, and noticeable hops. They have a deep rich color, and high alcohol. While many bocks and doppelbocks are brewed in France, Italy, and Scandinavia, not many are available in the United States, even those by the largest brewers in those countries. Again, no rating chart here, as these vary too much and you may be able to find only a few in the United States, though this may change in the future. For now, you might compare these to German Bocks. Refer to that scale and description on page 89.

European bocks to try:

❏ *Aass Bock (Norway)*
❏ *Birra Moretti La Rossa (Italy)*
❏ *Forst Sixtus Doppelbock (Italy)*

Porters and Other British Styles

The UK influences its neighbors too, and many European countries have their own versions of porters and stouts, not to mention bitters, IPAs, and other UK styles, although again, these are hard to find in the United States and vary too widely for a rating chart. You might compare these to British porters. Refer to that scale and description on page 67. The British influence is most evident in Scandinavia and in France and Italy.

European porters to try:

❑ *Carnegie Porter (Sweden)*
❑ *Sinebrychoff Porter (Finland)*

7

Eastern Europe

The birthplace of the pilsner style and a land that influences, and is influenced by, Germany, Eastern Europe has a vibrant and exciting beer culture centered primarily around pilsners. Some people believe that hops were first cultivated in Bohemia. While pilsner is the dominant style and the Czech Republic still produces some of the world's best (and certainly most authentic) pilseners, Eastern Europe boasts other beer achievements too.

You can find German-influenced styles from Eastern Europe, particularly dunkel (dark) lagers, a few bocks and doppelbocks, and Münchner-style helles (light) and Dortmunder-style lagers. The region's Baltic porters are dark, rich, winey, full-bodied, porterlike lagers primarily brewed in the Baltic States, or those countries surrounding the Baltic Sea—Estonia, Latvia, Lithuania, and Poland—and also Sweden and Finland. Not surprisingly, American microbrewers have also played around with this interesting style.

Because brewing is so often locally centered around small operations that don't export their beers, much of the beer in Eastern Europe isn't available in the United States. Doppelbocks, spiced ales, and other interesting interpretations of German brews and traditional ales all exist; we just don't get the benefit of most of them here in the United States. The northern provinces of Lithuania, for example, produce utterly obscure (to us) beers that rival the Belgian intensity. The Eastern European beers most notable and available in the United States are the pilsners and, to a lesser extent, the Baltic porters.

History and Current Trends

This land of pilsner is most famous for the birth of this now-ubiquitous and enthusiastically imitated style, but this didn't happen until 1842, when a Bavarian brewer named Josef Groll developed the style using pale malts, Noble hops, and the unusually soft water characteristic of the town of Pilzen in what was then Czechoslovakia. This clear, brilliant golden beer was an immediate hit in a country where dark, murky ales were the tradition. Obviously, the news didn't remain within the borders of Czechoslovakia for long. Soon, at least some variant of pilsner was available all over Europe, and Germany, of course, took this style and ran with it. The first brand of pilsner was Pilsner Urquell, and although a lot has happened to this brand in the last 150 years, the company claims it still uses the same recipe as the original style. Pilsner Urquell remains the quintessential standard by which all pilsner is measured.

The other famous and ongoing issue in Eastern Europe began in Czechoslovakia in 1265, with a beer called Ceske Budejovice. If you can't pronounce it, that helps explain why its more common name is Budweiser—and you probably can't help being familiar with *that* name. This popular golden lager inspired the Anheuser-Busch corporation—the world's second largest beer conglomerate—to imitation with its own Budweiser beer, and today the two companies have been involved for literally decades in numerous ongoing lawsuits about who can use the name Budweiser in which country. Currently, American Budweiser has rights to the name in the United States and most of Latin America, while Czech-based Budweiser has rights to the name in most of Europe. In America, Czech-based Budweiser is called Czechvar or Budvar, and in Europe, American-based Budweiser is called Bud. Czech-based Budweiser likes to use the slogan "The Original Budweiser," which probably irritates Anheuser-Busch but which is technically a correct statement.

Since the fall of Communism in Eastern Europe, Western European beer knowledge and products have increasingly filtered into Eastern Europe, and vice versa. Today, as disposable income increases in Eastern Europe and the beer industry turns its great eye increasingly toward some of Eastern Europe's less beer-saturated markets like Russia and the Ukraine, this region of the globe is expected to help drive beer sales in the global market. While nobody knows for sure what will happen in the coming decades in Eastern Europe, signs point to an increasing internal excitement about craft brews and an explosion of beer culture similar to what is happening in places like Italy and Denmark.

CZECH REPUBLIC AND SLOVAKIA

In 1989 the Communist Party of Czechoslovakia ended its control over Czechoslovakia, and in 1993 the country split into two separate nations: the Czech Republic and Slovakia. The Czech Republic consists of Bohemia and Moravia, and produces both Pilsner Urquell and its own Budweiser. Bohemia's capital city is Prague, home to a number of traditional breweries, including the Klaster (Czech for "Cloister") brewery, part of the baroque abbey of Strahov, founded in the twelfth century.

Slovakia is more a land of small-scale local brewers. Notable brewers include Zlaty, in Hurbanova, and Topvar, in Topolcany. Both export their lagers to the United States, but only in limited areas. Zlaty is the easiest to find—particularly Golden Pheasant, its pilsner—because Heineken owns it. In fact, most of the Eastern European beers available in the United States come from breweries owned by larger European conglomerates, but the beers still reflect much of what is going on in those countries and can give the beginner a sampling of representative Bohemian pilsners, Baltic porters, and Eastern Europe's interpretation of traditional German styles.

POLAND

Poland's most popular beer is a pale lager by the Zywiec brewery in the city of Zywiec. The brewery also makes a dark, rich, very strong (9.5% ABV) Baltic porter, despite being owned by the Heineken megalopoly, which might lead some to believe they would stick to more mainstream styles. Okacim and Piast are other well-known Polish breweries.

RUSSIA

While better known for its vodkas, Russia also has an interesting beer scene, and beer in Russia is nothing new. For centuries, Russians have enjoyed beer, and traditionally these were often flavored with honey, molasses, and berries. The 1894 creation of the Union of Russian Brewers did much to spread beer culture and knowledge around the country through beer exhibitions, brewing schools, tastings, and beer-oriented laboratories. The Communist Revolution brought an end to most organized brewing in Russia, and many breweries were destroyed, but since that party's fall, beer is again enjoying a revival.

Today in Russia, Baltic porters, lagers brewed with rye, and German-influenced styles like wheat beers and Märzens dominate. Russia's largest brewer and the brand most available in the United States is Baltika, but you may also be able to find Tinkov's pale lager or the occasional other odd import that manages to make the trip west.

PEA BEER?

In Lithuania, one variation on the pale lager theme is to include green peas as part of the grist, rather than pure malt. Brewers believe the protein in the peas adds flavor to the beer, and that the protein may improve head retention.

In many of the other, smaller countries of Eastern Europe—Lithuania, Estonia, Latvia, the Balkans—small-scale brewers continue to produce beer for the local market, but most of these beers aren't available in the United States. Who knows what the future may hold for these small countries as international borders increasingly blur due to travel, the Internet, and commerce? Small breweries could disappear, or they could expand into the global market.

Characteristic Types of Beer

BOHEMIAN PILSENERS/PALE LAGERS

Color: STRAW ▢▅▅▅▭▭▭▭ BLACK
Flavor: HOPS ▢▭▅▅▅▭▭ MALT
ABV: 4–5.5%
Serving temperature: 42–48° F

The original pilsener is slightly deeper gold and fuller bodied than its interpretations in most other European countries, including Germany. Bohemian pilseners should have noticeable and pleasing hop bitterness with a nice balance of malt. Both malt and hops should be present in the aroma as well as the taste of a Bohemian pilsener. Without this balance—and particularly without obvious hops in the aroma and palate—light lagers are really just light lagers, not pilseners. Some would argue that unless it comes from Pilzen, it isn't a pilsener, although many cities beyond Pilzen in Bohemia, as well as countries beyond the borders of Bohemia, have brewed excellent pilseners. Pilseners are, essentially, the crème of the light lager category—especially those from the Czech Republic.

Bohemian pilsners (and a few pale lagers) to try:

❏ *Baltika 3 Klassicheskoe (Russia)*
❏ *Czech Rebel (Czech Republic)*
❏ *Czechvar (aka Budvar, Czech Republic)*
❏ *Golden Pheasant (aka Zlaty Bazant, Slovak Republic)*
❏ *Okocim Mocne (Poland)*
❏ *Pilsner Urquell (Czech Republic)*
❏ *Radegast Premium (Czech Republic)*
❏ *Samson Premium Svetlý Ležák (Czech Republic)*

❑ *Starobrno Premium Lager (Czech Republic)*
❑ *Staropramen Lager (Czech Republic)*
❑ *Zywiec Beer (Poland)*

BALTIC PORTER

    Color: STRAW ▭▭▭▭▭▭ BLACK
    Flavor: HOPS ▭▭▭▭▭▭ MALT
    ABV: 6.5–9%
    Serving temperature: 53–58° F

A deep, rich, wine-dark lager ranging from black to garnet-reddish-black, Baltic porter is similar to imperial stout, but—unlike either the true stouts or porters of the UK made with ale yeasts—the Baltics are in general lagers, made with lager yeasts and lagering techniques. They are high in alcohol and appropriately warming considering their origin in the frigid upper regions of Eastern Europe. Richly malty with not-so-subtle coffee flavors and interesting undertones of oil, flowers, and wood, Baltic porter can be an acquired taste for those more accustomed to lighter lagers, but imperial stout lovers are bound to find Baltic porter attractive.

    Baltic porters to try:

❑ *Baltika 6 Porter (Russia)*
❑ *Pardubický Porter (Czech Republic)*
❑ *Sinebrychoff (or "Koff") Porter (Finland)*
❑ *Utenos Porter (Lithuania)*
❑ *Zywiec Porter (Poland)*

DORTMUNDER/EXPORT AND HELLES

Color: STRAW ⬜▬▭▭▭▭▭▭ BLACK
Flavor: HOPS ▭▭▬▬▬▭▭ MALT
ABV: 5–6%
Serving temperature: 42–48° F

This malt-accented pale lager style is less strictly de-
fined outside Germany than it is within the borders of
that country, so while the above ratings are those of the
German Dortmunder style, some Eastern European versions may fall slightly outside these guidelines. Helles is
typically lighter in color and alcohol content than Dortmunder, but the dividing line is a blurry one. In general,
however, both styles are pale to golden with about a
5–6% ABV, fuller-bodied and maltier than a pilsner or
generic pale lager. Beyond that, much depends on the
brewer.

Eastern European Dortmunder/export and helles to
try:

❏ *Kalnapilis Export (Lithuania)*
❏ *Svyturys Ekstra (Lithuania)*

EASTERN WIT

While many Eastern European countries make their own
versions of wheat or witbier, not many of these are available in the United States. One exception is Russia's answer
to Germany's hefeweizen:

❏ *Baltika 8 Pshenichnoe.* It is available in some U.S.
states.

Dunkel

Color: STRAW 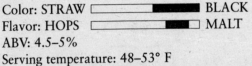 BLACK
Flavor: HOPS MALT
ABV: 4.5–5%
Serving temperature: 48–53° F

In Eastern Europe, pilsener may be a favorite, but many brewers also have a dark or dunkel lager. This widespread popular style is typically malty with a balancing crisp hop taste. It won't taste exactly like a German Dunkel because of regional ingredients differences, but will be similar enough to be recognizable. It should be light and smooth with a biscuity aroma, and while it may have chocolate and roasted flavors, these don't add a heaviness but a smooth full flavor.

Eastern European dunkels to try:

❏ *Baltika 4 Originalnoe (Russia)*
❏ *Kláster Tmavé Vycepni (Czech Republic)*
❏ *Lobkowicz Baron Premium Czech Dark Lager
(Czech Republic)*

♧ 8 ♧
Australia and New Zealand

In Australia, beer is a matter of national pride and no style is more widely beloved than pale lager. In the United States, we are familiar with Fosters, and this is indeed a popular brand in Australia, but other brands are also beloved. Australia is a large country and regional pride runs high too. While most of Australia's beer market is part of the gargantuan Carlton United Breweries (CUB), many small brewers with local followings produce styles outside the pale lager category. Witbiers, dunkels, stouts and porters, IPAs, doppelbocks, seasonal beers . . . you can get them all in the Land Down Under. You just can't get most of the Aussie-brewed beers in the United States.

In New Zealand, the situation is even more localized, with microbrewers selling their wares in the towns where they are located, but rarely making their brews available much beyond the local borders. This trend makes beer from Australia and New Zealand difficult to characterize, beyond the pale lager revolution. Yet lager's popularity in this hot, dusty continent makes sense. When the temperature soars and the residents are parched, what could taste better than an ice-cold, thirst-quenching lager? Sure, ales and darker German-influenced beers have their place, but for large-scale high-capacity drinking in the true Australian style, lagers win, hands down, and the lagers of Australia do tend to be light and mild, even compared to pale lagers from other countries. This is all in the service of Australia's great thirst.

NEW ZEALAND IS HOPPIN'

New Zealand is currently a leading global producer of organic hops, a crop difficult for most countries to produce. Because the New Zealand climate is just right for hop production and because crop pests of the hop plant have not yet been naturalized in New Zealand, this is one island where hops can thrive without pesticides. New Zealand grows hops for its own beer production, but also exports organic hops to the United States, Canada, Europe, and Asia.

History

When Captain James Cook first landed on the Australian shore in 1768, it was in a ship initially stocked with "four tonnes of beer." (This probably referred to a mash tun or large cask, not an actual ton as we know it today.) The ship docked a mere month after embarking on its journey because the beer was almost gone. Australia's great history of enthusiastic beer consumption was off to an excellent start. The same Captain Cook also brought beer to New Zealand in 1773, where it was similarly embraced . . . eventually. But first, these lands of the Southern Hemisphere had a long and exuberant flirtation with the demon rum.

From the time Europeans first began to settle in Australia into the early 1800s, rum was the most popular alcoholic drink in Australia—so popular, in fact, that public drunkenness became a huge problem. Even children, it was written, were drunk in the streets. Public officials considered rum a huge national problem, and so embarked on a campaign to convert this newly transplanted segment of the Australian population from rum to beer. Newspaper campaigns were waged. Brewers were given incentives. In 1796, Australia's first pub opened in Parramatta. In 1804, James Squire (honored today by Malt Shovel Brewery's James Squire Ale) first cultivated hops in Australia, and anyone who grew barley could trade it to the government for beer. The plan worked. Beer caught on fast, and by the mid-1800s, beer had displaced rum as the national beverage of choice. The Cascade Brewery opened in Hobart in 1822, Tooth's Brewery in Sydney in 1835, and suddenly brewing was a big industry.

Most of the beer produced at this time was ale: top-fermented, dark, and warm. The biggest challenge to brewing beer in Australia proved to be the climate. The heat and wild yeasts contaminated much of the local beer, which became notorious for its bad taste and hangover-inducing impurities. Australians called the lower-quality examples of their local beer colonial twang, and a handful of other colorful, derogatory names. Then, the lager revolution began. The more brewers learned, the better Australian ales became, but then lager came to the Land Down Under, and beer in Australia was never the same.

In the late 1800s, lager brewers began to move into Australia, with refrigeration equipment and new technology. Many of the smaller brewers were driven out of business. In 1901, the Federal Parliament passed the Beer and Excise Act, making home brewing illegal without an expensive license. This further reduced the smaller breweries and expanded the grasp of the larger breweries. In 1907, five large lager brewers joined together to become Carlton United Breweries Ltd. (CUB). This merger included Fosters, Victoria, Castlemaine, McCracken's, and Shamrock Breweries. In the 1970s, home brewing was made legal again without financial penalty, but lagers were firmly established in Australia, much to the delight of its population.

Current Trends

Today, Fosters is the most internationally known Australian beer, but the Fosters available in the United States is actually brewed in Canada. Steinlager is the most known New Zealand beer. In Australia, many people believe Victorias Bitter is superior to Fosters (it is actually very similar, but hoppier). While Victorias is very popular in Australia, it can be difficult to find in the United States. You might have better luck tracking it down in Canada.

In the northern regions of Queensland, Castlemaine XXXX Bitter has long been the local, passionate favorite, although it seems to be falling out of fashion in recent years. It is also very difficult if not impossible to find in the United States. Individual towns and regions also have their small brewers producing styles in the German and British traditions, but few of these make it beyond the country's borders. As with so many other countries, to really get a taste of what beer is like locally, you have to go there.

Characteristic Types of Beer

Small brewers produce many styles in Australia, but they aren't really Australian styles. Below are listed only those styles whose examples are available in the United States.

PALE LAGER

Color: STRAW 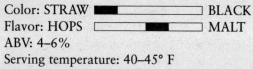 BLACK
Flavor: HOPS MALT
ABV: 4–6%
Serving temperature: 40–45° F

Australian pale lagers are straw to light gold with a light to medium body. Sometimes cane sugar is added. Low to moderate hops balanced by low malt and relatively low alcohol give these beers a thirst-quenching light body.

Australian pale lagers to try:

❏ *DB Export Gold (New Zealand)*
❏ *Fosters Lager (Australia, but what the United States gets is brewed in Canada)*
❏ *Fosters Special Bitter (Australia)*
❏ *King Lager (Australia)*
❏ *Lion Red Beer (New Zealand)*
❏ *Steinlager (New Zealand)*

FOREIGN STOUT/PORTER

Color: STRAW 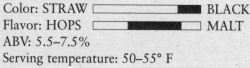 BLACK
Flavor: HOPS MALT
ABV: 5.5–7.5%
Serving temperature: 50–55° F

These classic dry stouts in the Irish tradition have a subtle initial toffee sweetness but finish with a coffee-flavored roasty bitterness. Australian examples are typically higher in alcohol than their Irish predecessors, with a dense mouthfeel and subtle suggestions of wood.

Australian foreign stouts/porters to try:

- ☐ *Carlton Sheaf Stout (Australia)*
- ☐ *Coopers Best Extra Stout (Australia)*
- ☐ *James Squire Porter (Australia)*
- ☐ *Old Australia Stout (Australia)*

GOLDEN/PALE ALE AND STRONG ALE

Color: STRAW ▭▬▭ BLACK
Flavor: HOPS ▭▬▭ MALT
ABV: 4–8%
Serving temperature 40–45° F

This English style is typically higher in alcohol when made in Australia than it is in England. Otherwise, though, both are gold to copper ales with medium to high hops and a fruity, malty flavor. The pale ales in Australia linger around 4.5-5% ABV, while the strong ales are nearer to 7.5%. Other ales, like Coopers Sparkling Ale (below, at 5.8%) fall somewhere in between the two.

Australian golden/pale ales and strong ales to try:

- ☐ *Coopers Original Pale Ale (Australia)*
- ☐ *Coopers Sparkling Ale (Australia)*
- ☐ *Coopers Vintage Ale (Australia)*

🍺 9 🍺
Asia

In Asia, as in much of the rest of the world, light, easy-drinking lager that complements warm climates and spicy foods is the most popular style of beer, but as beer culture continues to expand across the globe, small-scale craft brewers can be found all over Asia. Large conglomerates own many of the large and medium-sized breweries today in Asia, mostly producing pale and premium lagers. Large, populous countries like China and India import millions of tons of malt every year, just to keep up with the demand for beer.

As big as beer is in Asia today, it came to Asia relatively recently. Most Asian countries opened their first breweries around the turn of the twentieth century. In Japan, saké is the traditional alcoholic beverage, and for centuries, saké craft brewers have produced this rice-based fermented beverage. While saké is still a popular drink in Japan, beer has finally overtaken saké, to become the country's most popular alcoholic beverage.

History and Current Trends

Of all the Asian nations, Japan probably has the most evolved craft-brew culture. This is a recent development. Until the mid-1990s, a law forbidding small breweries kept the four giant beer producers in Japan from having any competition. When the law was repealed, Japan enjoyed an explosion of microbrew culture, called *ji-biru*, which means "local beer." This is a term borrowed from saké culture, and because small regional saké producers already have a devoted following, the term helped to nudge local brews into the comfort zone for a country previously accustomed to a mass-produced product. In fact, many small saké producers began brewing beer too, making both products in one facility.

IS SAKÉ BEER?

Saké is often called rice wine, but technically, it is a fermented beverage made from grain, making it much more akin to beer than wine. Saké can be sweet or dry and comes in five basic varieties, with subvarieties under each style. The styles are related to how processed the rice is and to the brewing techniques. Junmai saké is pure, with no added alcohol, and with rice that has been at least 30% polished. Honjozo is similar, but includes a small amount of added distilled alcohol. Daiginjo uses more highly polished rice, and may or may not have added distilled alcohol. Namazake refers to any type of unpasteurized saké. Some Japanese sakés available in the United States include the following:

☐ *Fu-Ki Saké*
☐ *Gekkeikan (Laurel Crown) Cap Ace Saké*
☐ *Hakutsuru (White Crane) Draft Saké*
☐ *Kikusakari (Blooming Chrysanthemum) Tarusaké*

While Kirin, Sapporo, Asahi, and Suntory still monopolize the light lager scene in Japan, small breweries all over Japan produce interesting interpretations of other styles, from witbiers to schwarzbiers, India pale ales to foreign stout. Most of these are not available for export, but you can probably find a few, mostly those produced by the larger of the craft brewers. Most of these will be lagers.

In Japan, there is an overriding idea that the only really quality beer in the world comes from Germany, and German techniques are superior. Japan's artful precision is a good fit for stringent German brewing techniques, and many Japanese craft brewers have their own versions of weizen (wheat beer), kölsch, bock, and other German styles. Some Japanese craft brewers also experiment with ale styles, including abbey styles, Scottish ales, pale ales, and seasonal beers. Dark beers labeled "stout" may actually be schwarzbiers brewed with lager yeast—as a true "stout" carries with it the implication of the UK-tradition ale brewing techniques.

JAPAN GOES BELGIAN

Belgian specialty beers have finally made their way to Tokyo, and there is at least one Belgian specialty bar currently operating in Tokyo, serving the international clientele. There have even been a few sighting of Japanese beer enthusiasts at the most recent Belgian Zythos festivals—a sure sign that the Japanese are ripe for broadening their brewing horizons.

In China circa 1903, Germans in Tsingtao set up a brewery, and today the brewery—now under Chinese ownership—is China's largest and most widely exported beer. It is the only Chinese beer reliably available in the United States. Tsingtao is a refreshing pale lager with higher hop content than most Chinese lagers. The brewery also makes a dark, rich, roasty version, Tsingtao black. beer, not generally available in the United States. China also has microbrewers producing interesting craft beer, some set up by German brewers, or in cooperation with (or in some cases imitation of) American brewers. These are rarely exported.

As is typical in hotter climates, India and southeast Asia aren't known for their beers, and produce primarily an international style lager good for thirst quenching. In the Philippines, San Miguel is the country's most famous brewery, producing darkish lagers. Tiger Beer is the favorite in Singapore, and the hoppy lager Singha is Thailand's most famous beer. Taj Mahal is a popular brand in India.

Characteristic Types of Beer

In general, the German influence looms large in Asia, and specialty beers are usually lagers, with some notable exceptions, particularly in Japan. Asian beers also tend to have evocative names that reflect each nation's identity and symbolism: Maharaja pale lager in India, Elegant Peak of Kuju in Japan, Black Tiger in Thailand, Yinpu Black Rice Beer and Red Dragon in China. Export versions of these may take a beating during their journey to the United States. Brewing conditions will not always allow these breweries to produce a Budweiserly-stable product. The combination of these two factors make for some pretty mediocre import products from Asia, which would taste much better in their homeland.

PALE/PREMIUM LAGER

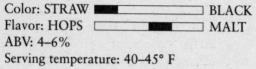

Color: STRAW ▆▆▆▆▆▆[＿＿＿＿＿] BLACK
Flavor: HOPS [＿＿＿＿▆▆▆＿] MALT
ABV: 4–6%
Serving temperature: 40–45° F

Pale and premium lagers in Asia are light, fizzy, hoppy, and generally similar to light lagers in other countries. Low to moderate in alcohol content, light in color, and thirst quenching, these beers are meant for general consumption, not the focused sipping of the connoisseur, but they are generally refreshing, crisp, clean, with a low flavor profile and no finish. Each country's variation of light lager tends to complement that country's cuisine.

Asian pale/premium lagers to try:

- ❑ *Asahi Super Dry (Japan)*
- ❑ *Beer Lao (Laos)*
- ❑ *Flying Horse Royal Lager Beer (India)*
- ❑ *Golden Eagle Lager (India)*
- ❑ *Hite Beer (South Korea)*
- ❑ *Hue Beer (Vietnam)*
- ❑ *Kingfisher Lager (India)*
- ❑ *Kirin Ichiban (Japan)*
- ❑ *Kirin Lager (Japan)*
- ❑ *Kirin Light (Japan)*
- ❑ *Lion Lager (Sri Lanka)*
- ❑ *Maharaja Premium Lager (India)*
- ❑ *San Miguel Premium Lager (Philippines)*
- ❑ *Sapporo Premium Draft (Japan)*

❑ *Sapporo Reserve (Japan)*
❑ *Singha (Thailand)*
❑ *Taiwan Beer (Taiwan)*
❑ *Taj Majal (India)*
❑ *Tiger Beer (Singapore)*
❑ *Tsingtao (Japan)*

SHOULDN'T BEER BE WET?

The Japanese invented a beer style called dry beer, based on a mild low-carb German adaptation of pilsner called Diat Pils. Dry beer became so popular in Japan that U.S. megabrewers have copied the style to capture the Japanese immigrant market on this side of the Pacific. Dry beer's distinguishing characteristic is to be almost tasteless (if you can call that a characteristic).

BELGIAN WITBIER
Color: STRAW ▰▰▱▱▱▱ BLACK
Flavor: HOPS ▱▱▱▰▱▱ MALT
ABV: 4.8–5.2%
Serving temperature: 45–50° F

Several Japanese brewers produce white ales in the Belgian style: pale, cloudy, and spiced with coriander, nutmeg, orange peel, and in the case of Hitachino—the one Japanese brewery whose white ale is available in the United States—orange juice. Their Celebration Ale also contains cinnamon and vanilla beans, and is really more a specialty wheat beer than a wit.

Asian witbiers to try:

❑ *Hitachino Nest New Year Celebration Ale (Japan)*
❑ *Hitachino Nest White Ale (Japan)*

HEFEWEIZEN

Color: STRAW ▬▬▬▬▭▭▭▭▭ BLACK
Flavor: HOPS ▭▭▭▭▭▬▭▭▭ MALT
ABV: 4.9–5.5%
Serving temperature: 45–50° F

Many Japanese brewers and a few in China (including German-based Paulaner's brewery in Shanghai) produce their own versions of German hefeweizen, with the characteristic banana and clove accents, and sometimes a mild citrus flavor. As with the witbier style, Hitachino Nest is the one brand typically available in the United States.

Asian hefeweizen to try:

❑ *Hitachino Nest Weizen (Japan)*

DORTMUNDER/HELLES

Color: STRAW ▭▬▬▭▭▭▭▭▭ BLACK
Flavor: HOPS ▭▭▭▬▬▭▭▭▭ MALT
ABV: 5–6%
Serving temperature: 45–50° F

This light golden lager, like its incarnation in Germany, is sweeter and fuller than pilsner, with a dry, mellow flavor. A few breweries in Japan and China make this style, but only Sapporo sends their version to the States.

Asian Dortmunder/helles to try:

❑ *Sapporo Yebisu (Japan)*

India Pale Ale

Color: STRAW ▭▬▭ BLACK
Flavor: HOPS ▭▬▭ MALT
ABV: 5–7.5%
Serving temperature: 50–55° F

No, India doesn't make any, but Japan does. Hitachino Nest bases their IPA on the original recipe for the pale ale sent to Japan from England in the nineteenth century. As is sometimes the custom in Japan, this ale ages in saké cedar casks.

Asian IPA to try:

❑ *Hitachino Nest Japanese Classic Ale (Japan)*

Traditional Ale

Traditional ales vary—as they do in any country—according to the ancient traditions of that country. In Japan, traditional ale may incorporate rice or saké into the brew. Traditional ales tend to be relatively high in alcohol in Asia, with unusual flavors. China makes its own ancient variation on barley wine in Lijiang, called Lijiang yinjiu, with 20% alcohol content, but it isn't exported.

Asian traditional ale to try:

❑ *Hitachino Nest Red Rice Ale (Japan)*

Dark Lager/Schwarzbier

Color: STRAW ▭▬ BLACK
Flavor: HOPS ▭▬▭ MALT
ABV: 4–5%
Serving temperature: 50–55° F

SAKÉ USA

Craft-brewed saké has become popular in the United States, as Japanese and American microbrewers consult with one another and share resources. Gekkeikan (Laurel Crown) Traditional Saké is brewed at Gekkeikan's North American saké brewery in Folsom, California. Other brands of traditional saké brewed in the United States by SakeOne Corporation in Forest Grove, Oregon, and Takara Saké USA, Inc., in Berkeley, California, include the following:

- [ ] *Momakawa (Peach River) Diamond Saké*
- [ ] *Momakawa (Peach River) Pearl Saké*
- [ ] *Momakawa (Peach River) Ruby Saké*
- [ ] *Moonstone Asian Pear Saké*
- [ ] *Moonstone Raspberry Saké*
- [ ] *Sho Chiku Bai (Pine Bamboo Plum) Classic Saké*
- [ ] *Sho Chiku Bai (Pine Bamboo Plum) Nigori Saké*
- [ ] *Sho Chiku Bai (Pine Bamboo Plum) Organic Nama Saké*
- [ ] *Sho Chiku Bai (Pine Bamboo Plum) Premium Ginjo Saké*

In China, when ordering a beer, you may be asked, "Yellow or black?" The answer "Black" may be likely to result in a dark lager. These vary in character from country to country but generally resemble the standard European-style dunkel or the lighter-bodied American-style dark lager. Their blackest, roastiest forms merge into schwarzbier. They are the dark alternative to the omnipresent pale lager.

Asian dark lagers/schwarzbiers to try:

- [ ] *Asahi Black (Japan)*
- [ ] *Sam Miguel Dark Lager (Philippines)*
- [ ] *Sapporo Black (Japan)*

SWEET STOUT

Color: STRAW ⬜▭▭▭▭▭◼️⬜ BLACK
Flavor: HOPS ⬜▭▭▭◼️▭⬜ MALT
ABV: 3–6%
Serving temperature: Minimum of 50° F

A few brewers in Japan and China brew this dark, rich, sweet style with relatively low alcohol, Asia's take on England's sweet stout (sometimes called milk stout or cream stout).

Asian sweet stout to try:

☐ *Hitachino Nest Lacto Sweet Stout (Japan)*

FOREIGN STOUT

Color: STRAW ⬜▭▭▭▭◼️⬜ BLACK
Flavor: HOPS ⬜▭▭◼️▭▭⬜ MALT
ABV: 5.5–7.5%
Serving temperature: 50–55° F

Dry, dark, and in the Irish style, foreign stout is typically higher in alcohol than in Ireland. Brewers in Sri Lanka make a few varieties, but only Lion exports theirs. Guinness also makes versions of its Foreign Extra Stout for various Asian countries, including a Malaysia/Singapore version brewed in Malaysia and a version brewed in Indonesia for Indonesia and China, but these are obviously made for foreign markets in the countries where the breweries reside and are not exported to the United States.

Asian foreign stout to try:

☐ *Lion Stout (Sri Lanka)*

🍺 __10__ 🍺
Africa and the Middle East

Thousands of years ago, the first brewers lived, farmed, and brewed in the Middle East and Africa. This ancient cradle of beer soon rocked in a northerly direction toward what is now Eastern Europe and Bavaria, where barley and wheat grew more readily than rice and millet, but beer has an ancient history in Africa and the Middle East. Today, as in so much of the world, pale thirst-quenching lagers dominate, but traditional ales as well as hearty, high-alcohol foreign stouts and the occasional riff on German styles like weizen and dunkel also play a small role. Not insignificantly, many countries in Africa and the Middle East are Muslim and don't make the production of alcoholic beverages a priority (or even a legality).

History and Current Trends

Even if beer originated in this region of the world, it has certainly blossomed more fully and dramatically elsewhere. However, Africa is a huge continent, and in sum, that means a lot of brewers. Some of the major international conglomerates have presences in the more populated African countries, and some smaller brewers produce traditional or traditionally influenced brews for local consumption. In general, however, African beers aren't easy to find in the United States.

In Morocco, pale lagers and pilsners dominate from the major breweries, and a beer named after Casablanca is probably Morrocco's most famous beer. Who wouldn't want to channel Humphrey Bogart as he swills this native brew? (Although didn't Bogey drink whiskey?)

In many African countries including Tunisia and Namibia, the German influence is strong and breweries produce weizens, dunkels, helles, Dortmunder/export, and other German styles. Hansa Urbock is one Namibian bock beer you might find in the United States, but most of Africa's German-style beers aren't available here.

Although a Muslim country, Egypt has produced a pale lager called Stella brewed by Al-Ahram, a Heineken-owned brewery (no relation to Belgium's Stella Artois). Along the Ivory Coast, Mamba is a popular premium lager that you can sometimes find in the United States. Kenya has brewed Tusker lager since 1922 and in Nigeria, Guinness owns four breweries, producing a Guinness stout unique in its recipe.

South Africa has the usual slew of light lagers but also a sweet milk stout, a selection of foreign stouts, bitters, pale ales, and pilsners, as well as a traditional Zulu beer made with sorghum.

While commercial brews are available in cities, in many small villages in Africa, people would rather brew their own. Africans have brewed their own beverages for centuries, based on the grains immediately available to them, and many of them still do this. Why pay good money for a bland pale lager when you can brew something truly native and interesting? Some of these brews use millet and sorghum in the mash, and may be flavored with fruits and vegetables immediately available.

Some of these traditional brews have caught the interest of commercial brewers. In Zambia, a traditional ale called chibuku is made with white maize, ground millet, and sorghum. The commercial version is called Chibuku Shake Shake and comes in a cardboard carton. You have to shake it up to mix up the sediment, and it is thick and sour and almost like a chunky yogurt drink, but as far as I know, you can't get it in the United States. Mongozo is an ale of Angolan descent brewed with African palm nuts and roasted malt. An Angolan refugee, Henrique Kabia, took his family's recipe for mongozo to the Netherlands. In 1999, he partnered with the Brouwerij Van Steenberge in Flanders (they also make Gulden Draak) to make Mongozo Palmnut, a 7% ABV ale traditionally served in a gourd. Mongozo means "cheers" in Swahili.

In general, many of the African beers from smaller brewers aren't exported to the United States. They would not survive the lengthy and erratic journey. These brewers don't have the stabilization techniques of larger-scale brewers, and the beers are specifically for local consumption. As with so many other countries less known for their beer, you really have to visit to get a true sense of the local beer.

As for the Middle East, even Muslim countries have the occasional brewery providing beer for tourists or export, but the Middle East simply isn't a land devoted to beer, at least not in the twenty-first century.

Characteristic Types of Beer

Most beer available in the United States from Africa is pale or premium lager, or an African take on pilsner. These, and a few exceptions, are listed below.

PALE/PREMIUM LAGERS
Color: STRAW ▰▱▱▱▱ BLACK
Flavor: HOPS ▱▱▰▱▱ MALT
ABV: 4–6%
Serving temperature: 40–45° F

Pale and premium lagers and the occasional pilsner are, as in other hot climates, straw colored to light gold with high carbonation and a balance of hops and malt.
African pale/premium lagers to try:

- ☐ *Carling Black Label (South Africa)*
- ☐ *Casablanca Beer (Morocco)*
- ☐ *Castle Lager (South Africa)*
- ☐ *Efes Pilsen (Turkey)*
- ☐ *Hansa Pilsner (South Africa)*
- ☐ *Mamba (Ivory Coast)*
- ☐ *Tusker Lager (Kenya)*
- ☐ *Windhoek Export (Namibia)*
- ☐ *Zambezi (Zimbabwe)*

FOREIGN EXTRA STOUT
Color: STRAW ▱▱▱▰▱ BLACK
Flavor: HOPS ▱▱▰▱▱ MALT
ABV: 5.5–7.5%
Serving temperature: 50–55° F

As in other countries far from the UK, foreign stout is dry, dark, and higher in alcohol than Ireland's dry stout version. A few African interpretations are available in the United States. In some countries, local Guinness Extra Stout breweries produce custom brews in accordance with that country's regulations, but not generally for export.

African foreign extra stouts to try:

❏ *Guinness Foreign Extra Stout (Nigeria)*
❏ *Hakim Stout (Ethiopia)*

HISTORICAL/INDIGENOUS BEERS

These usually home-brewed concoctions wouldn't normally be exported because they wouldn't survive the journey and are brewed only on a small scale, but they demonstrate the long tradition of brewing in Africa that has nothing to do with pale lager. As far as I know, you can't get any authentic examples of these in the United States, but if you ever do venture to Africa, be sure to give some of them a try.

🍺 11 🍺
Caribbean

While life in the Caribbean may conjure images of fruity rum drinks with umbrellas and big wedges of pineapple, people living in (and visiting) this part of the world love beer too. Whether pale lager or stout (the two most common styles in the Caribbean), Caribbean beers have a sweeter finish than similar styles in other parts of the world. Malt-flavored soda is a popular drink in the Caribbean too. Caribbean beer should also go well with Caribbean food, whether Jamaican jerk chicken or Cuban sandwiches.

History and Current Trends

Each Caribbean country has pale lager, and usually a favorite within that country that may or may not be available elsewhere: Banks Beer in Barbados is rarely seen in the United States, but Jamaica's Red Stripe is everywhere. The best-selling beer in the Bahamas, Kalik, is exported but not widely. Some brewers use local flavorings. The Carib brewery in Trinidad and Tobago makes a lager flavored with sorrel and another flavored with ginger.

Foreign stout is another popular style in the

Caribbean. Its history is similar to that of India pale ales, in that it was originally developed as a higher gravity (alcohol) style in order to export it to tropical climates occupied by the British Empire. Guinness brewed stout with a higher alcohol and hop content than its native version, so the stout would survive long journeys to steamy southern locales. Today Africa and the Caribbean are two of the world's biggest markets for Guinness Foreign Stout, and local brewers also compete with their own native versions, which can be sweet and fruity—what you might expect of a stout hailing from the islands.

Characteristic Types of Beer

Pale lager and foreign stout are the only Caribbean beers you can find in America, and even these can be elusive beyond the popular Red Stripe from Jamaica, Kalik from the Bahamas, and Presidente from the Dominican Republic.

PALE LAGER

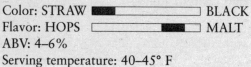

Color: STRAW ▆▆▆▆▆ BLACK
Flavor: HOPS ▆▆▆ MALT
ABV: 4–6%
Serving temperature: 40–45° F

Relatively malty with a sweet finish and sometimes brewed with corn in the mash, Caribbean lagers are made for the quick quaffing essential to the humid, hot climate.

Caribbean pale lagers to try:

❏ *Carib Lager (Trinidad and Tobago)*
❏ *Hatuey (Puerto Rico)*
❏ *Kalik (Bahamas)*
❏ *Medalla Light (Puerto Rico)*
❏ *Presidente (Dominican Republic)*
❏ *Red Stripe (Jamaica)*

FOREIGN STOUT

Color: STRAW ▭▬ BLACK
Flavor: HOPS ▭▬▭ MALT
ABV: 5.5–7.5%
Serving temperature: 50–55° F

Higher in alcohol than in the UK and sweeter than foreign stout in some countries like Australia, Caribbean foreign stout has a sweet, mouth-filling fruitiness. Guinness exports their foreign stout into most countries in the Caribbean.

Caribbean foreign stouts to try:

❏ *Dragon Stout (Jamaica)*
❏ *Jamaica Stout (Jamaica)*
❏ *Royal Extra Stout (Trinidad and Tobago)*
❏ *Stud Stout (Trinidad and Tobago)*

12

Mexico and Latin America

North Americans don't typically have much exposure to South American beer, but Mexico is a completely different phenomenon. Mexico's proximity to the United States, popularity as a tourist destination (dating from the 1960s), and large number of immigrants have contributed to a fondness for Mexican beer in the United States, and many brands are available here. The Mexican heat and spicy food make pale lagers as popular in Mexico as they are in other warm countries, but Mexico also produces many dark lagers in the American dark lager style, and many brewers produce amber to dark lagers inspired by—to varying degrees—Vienna lager.

Still, when most people think of Mexican beer, they think of those sweetish pale lagers that make ideal thirst quenchers and foils to spicy food. You're thinking of Corona, right? Mexican pale lagers are a light straw color, sparkling with carbonation, refreshing, and have a hint of corn flavor—or more than a hint. Corn is characteristic of many Latin American pale lagers. Corn as a component of the mash adds a creaminess and a distinct corn flavor connoisseurs can detect (and don't always care for), especially as the beers get closer to room temperature. Corn is a staple of the Latin American diet, so it makes sense that it would also figure in the beer.

The most popular pale lagers from Mexico have familiar names: Corona, Dos Equis, Tecate. In Mexico, two large companies own most of the breweries. Cervecería Modelo produces Corona, Mexico's number one selling beer and largest export. Corona was first brewed in 1925 in Mexico City, and today Grupo Modelo boasts that Corona is the fourth largest selling beer in the world. Corona sales pump a lot of money into the Mexican economy. This same company also owns the brewery that makes the full, rich, dark Negra Modelo and the light, increasingly popular Pacifico Clara.

The competing company is Cuauhtémoc-Monctezuma, a company that first opened a brewery in Mexico in 1890. They produce Tecate, Carta Blanca, Superior, Sol, Dos Equis, Indio, Bohemia, and Noche Buena, a dark, seasonal winter beer. Manuel Zambrano, a descendant of the family that founded this now-huge company, after living in the United States and learning from several brewers, moved back to Mexico and opened Mexico's largest microbrewery, Especialidades Cerveceras, in 1998. They produce the excellent Casta beers that are available in the United States. Casta makes ales instead of lagers, including some notable pale, golden, amber, wheat, and Belgian-style ales. Casta helped to set the stage for other craft brewers in Mexico.

But Mexico isn't the only Latin American country that brews beer. Many large international companies own breweries in the more populous areas of Latin America. For example, Heineken-controlled Quinsa

---

HANGOVER CURE

Too much Mexican beer? Try a steaming hot bowl of menudo, one of Mexico's favorite and traditional restorative cures for a hangover. This long-simmered, spicy soup contains tripe (cow stomach), calf's foot, lots of hot peppers, garlic, and meat broth. While your standard Mexican restaurant probably won't serve it, authentic Mexican restaurants in Mexican communities in the United States probably will.

---

controls companies producing beer in Argentina, Bolivia, Paraguay, Uruguay, and Chile. Molson-Coors-controlled Kaiser, in Brazil, makes the popular Xingu, a sweet, porterlike schwarzbier, and Palma Louca Pale Pils, a pilsner available in the United States, among many other beers not commonly exported. The colossal InBev has a Brazil location and makes, among other things, a pilsner called Sambadoro that is spottily available in the United States.

Grupo Empresarial Bavaria (GEB), the largest beverage company in Colombia and second largest brewery conglomerate in South America, has subsidiaries in Costa Rica, Panama, Colombia, Ecuador, Peru, Bolivia, and Chile. They produce many very popular brands in South America like Aguila, Cristal, Cusquena, and Atlas. They also claim Cristal is the most popular beer exported from South America to the United States.

This region of the world also hosts an increasing number of microbrewers and brewpubs. Some people believe that South America is in the infancy of its craft beer revolution, and that smaller breweries have a huge space in which to expand, especially in Argentina, Brazil, and Chile. Most of the products of these new microbrewers are not available in the United States—at least, not yet.

History

Modern beer (specifically lager) may be a relatively new phenomenon in Latin America, but fermented grain beverages have been around since the Aztecs. Mexico claims the first North American brewery, back in the days of the Spanish conquest. Deep in the heart of Latin America, archeologists have uncovered the oldest documented signs of a brewery.

The most ancient, traditional beerlike beverages in Latin America were probably made from native plants. They may have resembled pulque, a viscous drink made from maguey plant sap that is fermented with wild yeast and still widely available in Mexico, both as a hangover cure and as an aphrodisiac. Historically, Mexicans also made a kind of beer called tiswin, fermented from saguaro fruit boiled in water, then fermented in buried clay pots. Drinks from fermented corn, called chichi, also resembled beer. Many of these native brews played an important role in sacred ceremonies.

When the Spanish came to Mexico, they brought the technology for distilling liquor, and made the first mescal, but beer in Mexico today is really the result of more Germanic European influences. Austro-Hungary's brief occupation of Mexico in the 1860s brought lager technology (cold conditioning) to Mexico, and the thirst-quenching brew caught on quickly. The festive holiday Cinco de Mayo celebrates the Mexican ousting of European domination. Mexico may have rid itself of the presence of Archduke Maximillian of Austria, but didn't oust the beer influence (or the accordion music). Many brewers still produce Vienna-style amber lagers in Mexico.

Since the late 1990s, craft brewers have begun to produce some interesting alternatives to pale lager in Mexico, led by Casta. Whether mainstream pale lager or microbrewed ale, beer in Mexico tastes great with Mexican food. Elsewhere in Latin America, where megabrewers still control the scene, craft brewers are also gearing up to satisfy locals under the radar of the megaconglomerates, but where this will go remains to be seen.

Current Trends

As with other tropical climates, beer in Latin America doesn't travel well, so some of the tastiest examples aren't available in the United States. From this side of the border, Latin American beer can look fairly bland. A few breweries close to the Mexican-American border, like Cerveza Tijuana and the aforementioned Casta, are more successful at exporting their beers because the journey is a short one. Fortunately, Mexico is such a popular vacation spot that many Americans have the opportunity to try Mexican beer in Mexico, where it is freshest and best. South American beers are more elusive.

And what about that little wedge of lime in your Mexican beer bottle? Is that still trendy and cool? Corn is often served with lime in Mexican cuisine, and lime is often served with Mexican beer, but a new trend is brewing that rails against the use of lime. Beer connoisseurs turn up their noses in disgust at the wedge of lime nestled in the mouth of the bottle. Is lime a legitimate condiment for Mexican beer?

Both sides have their arguments. Some people say that lime cleared the dust from the dusty bottle. Others claim that lime is a nice foil for the pervasive flavor of corn so present in Mexican pale lager, and isn't lime also served with tequila? Why not beer? (Then again, not everyone agrees tequila should be served with lime, either.)

On the other side of the argument, rumors circulate that a marketer dreamed up the notion of lime in beer, and that such a combination certainly isn't authentic. Beer connoisseurs insist that lime simply masks the flavors of an inferior beer, and aren't we all better off drinking good beer that doesn't require a lime? The bottom line is simple. If you like your Mexican beer better with lime, use a lime. If you don't, don't use a lime. The jury is still out on this one, but don't be surprised if your friendly neighborhood beer connoisseur fails to be impressed by the lime in your Corona.

LIMEY BEER

If you like your Mexican beer with lime but still crave the authentic Mexican beer experience, look for limón agrios, the tiny Mexican lime available in Mexican grocery stores. One lime, cut in fourths, will service four bottles of Mexican beer. Cut a slice in the wedge and anchor it on the rim of your glass.

Characteristic Types of Beer

Not surprisingly, pale lagers dominate when considering what Latin American beers make it to the United States, but a few other examples, left over from Europe's influence on Latin America, are popular in Latin America and warrant a mention. When it comes to Mexico's lagers and ales, the styles more closely approximate American versions than their European counterparts. Traditional styles like pulque aren't really technically considered beer (they are fermented from plant sap, not grain), so they aren't included here.

PALE LAGER/PILSNER

Color: STRAW ▭▭▭▭▭▭ BLACK
Flavor: HOPS ▭▭▭▭▭▭ MALT
ABV: 4–6%
Serving temperature: 40–45° F

Pale lager in Latin America typically contains corn in the mash and has a characteristic sweetness, although some types taste hoppier than others. Pale to golden and refreshing, these lagers taste good very cold, as a foil to spicy food.

Latin American pale lagers to try:

❑ *Bahia (Guatemala)*
❑ *Bohemia (Mexico)*
❑ *Cabro (Guatemala)*
❑ *Carta Blanca (Mexico)*
❑ *Cerveza Cristal (Chile)*
❑ *Corona (Mexico)*
❑ *Cristal Lager (Peru)*
❑ *Cusquena (Peru)*
❑ *Dorado (Guatemala)*
❑ *Dos Equis XX Special Lager (Mexico)*
❑ *Famosa (Guatemala, where it is called Cerveza Gallo)*
❑ *Monte Carlo (Guatemala)*

- ☐ *Pacena (Bolivia)*
- ☐ *Pacifico (Mexico)*
- ☐ *Quilmes Cerveza (Argentina)*
- ☐ *Sambadoro (Brazil)*
- ☐ *Tecate (Mexico)*

PALE/GOLDEN ALE

Color: STRAW ▩▭▭▭▭ BLACK
Flavor: HOPS ▭▭▩▭ MALT
ABV: 4.5–5.5%
Serving temperature: 42–48° F

Closer to an American-style pale ale than anything out of England, pale and golden ale in Mexico isn't a common style, but more a function of the microbrewer revolution. Casta is the only version you can find in the United States.

Mexican pale/golden ales to try:

- ☐ *Casta Bruna (Mexico)*
- ☐ *Casta Dorada (Mexico)*

WHEAT BEER

Color: STRAW ▩▭▭▭▭ BLACK
Flavor: HOPS ▭▭▩▭ MALT
ABV: 4–6%
Serving temperature: 42–48° F

Casta makes an American-style wheat beer, which may prompt more microbrewers in Mexico to experiment with this style.

Mexican wheat beer to try:

- ☐ *Casta Triguera (Mexico)*

BELGIAN MEXICO?

Belgian ale certainly is not a typical style for Latin America, but Casta makes a bottle-conditioned and hand-crafted strong ale in the Belgian style. This unique offering from Casta may be their best beer yet. One can only hope they will inspire other brewers.

❑ *Casta Milenia (Mexico)*

AMBER LAGER/VIENNA LAGER/AMERICAN DARK LAGER
Color: STRAW ▭▬▭ BLACK
Flavor: HOPS ▭▬▭ MALT
ABV: 4–6%
Serving temperature: 48–54° F

Lagers in amber to deep bronze to dark brown are characteristic of Latin America, due to the German influence. Many countries have their lighter and darker lager options, and these can range from the amber, malty Vienna-influenced styles to those that more closely approximate the light-bodied American dark lager. A few are available in the United States.

Latin American amber and dark lagers to try:

❑ *Dos Equis XX Amber (Mexico)*
❑ *Negra Modelo (Mexico)*
❑ *Victoria (Mexico)*

Bock/Schwarzbier

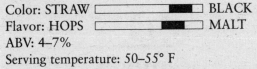

Color: STRAW [▬▬▬] BLACK
Flavor: HOPS [▬▬▬] MALT
ABV: 4–7%
Serving temperature: 50–55° F

Bock and schwarzbier styles in Latin America tend to be dark and sweet. Brazil's Xingu is widely available in the United States, and a good example of how Latin America likes to make schwarzbier—full of chocolate and coffee notes, but at the same time, with a surprisingly delicate body.

Latin American bocks/schwarzbiers to try:

☐ *Cusqueña Malta (Peru)*
☐ *Moza Bock (Guatemala)*
☐ *Xingu (Brazil)*

🍺 13 🍺
Canada

Our northern neighbors have brewed beer for centuries. Americans know mainstream names like Molson, Labatt, Moosehead, and Sleeman. Other brands based elsewhere have breweries in Canada, including Budweiser, Coors, Carlsberg, and Guinness. Many large breweries also brew what beer connoisseurs call stealth brands, more unusual styles manufactured in smaller batches that look and taste (more or less) like microbrewed beers, but that actually come from a large company like Labatt or Molson. Examples of Canadian stealth brands include Sleeman's Cream Ale, Rickard's Red Ale, and Alexander Keith's. (Stealth brands are a common phenomenon in the United States as well.)

Anyone who appreciates Belgian beer knows about Quebec-based Unibroue, Canada's world-famous Belgian-style brewery that produces Belgian ales of exceptional quality. Unibroue was recently purchased by Sleeman, striking fear into the hearts of its many fans worldwide, but so far Unibroue has maintained its integrity and continues to produce examples of abbey-style ales that will bring an appreciative tear to your eye.

Beyond Unibroue, microbrewing is mainly a local affair in Canada. Few microbrews are exported to the States, and the best ones are clustered in Quebec, with a few exceptions. Stay tuned, though. We may be hearing more from Canada on the international scene.

History

The Vikings loved their ale and wouldn't travel without it, so these Norse seafarers may have been the first to bring beer to Canada, but beer as we know it didn't take root in Canada until centuries later. The right ingredients simply didn't grow there. Today both barley and hops grow in Canada, but native people all over the North American continent made alcoholic beverages brewed from local ingredients long before agriculture was an established practice. In Canada, native Indians brewed their fermented beverages with spruce, an infusion they considered therapeutic. When explorer Jacques Cartier's crew developed a serious case of scurvy, spruce beer cured them.

In 1603, Samuel de Champlain colonized part of Canada for the French and recruited missionaries to join him in this new world. These Recollet missionaries already knew how to brew beer, and set up a brewery in 1620. Quebec's first official settler was an apothecary from Paris named Louis Hébert. In 1627, written records reveal that he (or his wife, Marie Rollet) were home brewers. In these early days, ale was the style. Quebec's brewing tradition remains special, small, and ale-oriented. Elsewhere in Canada, home brewing and making malt also served to sustain families and give farmers something to do during the colder months of the year.

The first commercial brewery in Canada opened in 1668 in Quebec City. In 1786, John Molson opened his brewery in Montreal. Alexander Keith founded his Nova Scotia brewery in 1829. The Brewing & Malting Company opened in 1840 in London, Ontario, spearheaded by Thomas Carling, and the Labatt brewery opened in London in 1847. Beer was a significant industry in Canada by the turn of the twentieth century.

While Prohibition, various world wars, and the depression hurt the brewing industry in Canada, it prospers today, with at least a handful of interesting breweries in every province except Prince Edward Island, which has just one small microbrewer. While large corporations have bought up many of Canada's smaller breweries, or microbreweries have merged to form medium-sized brewers, beer is alive and well in Canada. Canada's megabrewed crisp, refreshing pale lagers are a matter of national pride, and actually cost more than the country's microbrews in Canada. This is good news for connoisseurs who prefer the microbrewed craft beers to the products from the mainstream megabrewers.

Current Trends

The craft brew scene in Canada is gearing up, although none of the craft brewers in Canada have yet to approach the fame and prestige—not to mention global distribution—of Quebec-based Unibroue. This brewery creatively formulates new and original beers within the Belgian brewing tradition. Among those other breweries producing good microbrewed beer, most distribute only regionally within Canada, so you can't get most of these in the United States, let alone—in many cases—in other provinces. Unibroue, however, is widely available. Lucky us!

Some of the best artisanal brewers in Canada, from small to medium-sized and both breweries and brew-pubs, tend to cluster in Quebec and brew in the Belgian style. Unibroue is in Chambly. In Montreal, breweries include McAuslan, Les Brasseurs du Nord, and Brasseur RJ, the last formed from a 1998 merger of three Quebec microbreweries. Quebec's most popular brewpub is Brasserie Dieu du Ciel, and just over the border, in neighboring Ontario, Toronto is home to the acclaimed (and cleverly named) C'est What brewpub. These are just two of the interesting brewpubs, but the area has many.

BREWERY VERSUS BREWPUB

Some of the best beers in North America come from brew-eries, and some come from brewpubs. Brewpubs exist pri-marily for onsite draft consumption. They make beer to sell in their own pub. Breweries put more emphasis on bottle product, distributed via retailers.

In British Columbia, the microbrew revolution started in the mid-1980s. Granville Island in Vancouver began brewing in 1984, and Spinnaker's was Victoria's first brewpub, also opened in 1984. Both still operate today. Many small microbrews consolidated in the mid-to late 1990s, leading to more mainstream and arguably less interesting styles in British Columbia, but smaller brewers have recently began to emerge again. Vancou-ver has many interesting local, regional, and imported beers—arguably spurred on by the proximity of Seattle, one of the USA's most intense craft-brew cities. British

Columbia's environmentalism is reflected in their beer. Sorrento-based Crannog brews organic beer, and Pacific Western produced the first organic beer in Canada, called NatureLand Lager.

The Prairies, consisting of Alberta, Saskatechewan, and Manitoba, have the medium-sized Big Rock brewery and Great Western brewery. One notable brewpub is Bushwakker in Regina. In Ontario, Toronto is the center of the beer scene and home to micros Amsterdam, Brick, Steamwhistle, and Creemore Springs.

Atlantic Canada is home to the Moosehead brewery, and this beer, along with Labatt and Molson (contract-brewing their Canadian line at the Moosehead brewery) dominate this side of Canada. Nova Scotia has a few brewpubs and Labatt's Alexander Keith's brand is popular here. Newfoundland has just a few microbrewers.

BOP

In Canada, beer is more expensive than in the United States, largely due to high taxes. Approximately half the price of beer in Canada is tax. The microbrewed brands tend to be cheaper than the macros—the opposite of the United States. As a remedy, do-it-yourself breweries, called BOPs, or "brew on premises," allow you to "home brew" your own beer, using their equipment. This phenomenon is particularly popular in Vancouver. BOPs are, essentially, advanced home-brew rental labs. According to Canadian law, as long as you come in and add the yeast to the wort, the beer is your home brew. The operators take care of menial tasks like hucking spent grain as well as providing advanced knowledge in recipe formulation and the like, and you get your own "home-brewed" beer on the cheap. This takes some planning ahead, of course.

Characteristic Types of Beer

Megabrewed pale lagers and pilsners dominate the Canadian beer scene, with ales a mere blip on the radar. If not for Unibroue, Americans who haven't visited Canada would never know ales existed in the Great White North. While most of the examples of other styles listed below are from Unibroue, other breweries are making these styles too, particularly in Quebec. They just aren't available in the United States. Alexander Keith's and Rickard's are occasionally available, so are listed here, but aren't widely distributed. They are most likely found in those northern U.S. states bordering Canada.

In other chapters in this book, the beers listed are primarily those available in the United States. You'll find more Canada-only microbrews in this chapter's lists because Canada is so accessible. If you visit, you'll know what to look for. Just be sure to check the Internet for the latest brewery and brewpub information. Most breweries and brewpubs have websites, or check beer travel sites like *www.beertrips.com* or travel information on sites like *www.ratebeer.com* or *www.beeradvocate.com*, for the most current information before heading north.

PALE LAGER

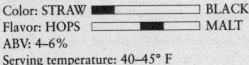

Color: STRAW ▆▬▬▬▬▬▬▬ BLACK
Flavor: HOPS ▭▭▭▭▬▬▭ MALT
ABV: 4–6%
Serving temperature: 40–45° F

Canada's megabrew style, mostly available from the big three in Canada: Labatt, Molson, and Moosehead

(Labatt owns Kokanee). Microbrewers like Steamwhistle and Creemore Springs make pale lagers (and pilsners), but don't export them to the United States. You can find Kokanee in the United States but mostly up close to the Canadian border.

These are fairly standard pale lagers and pilsners but they are worth a taste if you haven't tried them, just to get a taste of what so many Canadians value. See if you can tell a Molson from a Budweiser or a Labatt from a Miller Genuine Draft—if you like this style of beer.

Canadian pale lagers to try:

- ❏ *Kokanee (British Columbia)*
- ❏ *Labatt Blue (Ontario)*
- ❏ *Labatt Ice (Ontario)*
- ❏ *Molson Canadian (Quebec)*
- ❏ *Molson Dry (Quebec)*
- ❏ *Molson Golden (Quebec)*
- ❏ *Molson Ice (Quebec)*
- ❏ *Moosehead (Quebec)*

BELGIAN WITBIER

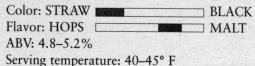

    Color: STRAW ▬▬▭▭▭▭ BLACK
    Flavor: HOPS ▭▭▭▬▭ MALT
    ABV: 4.8–5.2%
    Serving temperature: 40–45° F

Lots of Canadian microbrewers make their own interpretations of Belgian-style witbier, but all are cloudy, orange-gold, and brewed with wheat, with varying degrees of spicing. The only Belgian-style witbier from Canada reliably available in the United States comes from Unibroue.

Canadian Belgian witbier to try:

- ☐ *Charlevoix Dominus Vobiscum Blanche (Quebec)*
- ☐ *Dieu du Ciel Première Neige (Quebec)*
- ☐ *La Barberie Blanche aux Agrume (Quebec)*
- ☐ *L'Amère à Boire Blanche (Quebec)*
- ☐ *RJ Cheval Blanc Blanche de Blé (Quebec)*
- ☐ *Schoune Blanche de Quebec (Quebec)*
- ☐ *Unibroue Blanche de Chambly (Quebec)*

PALE ALE

Color: STRAW ▬▬▬⬜⬜⬜ BLACK
Flavor: HOPS ⬜⬜▬▬▬⬜ MALT
ABV: 4–8%
Serving temperature: Minimum of 43° F

The megabrewers in Canada also brew ales, but these aren't much different from their lagers in flavor and appearance. Microbreweries producing this style tend to have a more distinctive taste to their pale ales. As is typical for this style, Canadian pale ales are light straw to deep gold in color, lightly hopped and delicately malty. Good ones should have a malt/hop balance, with neither overwhelming. This listing includes pale ales, golden and blond ales, and India Pale Ales.

Canadian pale ales to try:

- ☐ *Alexander Keith's India Pale Ale (Nova Scotia)*
- ☐ *Alley Kat Full Moon Pale Ale (Alberta)*
- ☐ *Bièropholie Cascade (Quebec)*
- ☐ *Bièropholie Golding (Quebec)*
- ☐ *Bièropholie IPA (Quebec)*
- ☐ *Big Rock India Pale Ale (Alberta)*

- ❏ *Black Oak Pale Ale (Ontario)*
- ❏ *Boréale Blonde (Quebec)*
- ❏ *Boréale Dorée (Quebec)*
- ❏ *Brick Red Cap Ale (Ontario)*
- ❏ *Dieu du Ciel Paienne (Quebec)*
- ❏ *Dieu du Ciel Vaisseau des Songes (Quebec)*
- ❏ *Labatt 50 (Ontario)*
- ❏ *Le Chaudron Cobra (Quebec)*
- ❏ *Le Chaudron Coeur Dor (Quebec)*
- ❏ *McAuslan Griffon Extra Pale Ale (Quebec)*
- ❏ *Mill Street Tankhouse Ale (Ontario)*
- ❏ *Molson Export (Quebec)*
- ❏ *Niagara Falls Pale Ale (Ontario)*
- ❏ *Okanagan Extra Special Pale Ale (British Columbia)*
- ❏ *Rickards Pale (Quebec)*
- ❏ *St. Ambroise Pale Ale (Quebec)*
- ❏ *Scotch Irish Sgt. Majors IPA (Ontario)*
- ❏ *Sleeman Cream Ale (Ontario)*
- ❏ *Tree Hophead India Pale Ale (British Columbia)*

AMBER/DARK LAGER

Color: STRAW ▭▬▬▭ BLACK
Flavor: HOPS ▭▬▭ MALT
ABV: 4–6%
Serving temperature: 48–54° F

Amber to dark lagers are deep bronze to dark brown, and Canada has many choices, but again, most aren't exported, excepting Sleeman's versions. These tend to be malty and relatively light-bodied. In Canada, many versions are flavored with honey, or suggest honey in the flavor (and/or on the label).

Canadian amber/dark lagers to try:

- ☐ *Big Rock Honey Brown Lager (Alberta)*
- ☐ *Muskoka Honey Brown Lager (Ontario)*
- ☐ *Quidi Vidi Honey Brown (Newfoundland)*
- ☐ *Rickard's Honey Brown (Quebec)*
- ☐ *Sleeman Honey Brown Lager (Quebec)*
- ☐ *Sleeman Original Dark (Quebec)*
- ☐ *Steelback Tiverton Bear Honey Brown (Ontario)*

BELGIAN STRONG ALES

Just as with Belgian-style wits, microbrewers produce strong ales in Canada, primarily in Quebec, but only Unibroue exports theirs to the United States. These strong ales range in color and flavor from the pale gold and light body of a Belgian-style tripel to the deep, rich, brownish-garnet color and malty full-bodied flavor of a dubbel, but are all listed together here. For this reason, no color or flavor profile is listed above, but Belgian-style strong ales have one thing in common: they are all high in alcohol and warming. Expect an ABV of 7–12% for these strong ales, and serve them at a cellar temperature of around 50–55° F. Incidentally, La Fin du Monde, Maudite, and Trois Pistoles are among my very favorite beers of all time.

Canadian Belgian strong ales to try (all from Quebec):

❑ *Dieu du Ciel Rigor Mortis Double*
❑ *La Trip des Schoune*
❑ *RJ Le Cheval Blanc Blonde d'Achouffe*
❑ *RJ Le Cheval Blanc Brune d'Achouffe*
❑ *RJ Le Cheval Blanc Snoreau*
❑ *Schoune Rebs Ale*
❑ *Unibroue Don de Dieu*
❑ *Unibroue Eau Bénite*
❑ *Unibroue La Fin du Monde*
❑ *Unibroue La Terrible*
❑ *Unibroue Maudite*
❑ *Unibroue Trois Pistoles*

Stout

Color: STRAW ▭▬ BLACK
Flavor: HOPS ▭▬▭ MALT
ABV: 3–6%; imperial stout: 7–12%
Serving temperature: 50–55° F

The cold climate works well with a dark, rich stout, and Canada offers many. Most notably for the United States, much Guinness available in North America is actually brewed in Canada, not Ireland, even though the bottle or pub can of Guinness may give no clear indication of this fact. Other stouts available in Canada include smooth oatmeal stouts, sweet cream stouts, high-alcohol imperial stouts, and dry stouts in the Irish style. Most Canadian stouts are not exported to the United States. You might be able to find St. Ambroise Oatmeal Stout in the States.

Canadian stouts to try:

☐ *Amsterdam Irish Stout (Ontario)*
☐ *Bedondaine et Bedons Ronds Le Bedon (Quebec)*
☐ *Big River Dry Irish Stout (British Columbia)*
☐ *Big Rock McNallys Reserve (Alberta)*
☐ *Boréale Noire (Quebec)*
☐ *Charlevoix Vache Folle Milk Stout (Quebec)*
☐ *Dieu du Ciel Déesse Nocturne (Quebec)*
☐ *Granite Brewery Keefes Irish Stout (Nova Scotia)*
☐ *Granville Island Killarney Stout (British Columbia)*
☐ *Le Cheval Blanc Noire (Quebec)*
☐ *Le Sergent Recruteur Ténébreuse (Quebec)*
☐ *Réservoir Noire (Quebec)*
☐ *St. Ambroise Oatmeal Stout (Quebec)*
☐ *Yukon Midnight Sun Espresso Stout (Yukon)*

SPECIALTY BEERS

Whether smoked, fruited, spiced, or brewed with the ever-popular hemp, Canada produces some interesting specialty beers. Not surprisingly, the ones available in the United States come from Unibroue, but in Canada, brewers definitely like to experiment, producing hundreds of specialty brews with ingredients you might never before have considered beer-worthy, like garlic or cranberry. Just to get an idea of what Canada has to offer in this style, check out this following list, although, once again, you will probably be able to find only Unibroue's offerings in the States. Because the base of these specialty beers varies so much, I won't try to scale them.

Canadian specialty beers to try:

- ☐ *Amsterdam Framboise (raspberry flavored) (Ontario)*
- ☐ *Bear Brewing Black Bear Ale (blackberry flavored) (British Columbia)*
- ☐ *Biéropholie Calume (smoked) (Quebec)*
- ☐ *Bowen Island Hemp Cream Ale (British Columbia)*
- ☐ *Brew Brothers Antonios Original Garlic Pils (Alberta)*
- ☐ *C'est What (hemp ale) (Ontario)*
- ☐ *C'est What Chocolate Ale (Ontario)*
- ☐ *Church Key Cranberry Maple Wheat (Ontario)*
- ☐ *Church Key Ginger & Rosemary (Ontario)*
- ☐ *Church Key Holy Smoke (Ontario)*
- ☐ *Cool Beer Millennium Buzz (hemp lager) (Ontario)*
- ☐ *Dieu du Ciel Charbonnière (Quebec)*
- ☐ *Dieu du Ciel Fumisterie (hemp ale with smoked hazelnuts) (Quebec)*
- ☐ *Dieu du Ciel La Route des Épices (spiced with black pepper) (Quebec)*

- ❑ Garrison Jalapeno Ale (Nova Scotia)
- ❑ Granite Brewery Ringberry Ale (raspberry flavored) (Nova Scotia)
- ❑ Kawartha Lakes Raspberry Wheat (Ontario)
- ❑ Les Trois Mousquetaires La Folle du Roi (hemp red ale) (Quebec)
- ❑ McAuslan Apricot Wheat Ale (Quebec)
- ❑ Niagara Falls Apple Ale (Ontario)
- ❑ RJ Le Cheval Blanc Sainte-Paix aux Pommes (apple flavored) (Quebec)
- ❑ Unibroue Ephemere (each year, Unibroue does something different with this one—past examples include apple, cranberry, pear, and cassis) (Quebec)
- ❑ Unibroue Quelque Chose (cherry-flavored ale) (Quebec)
- ❑ Unibroue Raftman (smoked) (Quebec)

☗ 14 ☗
United States: Northeast

The northeast corner of the United States has a colorful colonial history, from the *Mayflower*'s landing at Plymouth because of a beer shortage on board, to maltster Samuel Adams's Boston legacy, to great brewpubs today from Portland, Maine, to Providence, Rhode Island. This region gets its character and reputation, probably most famously, from the Massachusetts-based Samuel Adams brewery, with its widely distributed and well-advertised ales and lagers. The Northeast has many interesting craft brewers, too.

The northeastern United States has always maintained a sense of history and a British influence, since the first colonists began to settle up and down the Eastern Seaboard, and this is still evident today, even in the beers of the region. Northeastern beer tends to be in the English style—lots of brown ales, IPAs, stouts, and porters. They also tend to have names that evoke Ye Olde England, or at least Charles Dickens (Thomas Hooker Old Marley Barleywine and Samuel Adams Old Fezziwig Ale come to mind).

There are some notable exceptions to the British bent of the Northeast, however, such as the Belgian-influenced Allagash brewery in Portland and the inter-

esting German-style offerings by some of the more di-
versified craft brewers like Smuttynose or the mid-sized
Samuel Adams, that make a wide range of British and
German styles.

History

Beer in America didn't originate in the northeastern
United States. Native Americans brewed beverages
made from corn and other substances long before the
Pilgrims arrived at Plymouth. But beer as we know it
today started on America's East Coast, and the Pilgrims
on the *Mayflower*, though not the first Brits to land on
American shores, landed where they did in the Northeast because of beer.

The *Mayflower*'s records indicate that the crew was
running low on provisions, and "especially beere," so
they dumped the Pilgrims off early and headed home,
presumably to their local pubs. The plan had been to
land at the mouth of the Hudson River; the Pilgrims—
left without any beer—had to settle for Plymouth.

Obviously, a group of thirsty Pilgrims without beer
had to begin brewing, and so began a long tradition of
beer in the northeastern United States. One of the most
famous names in beer during colonial times was Samuel
Adams himself, who was actually a maltster, not a
brewer, according to most beer historians. Adams came
from a line of maltsters who malted barley and sold it
to brewers. He was also a radical, a revolutionary, and
one of the foremost proponents of breaking from England. While the dominant beer styles in Massachusetts
(home to the Samuel Adams brewery) imitate those
from the UK, they also imitate those from Germany,

ALE-LAGER MULTITASKING

One unique quality of American microbrewers is the tendency to make both ale and lager. In other parts of the world, brewers—indeed, entire countries—tend to specialize in one or the other. Making both out of a single brewery certainly happens in Europe, but to do it as much as the U.S. microbrewers do it is a unique characteristic of craft beer in America. This practice is unusual because of the differences in both raw materials and process variables required for brewing ale versus lager. It's difficult to set up a do-it-all brewery. Then again, Americans love to pioneer, and can't resist a challenge. Whether this kind of multitasking makes beer more interesting or makes American brewers "jacks of all trades, masters of none" is a matter of opinion.

and put their own, all-American twist on those borrowed styles, making them into something entirely new. Even though the Samuel Adams brewery itself can hardly be called a microbrewery or craft brewery, its beers are distinct from the beers of Britain as well as (for the most part) the mainstream pale lagers of the United States.

For many years after brewing began in America, through wars both national and international, through economic depressions and the tidal wave of pale lagers that enveloped the brewing scene in the mid-1840s, through the rise of midwestern brewers as the megabrewers of the nation, through the devastating effects of Prohibition, northeastern brewers continued to brew beer (on and off) in their own quiet way.

Not until the microbrew revolution of the late 1980s and early 1990s, however, did the beer of the northeastern United States begin to take on a character all its own. In an interesting reversal/replaying of history, brewing was reinvented in America, but this time, it all started on the West Coast and worked east, rather than the other way around, as it had three centuries earlier. Reintroduced to the old ale styles and variations on the pale lager theme, Americans began to appreciate beer anew.

In the twenty-first century, the rate of new brewery inception has slowed somewhat, but northeastern brewers continue to produce interesting, experimental, or historical ales and lagers in their microbreweries and brewpubs, with local and regional pride.

Current Trends

For the purposes of this book, the Northeast includes Maine, New Hampshire, Vermont, Massachusetts, Connecticut, and Rhode Island. Each state has its own breweries and brewpubs of note, mostly originating in the late 1980s and early 1990s, with the craft-brew explosion. The following state-by-state look at some of the most interesting breweries and brewpubs in each major beer-producing region reveals the Northeast's unique character. That includes a love of ales, of the rarer German styles, of colonial history, and of local character. Northeastern brewers often choose brewery and beer names that suggest the local climate, ships at sea, storms in the Atlantic, and cozy British pubs.

Try to find some of these for your own beer-tasting experience. Some are widely distributed, others may require a visit to the Northeast.

MAINE

In Portland, Maine, the Allagash brewery is one of the few breweries in the United States to specialize in Belgian-style beer only. Shipyard is another Portland-based brewery, and Maine's largest. They specialize in handcrafted English-style ales and seasonal brews, and have a wide distribution. D. L. Geary brewing company also specializes in English-style and seasonal ales, but on a smaller scale. Brewer David Geary trained in England and Scotland before opening his own microbrewery, and began brewing in 1986.

Also in Portland, Casco Bay Brewing Company makes ales and lagers, and they also produce beers with the Carrabassett prefix (they used to make Katahdin beers too, but discontinued this line). Gritty McDuffs is a brewpub with locations in Portland and Freeport. They also specialize in English-style ales and seasonals.

Sea Dog Brewing Company operates two brewpubs, one in Camden and one in Bangor. They make a variety of ales and lagers for consumption in their brewpubs. Their Blue Paw Wheat Ale incorporates Maine wild blueberries.

The Atlantic Brewing Company in Bar Harbor has a brewery, tavern, and beer garden, and they also specialize in English-style ales. The tiny Bar Harbor Brewing Company in Bar Harbor produces an award-winning dry stout and makes just 260 barrels of beer each year. They call themselves a cottage brewery.

NEW HAMPSHIRE

The biggest microbrewery name in New Hampshire is Smuttynose, craft brewing since 1994 in Portsmouth. Don't miss these great, award-winning beers, if you can get them—distributed in the Northeast and Mid-Atlantic. Also look for the Nutfield Brewery Company, craft-brewery British style ales in Derry.

VERMONT

In Vermont, Magic Hat brewery, in South Burlington, produces fanciful, quirky interpretations of English ales. They also have a killer website (*www.magichat.net*). Also in Burlington, three great brewpubs are within walking distance: Three Needs Brewery and Taproom, American Flatbread/Zero Gravity, and Vermont Pub and Brewery. Vermont is also home to Green Mountain Cidery in Middlebury. They make the popular Wood-chuck hard cider, including many flavor variations like Granny Smith, Pear, and Raspberry. Also in Middle-bury, Otter Creek Brewing Company makes a line of craft beers and also the Wolaver line of certified organic ales. In Bridgewater Corners, Long Trail Brewery makes a small group of ales available in the Northeast and several distinctive beers in the German altbier style. McNeill's in Brattleboro makes a wide selection of ales and lagers for sale in their own brewpub. Other notable brewpubs: Shed Restaurant and Brewery in Stowe and The Alchemist in Waterbury.

MASSACHUSETTS

Massachusetts is Sam Adams territory, and the many beers available from the Samuel Adams brewery, owned by the Boston Beer Company, are known to beer drinkers in every corner of the United States. The Boston Beer Company is a medium-sized company and claims that its beers have won more awards than those of any other company in history. Samuel Adams has a wide range of styles in both the British and German tradition. Its best-selling lager is a premium pale lager—not surprisingly, as it is designed to appeal to the masses that prefer pale lager. It may be a step up from the pale lagers produced by the three megaconglomerates in the United States, but is standard pale lager nevertheless. Try some of Samuel Adams's other styles for a different taste experience.

But Samuel Adams isn't the only notable beer in Massachusetts, even if it is the most famous. Look for beer from the Harpoon Brewery in Boston (they also have a Windsor, Vermont, location). They make both ales and lagers in traditional British and German styles. They even have a Belgian-style tripel. Cisco Brewers Inc. in Nantucket has a brewery, vineyard, and distillery. They make just a few ales all year, and a few more seasonal offerings. Mercury Brewing, formerly the Ipswich Brewing Company, produces distinctive ales and lagers, including Ispwich Ale and the Stone Cat ales.

CONNECTICUT

Most of the beer action in Connecticut centers around the city of Hartford. The Troutbook Brewing Company in Hartford produces Thomas Hooker ales and lagers, available in Connecticut and Rhode Island. Also in Hartford, City Steam Brewing Company brews beer, serves food, and has a comedy club. The Old Burnside Brewing Company in East Hartford brews Scottish-style ales. The Willimantic Brewing Company in Willimantic, housed in a former post office building, names all its brews with post-office-themed names like Mail Carrier Maibock and Postage Porter.

RHODE ISLAND

Coastal Extreme Brewing Company in Middleton makes the line of Newport Storm ales, plus one Oktoberfest lager. Their beers all have storm-themed names: Hurricane Amber Ale and Maesltrom IPA, for example. In Providence, the Trinity brewpub brews its own award-winning ales and lagers.

Characteristic Types of Beer

American microbrewers make just about every type of beer, including pale lager, which some see as a way to draw more people to their brands. The Northeast's mid-sized Samuel Adams makes a premium lager (its best-selling Boston Lager), but craft brewers in the area otherwise largely ignore this style for the less common British and German styles (why compete with the big guys if you don't have to?). The styles listed below are those with at least two representative examples from northeastern brewers.

HEFEWEIZEN

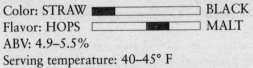

Color: STRAW ▄▬▬▬▬▬▬ BLACK
Flavor: HOPS ▭▬▬▬▬ MALT
ABV: 4.9–5.5%
Serving temperature: 40–45° F

In the old German style, this is a cloudy white ale that tastes of wheat, yeast, and fruit. American hefeweizens tend to be more citrusy than their German counterparts, but both share spicy notes of nutmeg and cloves. Drink this with the yeast sediment. It's good for you.

Northeastern hefeweizens to try:

❑ *Harpoon UFO Hefeweizen (Massachusetts)*
❑ *Samuel Adams Weissbier (Massachusetts)*
❑ *Smuttynose Weizenheimer (New Hampshire)*

PALE ALES, BITTERS, ESBS, MILDS

Color: STRAW ▉▉▉▉▉▭▭▭▭▭ BLACK
Flavor: HOPS ▭▭▭▉▉▭▭▭▭▭ MALT
ABV: 3–5%
Serving temperature: 45–50° F

If it's an ale and it's pale, you'll find it listed below, despite the fact that many people distinguish between English pale ales, American pale ales, Bitters, ESBs, and milds with slightly different qualities. (IPAs are listed separately.) Gold to light bronze and easy to drink with noticeable to potentially outrageous hops balanced with a substantial blush of maltiness, this range of pale ale styles is low in alcohol and perfect for sharing with friends over the course of an evening— "session beers," as the Brits would say. In general, USA styles will be more aggressively hopped than those from the UK.

Northeastern pale ales (and their relatives) to try:

❑ *Casco Bay Carrabassett Pale Ale (Maine)*
❑ *Cisco Bailey's Ale (Massachusetts)*
❑ *Cisco Whales Tail Pale Ale (Massachusetts)*
❑ *City Steam Ale (Connecticut)*
❑ *Geary's Pale Ale (Maine)*
❑ *Gritty McDuff's Best Bitter (Maine)*
❑ *Gritty McDuff's Original Pub Style Pale Ale (Maine)*
❑ *Ipswich Original Ale (Massachusetts)*
❑ *Magic Hat Fat Angel (Vermont)*

❑ *McNeill's Extra Special Bitter (Vermont)*
❑ *Nutfield Old Man Ale (New Hampshire)*
❑ *Otter Creek Pale Ale (Vermont)*
❑ *Ringwood Old Thumper (Maine)*
❑ *Shipyard Export Ale (Maine)*
❑ *Smuttynose Shoals Pale Ale (New Hampshire)*
❑ *Thomas Hooker American Pale Ale (Connecticut)*
❑ *Trinity Point Break Pale Ale (Rhode Island)*
❑ *Willimantic Rail Mail Rye (Connecticut)*
❑ *Wolaver's Pale Ale (Vermont)*

SESSION BEER

If you start educating yourself about beer and reading beer books and beer websites, you will probably run into the term "session beer." This simply means a relatively low alcohol, easy-to-drink beer that you can drink several of in a row, as opposed to a higher alcohol or more intensely flavored beer that is meant more as an aperitif or for after-dinner sipping. Sessions beers are the sociable beers made for talkative evenings at the pub or—in America, at least—the aptly named Happy Hour.

INDIA PALE ALE

Color: STRAW ▭ BLACK
Flavor: HOPS ▭ MALT
ABV: 5–7.5%
Serving temperature: Minimum of 45° F

IPA has been a familiar style in the United States since colonization. Today many microbrewers imitate this style. American microbrewers often attempt to imitate their vision of the traditional IPA, but that vision differs from brewer to brewer and region to region. The best way to understand this style is to try as many versions as you can.

One variation on the IPA that is uniquely American is the imperial or double IPA. Americans like to do everything big, with loud, obvious flavors. This is even more so on the West Coast, so "big" on the East Coast may be slightly more understated than "big" on the West Coast when it comes to beer. New Hampshire-based Smuttynose's Big A IPA—with its 9% alcohol—is pretty darned big. See if you can distinguish Northeastern U.S. IPAs from Northwestern U.S. IPAs.

Northeastern IPAs to try:

❑ *Harpoon IPA (Massachusetts)*
❑ *Magic Hat Blind Faith (Vermont)*
❑ *Newport Storm Maelstrom IPA (Rhode Island)*
❑ *Samuel Adams India Pale Ale (Massachusetts)*
❑ *Sea Dog Old East India Pale Ale (Maine)*
❑ *Shipyard Fuggles IPA (Maine)*
❑ *Smuttynose Big A IPA (New Hampshire)*
❑ *Smuttynose IPA (New Hampshire)*
❑ *Trinity RI IPA (Rhode Island)*
❑ *Wolaver's India Pale Ale (certified organic, Vermont)*

AMBER ALE

Color: STRAW ▭ BLACK
Flavor: HOPS ▭ MALT
ABV: 4.3–5.0%
Serving temperature: Minimum of 45° F

These copper-colored, malty ales inspired by beers ranging from the UK copper ales through the altbier of Düsseldorf are balanced and smooth, with a maltier taste than a pale ale but less sweetness than a typical German dunkel. As is typical for American microbrewers, this category contains many examples of brewers taking grand liberties with the classic ale/lager distinction and fiddling with new ways of blurring the line between those categories.

Northeastern amber ales to try:

- ☐ *Harpoon Ale (Massachusetts)*
- ☐ *Harpoon Hibernian Ale (Massachusetts)*
- ☐ *Longtrail Double Bag (Vermont)*
- ☐ *Newport Storm Hurricane Amber Ale (Rhode Island)*
- ☐ *Ottercreek Copper Ale (Vermont)*
- ☐ *Samuel Adams Boston Ale (Massachusetts)*

SCOTTISH-STYLE ALE

Color: STRAW ▭▬▭ BLACK
Flavor: HOPS ▭▬▭ MALT
ABV: 2.8–7%
Serving temperature: Minimum of 45° F

Scottish-style ales can be fruity and sweet or rich, dark, and peaty. Typically, American Scottish-style ales have strong flavors and can be too earthy for some tastes. Smuttynose brews their Scotch ale with candy sugar, upping the alcohol content and the sweetness. Those called Scotch ale are of the darker, sweeter, stronger, higher-alcohol variety.

Northeastern Scottish-style ales to try:

- ☐ *Long Trail Hibernator (Vermont)*
- ☐ *Olde Burnside Ten Penny Ale (Connecticut)*
- ☐ *Samuel Adams Scotch Ale (Massachusetts)*
- ☐ *Smuttynose Scotch Ale (New Hampshire)*

IRISH/RED ALE

Color: STRAW 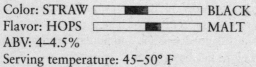 BLACK
Flavor: HOPS MALT
ABV: 4–4.5%
Serving temperature: 45–50° F

Reddish-bronze with a malt/hop balance and relatively low alcohol, Irish ales are easy-drinking session beers.

Northeastern Irish-style ales to try:

☐ *Casco Bay Riptide Red Ale (Maine)*
☐ *Harpoon Hibernian Ale (Massachusetts)*
☐ *Newport Storm Thunderhead Irish Red (Rhode Island)*
☐ *Nutfield Auburn Ale (New Hampshire)*
☐ *Thomas Hooker Irish Style Red Ale (Connecticut)*

A BIT OF BELGIUM

The Belgian style isn't characteristic of craft brewers in the Northeast, except for a few exceptions, most notably the Allagash brewery in Portland, Maine. This brewery specializes in Belgian-style ales. Allagash not only brews exclusively in the Belgian style, but also barrel ages some of their beers in wooden bourbon barrels from the Jim Beam distillery, giving their Allagash Curieux, in particular, a compelling complexity. This tripel's second fermentation in the barrel lasts eight weeks. This and other Belgian-style offerings from Allagash include the following:

☐ *Allagash Abbey Tripel Reserve*
☐ *Allagash Bruin (a Flemish sour)*
☐ *Allagash Curieux (a Belgian strong ale with 9.5% ABV)*

❑ *Allagash Double Ale (an abbey dubbel)*
❑ *Allagash Dubbel Reserve*
❑ *Allagash Four (an abbey quadruple with 10% ABV)*
❑ *Allagash Grand Cru (a Belgian strong ale with 7.2% ABV)*
❑ *Allagash Summer Ale*
❑ *Allagash White (a Belgian witbier)*

OKTOBERFEST-MÄRZEN

Color: STRAW ▭ BLACK
Flavor: HOPS ▭ MALT
ABV: 4.5–5%
Serving temperature: 45–50° F

Like its German counterpart, these American Oktoberfest-Märzens are medium-weight lagers ranging from deep golden to a rich bronze with just a suggestion of hoppiness but with lightly caramelized or bready malt dominating the flavor. Many are quite malty.

Northeastern Oktoberfest-Märzens to try:

❑ *Harpoon Oktoberfest (Massachusetts)*
❑ *Newport Storm Regenschauer Oktoberfest (Rhode Island)*
❑ *Samuel Adams Oktoberfest (Massachusetts)*
❑ *Smuttynose Oktoberfest/Märzen (New Hampshire)*

BROWN ALE

Color: STRAW ▭ BLACK
Flavor: HOPS ▭ MALT
ABV: 4–5.5%
Serving temperature: 45–50° F

Bronze to toasty brown, these ales are a medium-weight, malty beer with fruitiness, nuttiness, and a low alcohol content. Brown ales from the Northeast tend to be pleasantly similar to British brown ales, but may have a little more of a forwardly malty taste. Like many foreign styles that Americans imitate, the American versions tend to be more exaggerated, but this is yet another easy-drinking session-style ale.

Northeastern brown ales to try:

❏ *Atlantic Bar Harbor Real Ale (Maine)*
❏ *Ipswich Dark Ale (Massachusetts)*
❏ *Shipyard Brown Ale (Maine)*
❏ *Smuttynose Old Brown Dog (New Hampshire)*
❏ *Wolaver's Brown Ale (certified organic, Vermont)*

PORTER

Color: STRAW ▭▭▬▭ BLACK
Flavor: HOPS ▭▭▬▭ MALT
ABV: 4.5–6.5% (darker, robust porters or so-called imperial porters are on the higher side)
Serving temperature: 50–55° F

Deep, dark, and full-bodied with reddish jewel tones behind the dark brown to ebony color and flavors of espresso, chocolate, and roasted grain Porters are a popular style in the Northeast, and many craft brewers make their own versions in varying strengths and often with clever names (like Atlantic Brewing's Coal Porter). Technically, Thomas Hooker Imperial Porter is actually a lager and more akin to a Baltic porter, with its high ABV of 8%, but I've included it here anyway, for simplicity.

Northeastern porters to try:

- ☐ *Atlantic Brewing Coal Porter (Maine)*
- ☐ *Geary's London Porter (Maine)*
- ☐ *Magic Hat Ravell (Vermont)*
- ☐ *Newport Storm Blizzard Porter (Rhode Island)*
- ☐ *Otter Creek Stovepipe Porter (Vermont)*
- ☐ *Samuel Adams Holiday Porter (Massachusetts)*
- ☐ *Sea Dog River Driver Hazelnut Porter (Maine)*
- ☐ *Smuttynose Robust Porter (New Hampshire)*
- ☐ *Thomas Hooker Imperial Porter (Connecticut)*

STOUTS

Color: STRAW ▭▬ BLACK
Flavor: HOPS ▭▬▭ MALT
ABV: 3–6%; imperial or "extra" stout and strong ale: 6.5–12%
Serving temperature: Minimum of 50° F

As in the UK, the term "stout" encompasses several styles: dry, Irish-style stout (in the Guinness family), sweet stout brewed with lactose (sometimes called milk stout or cream stout) or with oatmeal in the grist schedule (adding a silky smoothness), and imperial stout or "extra stout," with an above-average alcohol content. In general, stout is dark, rich, and similar to porter (consider them two abutting regions on the dark ale spectrum), with roasted coffee and bittersweet chocolate flavors. American microbrewers make hundreds of stouts, sometimes almost indistinguishable from those in the UK, sometimes with some pretty funky variations, such as the addition of real coffee, chocolate, hazelnuts, or whatever might strike the creative brewer's fancy.

Northeastern stouts to try:

- ❑ *Bar Harbor Cadillac Mountain Stout (Maine)*
- ❑ *Cisco Captain Swain's Extra Stout (Massachusetts)*
- ❑ *Gritty McDuff's Black Fly Stout (Maine)*
- ❑ *Ipswich Oatmeal Stout (Massachusetts)*
- ❑ *Magic Hat Heart of Darkness Stout (an oatmeal stout, Vermont)*
- ❑ *McNeill's Imperial Stout (Vermont)*
- ❑ *Samuel Adams Cream Stout (Massachusetts)*
- ❑ *Shipyard Blue Fin Stout (Maine)*
- ❑ *Smuttynose Imperial Stout (New Hampshire)*
- ❑ *Trinity Russian Imperial Stout (Rhode Island)*
- ❑ *Wolaver's Oatmeal Stout (certified organic, Vermont)*
- ❑ *Z Street Mocha Java Stout (Massachusetts)*

STRONG ALE

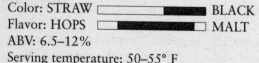

Color: STRAW ▭▬▬ BLACK
Flavor: HOPS ▭▬▭ MALT
ABV: 6.5–12%
Serving temperature: 50–55° F

In general, this category includes the English strong ales and English old ales, although those listed in this chapter are in the English old ale style. This latter style often has suggestions of port, sherry, or whiskey. Don't forget to let these warm up a bit—they will taste much better closer to cellar temperature than if you drink them straight out of the fridge.

Northeastern strong ales to try:

- ❑ *Casco Bay Old Port Ale (Maine)*
- ❑ *City Steam Dexter Gordon Old School Strong Ale (Connecticut)*

☐ *Geary's Hampshire Special Ale (Maine)*
☐ *McNeill's Duck's Breath Ale (Vermont)*
☐ *McNeill's Old Ringworm (Vermont)*
☐ *Shipyard Prelude Ale (Maine)*

DOPPELBOCK/MAIBOCK

Color: STRAW ▭ BLACK
Flavor: HOPS ▭ MALT
ABV: 7–10%
Serving temperature: Minimum of 50° F

A potent lager in the bock style, Doppelbock (which means "double bock") is usually (but not always) dark in color and is (always) high in alcohol, usually over 7%. Maibocks may be lighter in color, but Smuttynose's version still boasts a respectable 7.7% ABV, and watch out for their Smuttonator, at a potent 9.6% alcohol! Like their German counterparts, American microbrewed doppelbocks often have names that end in "-ator."

Northeastern doppelbocks (and one Maibock) to try:

☐ *Samuel Adams Doppelbock (Massachusetts)*
☐ *Smuttynose Maibock (New Hampshire)*
☐ *Smuttynose Smuttonator (New Hampshire)*
☐ *Thomas Hooker Liberator Doppelbock (Connecticut)*
☐ *Willimantic Mail Carrier Maibock (Connecticut)*

BARLEY WINE

Color: STRAW ▭ BLACK
Flavor: HOPS ▭ MALT
ABV: 7–12%
Serving temperature: 50–55° F

This high-gravity style is just right for the cold, icy northeastern winters. Sweet, rich, and complex, these warmers are usually amber to medium brown with suggestions of rich toffee and undertones of port or sherry (this can be accentuated via cask conditioning). You can cellar these for a few years to help them mellow and develop even more complexity. The following northeastern microbrewers obviously enjoyed choosing creative, British-inspired names for their barley wines. Samuel Adams's version might surprise you.

Northeastern barley wines to try:

❑ *Cisco Baggywrinkle Barleywine (Massachusetts)*
❑ *Harpoon Triticus (Massachusetts)*
❑ *Magic Hat Chaotic Chemistry (Vermont)*
❑ *Samuel Adams Utopias (Massachusetts)*
❑ *Smuttynose Barleywine Style Ale (New Hampshire)*
❑ *Smuttynose Wheat Wine (actually a wheat wine, not a barley wine, but the styles are similar, New Hampshire)*
❑ *Stone Cat Barleywine (Massachusetts)*
❑ *Thomas Hooker Old Marley Barleywine (Connecticut)*

SEASONAL AND SPECIALTY BEERS

The northeasterners love seasonal beers for any occasion. Because wild blueberries grow in Maine, many local brews also incorporate them, especially into their wheat beers and summer ales. Winter seasonals are typically higher in alcohol, for those chilly winter evenings when the nor'easters are blowing in. Each is different (too different for a scale), so if you enjoy specialty beers, take the opportunity to indulge in the unique experience of each brewer's vision.

Northeastern seasonal and specialty beers to try:

- ❏ *Atlantic Bar Harbor Blueberry Ale (Maine)*
- ❏ *Atlantic Mount Desert Island Ginger (a ginger-flavored wheat beer, Maine)*
- ❏ *Geary's Autumn Ale (Maine)*
- ❏ *Geary's Summer Ale (a kölsch, Maine)*
- ❏ *Geary's Winter Ale (an IPA, Maine)*
- ❏ *Harpoon Winter Warmer (Massachusetts)*
- ❏ *Long Trail Blackberry Wheat (Vermont)*
- ❏ *Magic Hat Jinx (a smoked beer, Vermont)*
- ❏ *Magic Hat #9 (a fruit beer, but Magic Hat won't tell you what fruit they use, but it tastes like apricot, Vermont)*
- ❏ *Samuel Adams Cherry Wheat (Massachusetts)*
- ❏ *Samuel Adams Chocolate Bock (Massachusetts)*
- ❏ *Samuel Adams Cranberry Lambic (Massachusetts)*
- ❏ *Samuel Adams Old Fezziwig Ale (Massachusetts)*
- ❏ *Samuel Adams Spring Ale (Massachusetts)*
- ❏ *Samuel Adams Summer Ale (Massachusetts)*
- ❏ *Samuel Adams Winter Lager (a wheat bock, Massachusetts)*
- ❏ *Sea Dog Blue Paw Wild Blueberry Wheat Ale (Maine)*
- ❏ *Shipyard Longfellow Winter Ale (Maine)*
- ❏ *Shipyard Winter Ale (a wheat beer, Maine)*
- ❏ *Smuttynose Pumpkin Ale (brewed with pumpkin and spices, New Hampshire)*
- ❏ *Willimantic First Class Festive Ale (Massachusetts)*

☕ 15 ☕
United States: Mid-Atlantic

The mid-Atlantic United States spawned some of the most exciting beer activity during the early days of Colonial America, and today produces some of the best craft beer in the entire country. Beer lore tells us that in New Amsterdam—now Manhattan—the first European-descended American was born in what was probably the first brewery in North America, Block & Christiansen's brewhouse. Appropriately, Jean Vigne grew up to become a brewer, a few years before the *Mayflower* ever docked at Plymouth. Today New York is home to the influential Brooklyn Brewery, Pennsylvania calls Victory Brewing Company its own, and Delaware has the notably superb Dogfish Head Brewery. These are just a few of the craft brewers spread over this region, which includes New York, Pennsylvania, New Jersey, Maryland, Washington, D.C., and Delaware.

Breweries of the Mid-Atlantic—colonial home to most of the patriots responsible for directing America toward liberation from the British—still reveal their colonial roots. Early American symbolism and eighteenth century-style patriotic fervor still echo from the tourist attractions in these states. The names of breweries and their beers reflect American liberation (Victory) proximity to the country's capital (Capitol City,) and a grounded sense of place. You'll also find a quirky, dry, even irreverent sense of humor in this region's beer names and even in the styles themselves (Weyerbacher Blithering Idiot, Middle Ages ImPaled Ale, Heavyweight Old Salty, Bethlehem Brew Works Stumbling Monk). Finally, as with the Northeast, the mid-Atlantic states love an excuse to produce seasonal and specialty beers.

An area this populous also must produce a wide variety of styles, and the Mid-Atlantic does just that, with examples of just about every British, German, and Belgian style ever recorded (only those styles with a significant number of examples are listed here, due to space limitations). Many of the beers from these breweries are widely distributed and available in many states.

History

In 1612, Adrian Block and Hans Christiansen opened the first brewery on the North American continent on the island of New Amsterdam, now Manhattan. For approximately two and a half centuries from this date, the brewing center of the North American continent flipped back and forth between New York and Pennsylvania. Throughout the 1600s, breweries opened in New Amsterdam, one after the other, and the Rutgers family—who would later endow Rutgers University—held a heavy influence on the brewing scene in that city. Philadelphia was home to some of George Washington's favorite brewers. Washington often requested shipments of porter from brewer Robert Hare, an English expatriate who brewed some of the earliest porter in America.

Thomas Jefferson favored a brewer named Henry Pepper (formerly Heinrich Pfeiffer of Germany), who owned a brewery in Philadelphia.

Another European expatriate and Pittsburgh brewer named Joseph Coppinger believed the United States should create a national brewery, to officially attempt to sway the masses away from the consumption of hard liquor. Coppinger believed that a regulated national brewery would encourage people to choose beer instead, with its more moderate alcohol content and higher nutrition. Coppinger's plan never came to fruition, in part because former president Thomas Jefferson advised Coppinger that such an enterprise was unnecessary because beer would catch on anyway. He was right, of course. Beer caught on so well that a segment of the population took up the cause of temperance. In 1808, some of the members of the Congregational Church in Saratoga County, New York, formed a temperance society. In 1826, the American Society for the Promotion of Temperance formed in Boston, and by 1829 had 100,000 members.

In 1829, David Yuengling, a German brewer, moved to Pottsville, Pennsylvania, and established the Eagle Brewery. This brewery still operates today under the name D. G. Yuengling, and is the oldest brewery in the United States. Look for their Traditional Lager and their Dark Brewed Porter. Yuengling has produced Porter since the beginning and was one of the few breweries to continue producing this style when pale lager changed the face of beer in America in the mid-1800s.

While not everybody agrees how lager first came to America, it may have been in the hands of John Wagner, a Bavarian brewer who immigrated to Philadelphia and started brewing in 1840. Wagner produced lager and taught others how to produce it too. The style caught on quickly, especially in neighboring New York, with its large German population. But everybody seemed to love lager, not just Germans, and the style spread all over the country. Beer gardens and lager breweries proliferated in New York, and then spread west. Still, the mid-Atlantic region of the country was the center of beer.

Just after the Civil War, the largest brewery in the United States was still in New York City, owned by George Ehret, a German brewer whose lager brewery on Ninety-second Street became a center for New York City's German-American community. Hell Gate Brewery began brewing in 1867. Other significant brewers included Peter Ballantine, from England, and Frederick Schaefer, from Germany. As New York City breweries grew, so did those in Milwaukee. Then the temperance movement geared up and Prohibition hit.

Prohibition activist Carrie Moore Nation, notorious for her violent attitude toward drinking and her purported divine mission to literally destroy saloons with axes, moved to New York City to attract media attention to her temperance mission. She died eight years before Prohibition became law in 1917, when Congress passed a constitutional amendment prohibiting the manufacture or sale of alcoholic beverages. This spurred not only the soft drink industry, but all kinds of illegal alcohol activity, from bootlegging to speakeasies. You can still visit Chumley's, a beer pub and former speakeasy, in Manhattan, with its false entrance and Prohibition-era decor.

One of the few breweries to thrive after Prohibition was the Ruppert Brewery in New York City, which expanded into New Jersey, Virginia, and Massachusetts even during World War II. The first beer can with a flat top (as they are today) came from Krueger Brewing of Newark, New Jersey, in 1935. In 1949, Schlitz bought the George Ehret Brewery in Brooklyn, and in 1951, Anheuser-Busch built a plant in Newark, New Jersey. The larger companies were beginning to consolidate, buying up smaller facilities. More and more smaller breweries disappeared and most of the styles other than pale lager suffered a similar fate. By the 1980s, three major corporations owned almost all the breweries in the United States.

But in the early 1980s, as the Microbrew Revolution was just gearing up on the West Coast, New York City spawned the first new microbreweries on the East Coast, and by the late 1980s, microbrews began to pop up all over the East Coast. In the twenty-first century, the number of new breweries opening has slowed down, but mid-Atlantic brewers continue to produce some of the most interesting ales and lagers in the country.

Current Trends

The following state-by-state look at some of the most interesting breweries and brewpubs mostly excludes megabrewers to focus on the more interesting and influential craft brewers in the Mid-Atlantic. Keep in mind, however, that the brewpub scene is volatile and this information can change quickly, so before visiting an area with the hope of touring a brewpub or microbrewery, search the Internet or call to make sure they are still in operation.

NEW YORK

In New York, the Brooklyn Brewery is probably the state's most famous microbrewery. Headed by brewer and beer writer Garrett Oliver, this microbrewery produces a wide variety of ales and lagers. The Ommegang brewery in Cooperstown specializes in Belgian-style ales and produces some impressive examples. They cave-age their Abbey Ale 156 feet below ground.

A regional brewing company in Utica, Matt Brewing Company, makes the Saranac brand and owns the Pete's Wicked line, and almost-megabrewer High Falls Brewing Company owns several brands, including J. W. Dundees and the canned pale lager Genesee. In Lakewood, Southern Tier makes small-batch beers, often seasonal. Middle Ages Brewing Company in Syracuse has pleasingly medieval beer names (if such things please you), such as Middle Ages Druid Fluid. Sixpoint Craft Ales in Brooklyn brews interesting and experimental ales that can defty categorization.

New York City has many notable brewpubs and I can't help listing many of my favorites. A few of the best include the aforementioned former speakeasy Chumley's, cozy upscale d.b.a, The Ginger Man, Heartland Brewery with five locations around Manhattan, the attractively divey Peculiar Pub, Times Square Brewery, the Chelsea Brewing Company, and, of course, the Brooklyn Brewery, with its large, crowded brewpub scene. As of this writing, the much-beloved Blind Tiger Ale House is closing its doors, something Manhattan beer lovers lament. (I was lucky enough to make there before this happened.)

PENNSYLVANIA

Pennsylvania-based larger regional craft brewers include Victory, in Downington, which makes some excellent examples of German styles and a few ales too, and Yuengling, the longest-surviving brewer in the United States. The more obviously conglomerate Latrobe Brewing Company, which makes Rolling Rock Extra Pale, and Pittsburgh Brewing Company, which makes Iron City pale lager, are really megabrewers. Also in Pittsburgh is the Pennsylvania Brewing Company. Smaller craft brewers of note include Stoudts Brewing Company in Adamstown, which claims to be Pennsylvania's first craft brewer, as well as Weyerbacher Brewing Company in Easton, Tröegs Brewing Company in Harrisburg, Lancaster Brewing Company in Lancaster, McKenzie Brew House in Glen Mills, and Philadelphia-based Yards Brewing Company. The Sly Fox brewery in Philadelphia's western suburbs began bottling in 2005, to expand their distribution beyond Pennsylvania.

NEW JERSEY

Notable New Jersey microbrewers include Heavyweight Brewing Company in Ocean Township, English and Belgian ale brewer Flying Fish Brewing Company in Cherry Hill, River Horse Brewing Company in Lambertville, and High Point Brewing Company in Butler, makers of convincingly authentic Ramstein German-style lagers.

MARYLAND

In Maryland, regional brewers include the Frederick Brewing Company which brews and distributes their

Blue Ridge, Brimstone, and Wild Goose brands regionally, and Clipper City Brewing Company which brews handcrafted beers in Baltimore. Unfortunately, the Baltimore Brewing Company recently went out of business. Popular DuClaw Brewing Company has four locations, in Bel Air, Fell's Point, Arundel Mills, and Bowie.

WASHINGTON, D.C.

Our nation's capital's craft brewer is Capitol City Brewing Company. They make many different British, German, and Belgian-style ales and lagers. Besides having locations on Capitol Hill and in downtown D.C., they also have sites in Arlington, Virginia, and Baltimore, Maryland.

DELAWARE

Dogfish Head, in Milton, is Delaware's premiere craft brewer. Their wide selection of ales are among the very best in the entire eastern United States, and Dogfish Head is truly a trendsetter on the craft beer scene. Other notable Delaware brewpubs include Iron Hill in Newark and Fordham, which owns the Ramshead Tavern, with one location in Rehoboth Beach, and two Maryland locations (Annapolis and Savage).

Characteristic Types of Beer

American microbrewers make just about every type of beer in the Mid-Atlantic. You'll find a wide variety of British, German, and Belgian styles, with a particular emphasis on full-bodied, high-alcohol styles like imperial stouts and double IPAs.

BELGIAN-STYLE WITBIER

Color: STRAW ▭▬▭ BLACK
Flavor: HOPS ▭▬▭ MALT
ABV: 4.8–5.2%
Serving temperature: 45–50° F

Several craft brewers in the Mid-Atlantic produce good interpretations of Belgian beers. This particular style is cloudy, pale, made with wheat or barley, and typically flavored with coriander and orange peel, as in the Belgian tradition. The moderate alcohol content makes these beers a good option for summer thirst-quenching.

Mid-Atlantic Belgian-style witbiers to try:

❑ *Blanche de Brooklyn (New York)*
❑ *Dogfish Head WeedWacker Wit (Delaware)*
❑ *Du Claw Sawtooth (Maryland)*
❑ *Ommegang Witte (New York)*
❑ *Saranac Belgian White (New York)*
❑ *Southampton Double White Ale (New York)*
❑ *Sterkens White Ale (New York)*
❑ *Victory Whirlwind Witbier (Pennsylvania)*
❑ *Weyerbacher Blanche (Pennsylvania)*

HEFEWEIZEN

Color: STRAW ▬▭ BLACK
Flavor: HOPS ▭▬▭ MALT
ABV: 4.9–5.5%
Serving temperature: 40–45° F

In the old German style, this is a cloudy white ale that tastes of wheat, yeast, and fruit. American hefeweizens tend to be more citrusy than their German counterparts, but both share spicy notes of nutmeg and cloves. Mid-Atlantic brewers often experiment with this style.

Mid-Atlantic hefeweizens to try:

- ☐ *Brooklyner Weisse (New York)*
- ☐ *Capitol City Hefeweizen (Washington, D.C.)*
- ☐ *DeGroens Weizen (Maryland)*
- ☐ *Penn Weizen (Pennsylvania)*
- ☐ *Ramstein Blonde (New Jersey)*
- ☐ *Saranac Hefeweizen (New York)*
- ☐ *Stoudts Weizen (Pennsylvania)*
- ☐ *Victory Sunrise Weissbier (Pennsylvania)*

PALE LAGER, PREMIUM LAGER, AND PILSNER

Color: STRAW ▬▬▬▭▭▭▭ BLACK
Flavor: HOPS ▭▬▬▭▭▭▭ MALT
ABV: 4–5.5%
Serving temperature: 40–45° F

American microbrewed pale/premium lagers and pilsners sometimes resemble the original pilsners of Bohemia, and sometimes come closer to the German variation (lighter in color and body), depending on the brewer. Others taste all-American, and unique to the brewer. Light to deep gold with pleasing hop bitterness and a nice balance of malt, they tend to have a pleasant fruity, flowery aroma and easy drinkability. Mid-Atlantic premium lagers and pilsners aren't particularly different than those in other regions, varying more by individual brewer than anything else.

Mid-Atlantic pale/premium lagers and pilsners to try:

☐ *Brooklyn Lager (New York)*
☐ *Brooklyn Pilsner (New York)*
☐ *Fordham Helles Lager (Delaware)*
☐ *Heartland Cornhusker Lager (New York)*
☐ *Penn Pilsner (Pennsylvania)*
☐ *Saranac Pilsner (New York)*
☐ *Victory Prima Pils (Pennsylvania)*
☐ *Yuengling Traditional Lager (Pennsylvania)*

PALE ALES

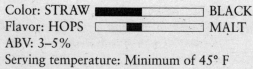

Color: STRAW ■■■■■■   BLACK
Flavor: HOPS ☐■■☐   MALT
ABV: 3–5%
Serving temperature: Minimum of 45° F

Gold to light bronze and easy to drink with noticeable but not overwhelming hops well balanced with
malt, this category is easy to drink, low in alcohol, and
perfect for sharing with friends over the course of an
evening. In general, U.S. styles will be more aggressively
hopped than those from the UK. Some Mid-Atlantic
styles are particularly hoppy.

Mid-Atlantic pale ales to try:

☐ *Brooklyn Ale (New York)*
☐ *Capitol City Pale Rider Ale (Washington, D.C.)*
☐ *Chelsea Checker Cab Blonde Ale (New York)*
☐ *Clipper City Pale Ale (Maryland)*
☐ *Dogfish Head Shelter Pale Ale (Delaware)*
☐ *Flying Fish ESB (New Jersey)*
☐ *Flying Fish Extra Pale Ale (New Jersey)*
☐ *Foggy Bottom Ale (New York)*

- [ ] *Iron Hill Ironbound Ale (Delaware)*
- [ ] *JW Dundees American Pale Ale (New York)*
- [ ] *River Horse Hop Hazard Pale Ale (New Jersey)*
- [ ] *Saranac Pale Ale (New York)*
- [ ] *Southern Tier Phin & Matts Extraordinary Ale (New York)*
- [ ] *Stoudts American Pale Ale (Pennsylvania)*
- [ ] *Yuengling Lord Chesterfield Ale (Pennsylvania)*

INDIA PALE ALE

Color: STRAW [▭▬▭] BLACK
Flavor: HOPS [▬▭▭] MALT
ABV: 5–7.5%, up to 20% for double/imperial IPAs
Serving temperature: Minimum of 45° F

American microbrewers often have their unique visions of what an IPA should be, so IPAs in the American style differ from brewer to brewer. Mid-Atlantic versions tend to be appropriately hop-heavy.

HOPPIER HOPS

One reason that the American versions of classic British and German styles tend to be "hoppier" than their counterparts across the pond may be that hops grown in America have a higher level of alpha acid—the critical bitter component—than hops grown in the Old World (that is, Europe). Through agricultural evolution, these levels have increased, so that the newer varieties simply taste hoppier, giving beer made with North American–grown hops one facet of its unique character.

One variation on the IPA that is uniquely American is the imperial or double IPA. Americans like to do everything big, with loud, obvious flavors. This is even more so on the West Coast, but mid-Atlantic double or imperial IPAs are pretty huge. Just try Dogfish Head's 120 Minute IPA, with its alcohol percentage at over 20%. That has to break some kind of record.

Mid-Atlantic IPAs to try:

☐ *Brooklyn East India Pale Ale (New York)*
☐ *Chelsea Henry Hudson IPA (New York)*
☐ *Clipper City Heavy Seas Winter Storm (Maryland)*
☐ *Dogfish Head ApriHop (brewed with apricots, Delaware)*
☐ *Dogfish Head 120 Minute IPA (beware, 20% ABV! Delaware)*
☐ *Dogfish Head 90 Minute Imperial IPA (Delaware)*
☐ *Dogfish Head 60 Minute IPA (Delaware)*
☐ *Heartland Indiana Pale Ale (New York)*
☐ *Lancaster Hop Hog IPA (Pennsylvania)*
☐ *Middle Ages ImPaled Ale (New York)*
☐ *Saranac IPA (New York)*
☐ *Southern Tier IPA (New York)*
☐ *Stoudts Double IPA (Pennsylvania)*
☐ *Victory Hop Devil IPA (Pennsylvania)*
☐ *Victory Hop Wallop (Pennsylvania)*
☐ *Weyerbacher Hops Infusion (Pennsylvania)*
☐ *Wild Goose India Pale Ale (Maryland)*
☐ *Yards India Pale Ale (Pennsylvania)*

BELGIAN-STYLE ALES/STRONG ALES/ABBEY-STYLE TRIPELS

Color: STRAW ⬜▬▬▬▬⬜ BLACK
Flavor: HOPS ⬜▬▬▬▬⬜ MALT
ABV: 6.5–12%
Serving temperature: Minimum of 45° F

American craft brewers often imitate Belgian abbey styles, in those states where the brewing of high-alcohol beers is allowed. Tripels are a popular style because they are light-bodied and pleasant to drink, yet high in alcohol and warming. Belgian-style ales, strong ales, and tripel ales are generally a light brilliant gold in color and lightly hopped using only lightly kilned malts to impart subtle nuances of malt character and color. To achieve a light body and a higher ultimate ABV, these strong ales are often brewed with Belgian candy sugar, softening any sense of hop bitterness and accentuating this ale's natural fruity and caramelized characters. Dubbels are typically lower in alcohol and darker in color. Quadruples are the most potent of the abbey ales, encompassing those with an ABV above 10%. Like dubbels, these are often darker in color than the pale tripels.

Mid-Atlantic Belgian-style and abbey-style ales to try:

❏ *Dogfish Head Snowblower Belgian Ale (Delaware)*
❏ *Flying Fish Abbey Dubbel (New Jersey)*
❏ *Flying Fish Grand Cru (New Jersey)*
❏ *Heavyweight Baltus O.V.S. (New Jersey)*
❏ *Heavyweight Lunacy (New Jersey)*
❏ *McKenzie Trappist Pale Ale (Pennsylvania)*
❏ *Ommegang (New York)*

❑ *Ommegang Three Philosophers (New York)*
❑ *Ommegang Vos (New York)*
❑ *River Horse Belgian Frostbite Winter Ale (New Jersey)*
❑ *Sixpoint Encore (New York)*
❑ *Sixpoint Sweet Action (New York)*
❑ *Southampton Grand Cru (New York)*
❑ *Stoudts Abbey Double (Pennsylvania)*
❑ *Stoudts Abbey Triple (Pennsylvania)*
❑ *Victory Golden Monkey (Pennsylvania)*
❑ *Victory Grand Cru (Pennsylvania)*
❑ *Victory V12 (Pennsylvania)*
❑ *Weyerbacher Merry Monks Ale (Pennsylvania)*
❑ *Weyerbacher Quad (Pennsylvania)*

AMBER ALE

Color: STRAW ▭▬▭ BLACK
Flavor: HOPS ▭▬▭ MALT
ABV: 4.3–5%
Serving temperature: Minimum of 45° F

These copper-colored, malty ales inspired by beers ranging from the UK copper ales through the altbier of Düsseldorf are balanced and smooth, with a maltier taste than a pale ale but less sweetness than a typical German dunkel. As is typical for American microbrewers, this category contains many examples of brewers taking grand liberties with the classic ale/lager distinction and fiddling with new ways of blurring the line between those categories. Amber ales abut the pale ales in style and color, following them on the darker end, and also abut the Belgian tripels on the lower end of the gravity scale.

Mid-Atlantic amber ales to try:

- ☐ *Capitol City Amber Waves Ale (Washington, D.C.)*
- ☐ *Dock Street Amber (New York)*
- ☐ *Fordham Copperhead Ale (Delaware)*
- ☐ *Heavyweight Stickenjab Altbier (New Jersey)*
- ☐ *Middle Ages Wailing Wench (really a strong ale, at 8% ABV, New York)*
- ☐ *Tröegs HopBack Amber Ale (Pennsylvania)*
- ☐ *Wild Goose Amber (Maryland)*

OKTOBERFEST-MÄRZEN

Color: STRAW ▭▬▭ BLACK
Flavor: HOPS ▭▬▭ MALT
ABV: 4.5–5%
Serving temperature: 45–50° F

Like its German counterpart, these American Oktoberfest-Märzens are medium-weight lagers ranging from deep golden to a rich bronze, with just a suggestion of hoppiness, but with lightly caramelized or bready malt dominating the flavor. Many are quite malty.

Mid-Atlantic Oktoberfest-Märzens to try:

- ☐ *Brooklyn Oktoberfest (New York)*
- ☐ *Clipper City Balto MärzHon (Maryland)*
- ☐ *Penn Oktoberfest (Pennsylvania)*
- ☐ *Pete's Wicked Oktoberfest (New York)*
- ☐ *Saranac Octoberfest (New York)*
- ☐ *Stoudts Fest (Pennsylvania)*
- ☐ *Victory Festbier (Pennsylvania)*

BROWN ALE AND PORTER

Color: STRAW `[======█======]` BLACK
Flavor: HOPS `[=====█=====]` MALT

ABV: 4.5–6.5% (darker, robust porters or so-called imperial porters are on the higher side)

Serving temperature: Minimum of 45° F

Bronze to toasty to deep and dark with reddish jewel tones, brown ales and porters are medium-weight, malty beers with fruitiness, nuttiness, and a low alcohol content. Brown ales from the Mid-Atlantic tend to be pleasantly similar to British brown ales, but may have a little more of a forwardly malty taste. The darker porters have flavors of espresso, chocolate, and roasted grain. So-called imperial porters like Southampton's are really more akin to Baltic porters, with their high ABVs of 8% or more.

Mid-Atlantic brown ales and porters to try:

- ❑ *Brooklyn Brown Ale (New York)*
- ❑ *Brooklyn Sustainable Organic Porter (New York)*
- ❑ *Capitol City Prohibition Porter (Washington, D.C.)*
- ❑ *Dogfish Head Indian Brown Ale (Delaware)*
- ❑ *Flying Fish Porter (New Jersey)*
- ❑ *Heavyweight Perkunos Hammer Imperial Porter (New Jersey)*
- ❑ *Iron Hill Pig Iron Porter (Delaware)*
- ❑ *Mississippi Mud Black and Tan (New York)*
- ❑ *Pete's Wicked Ale (New York)*
- ❑ *Saranac Caramel Porter (New York)*
- ❑ *Southampton Imperial Baltic Porter (New York)*
- ❑ *Wild Goose Porter (Maryland)*

❑ *Yuengling Dark Brewed Porter (Pennsylvania)*
❑ *Yuengling Original Black and Tan (Pennsylvania)*

STOUTS AND IMPERIAL STOUTS

Color: STRAW ▭▬▬ BLACK
Flavor: HOPS ▭▬▬▭ MALT
ABV: 3–6%; imperial or "extra" stout and strong ale: 6.5–12% or even higher for certain specialty releases
Serving temperature: Minimum of 50° F

As in the UK, the term "stout" encompasses several styles: dry, Irish-style stout (in the Guinness family), sweet stout brewed with lactose (sometimes called milk stout or cream stout) or with oatmeal in the grit schedule (adding a silky smoothness), and imperial stout or "extra stout," with their higher-than-average, warming alcohol content. In general, stout is dark, rich, and similar to porter (they are often lumped together), with roasted coffee and bittersweet chocolate flavors. Watch out for Dogfish Head World Wide Stout, which comes out in annual editions featuring ABVs of a staggering 18 to 19%.

Mid-Atlantic stouts and imperial stouts to try:

❑ *Brooklyn Black Chocolate Stout (imperial stout, New York)*
❑ *Clipper City Heavy Seas Peg Leg (imperial stout, Maryland)*
❑ *Dogfish Head Chicory Stout (Delaware)*
❑ *Dogfish Head World Wide Stout (imperial stout, Delaware)*

❑ *DuClaw Black Jack Stout (Maryland)*
❑ *Heartland Farmer Jons Oatmeal Stout (New York)*
❑ *Iron Hill Russian Imperial Stout (Delaware)*
❑ *Lancaster Milk Stout (Pennsylvania)*
❑ *McKenzie 5 Czars Imperial Stout (Pennsylvania)*
❑ *Saranac Black and Tan (New York)*
❑ *Saranac Stout (New York)*
❑ *Tröegs Oatmeal Stout (Pennsylvania)*
❑ *Victory Storm King Imperial Stout (Pennsylvania)*
❑ *Weyerbacher Heresy (imperial stout, Pennsylvania)*
❑ *Weyerbacher Old Heathen (imperial stout, Pennsylvania)*
❑ *Weyerbacher Raspberry Imperial Stout (Pennsylvania)*
❑ *Wild Goose Oatmeal Stout (Maryland)*
❑ *Yards Love Stout (Pennsylvania)*

DOPPELBOCK/WEIZENBOCK

Color: STRAW ▭▬▭ BLACK
Flavor: HOPS ▭▬▭ MALT
ABV: 7–10%
Serving temperature: 48–53° F

A potent lager in the bock style, doppelbock (which means "double bock") is usually dark in color and always high in alcohol, usually over 7%. Weizenbocks are brewed with wheat. Like their German counterparts, American microbrewed doppelbocks often have names that end in "-ator."

Mid-Atlantic doppelbocks/weizenbocks to try:

❑ *Ramstein Classic (actually a Dunkelweizen, New Jersey)*
❑ *Ramstein Winter Wheat (New Jersey)*

❑ *Saranac Black Forest (New York)*
❑ *Tröegs Trogenator Doppelbock (Pennsylvania)*
❑ *Victory Moonglow Weizenbock (Pennsylvania)*

BARLEY WINE

Color: STRAW ▭▭▭▬▬▬▭▭ BLACK
Flavor: HOPS ▭▭▭▭▬▬▭ MALT
ABV: 7–12%
Serving temperature: 50–55° F

This high-gravity style is just right for the cold, icy mid-Atlantic winters. Sweet, rich, and complex, these warmers are usually amber to medium brown with suggestions of rich toffee and undertones of port or sherry (this can be accentuated via cask conditioning). You can cellar these for a few years to help them mellow and allow flavors to mature even more.

Mid-Atlantic barley wines to try:

❑ *Brooklyn Monster Ale (New York)*
❑ *Dogfish Head ImmortAle (Delaware)*
❑ *Dogfish Head Olde School Barleywine (Delaware)*
❑ *DuClaw Devil's Milk (Maryland)*
❑ *Heavyweight Old Salty (New Jersey)*
❑ *Middle Ages Druid Fluid (New York)*
❑ *Victory Old Horizontal (Pennsylvania)*
❑ *Weyerbacher Blithering Idiot (Pennsylvania)*

SEASONAL AND SPECIALTY BEERS

The brewers in the mid-Atlantic United States, like many American craft brewers, enjoy brewing seasonal beers for any occasion. Winter warmers are popular and so are unusual ingredients like raisins and saffron, but in this category, anything goes and creative brewers can really have fun. Flavor, color, etc. are too varied to justify a scale for this style.

Mid-Atlantic seasonal and specialty beers to try:

- ❑ *Clipper City Heavy Seas Red Sky at Night (Maryland)*
- ❑ *Dogfish Head Au Courant (brewed with black currants, Delaware)*
- ❑ *Dogfish Head Midas Touch Golden Elixir (a traditional ale brewed with white Muscat grapes, honey, and saffron, Delaware)*
- ❑ *Dogfish Head Punkin Ale (Delaware)*
- ❑ *Dogfish Head Raison d'Etre (brewed with beet sugar, green raisins, and Belgian yeast, this ale really is—as the name implies—one very good reason to exist, Delaware)*
- ❑ *Flying Fish Farmhouse Summer Ale (New Jersey)*
- ❑ *Heavyweight Biere d'Art (New Jersey)*
- ❑ *Heavyweight Cinderblock Lager (smoked, New Jersey)*
- ❑ *Heavyweight Two Druids Gruit Ale (a traditional-style ale flavored with herbs like yarrow and wild rosemary instead of hops, New Jersey)*
- ❑ *Ommegang Hennepin (New York)*
- ❑ *Pete's Wicked Strawberry Blonde Ale (New York)*
- ❑ *Pete's Wicked Summer Brew (New York)*
- ❑ *Pete's Wicked Winter Brew (New York)*
- ❑ *Post Road Pumpkin Ale (New York)*
- ❑ *Sixpoint S.M.P. (smoked Baltic Porter, New York)*
- ❑ *Southampton Biere de Garde (French country Christmas ale, New York)*
- ❑ *Southampton Saison (New York)*

❑ *Southampton Secret Ale (New York)*
❑ *Tröegs Mad Elf (brewed with cherries, honey, chocolate malt, and an 11% ABV, Pennsylvania)*
❑ *Wild Goose Snow Goose Winter Ale (Maryland)*
❑ *Yards Saison (Pennsylvania)*

☕ 16 ☕
United States: Southeast

South of the Mason-Dixon line, the beer landscape changes. Not immediately, but gradually, beer becomes less a craft than a simple warm-climate quencher (read: pale lager). Just over that famous line dividing North and South, Virginia still seems like part of the Mid-Atlantic, with a colonial beer history linked to that of the states just above it. The farther south you travel, however, the less extensive the beer history becomes. With the exception of metropolitan areas like Atlanta, beer simply hasn't thrived in the Southeast the way it has in the Northeast, Northwest, and Midwest. (Later on in this book, you'll see that the southwest shares this paucity of good beer with the southeast.)

That's not to say the Southeast is completely bereft of beer knowledge, resources, or history. Larger southern cities like Atlanta, Richmond, Nashville, Tampa, Raleigh, and even New Orleans have vibrant microbrew scenes. Many southern cities, however, have just a handful of breweries or brewpubs, if that, and many still have laws prohibiting the sale of any beer above 6% ABV, which severely limits the choice of beer in these states. Mississippi, notably, was the last state to legalize commercial brewing, and as of this writing, has just one microbrewer, Lazy Magnolia Brewery Company, and this brewery sustained quite a lot of hurricane damage (and the brewers lost their home). The state also has a few brewpubs. Some local brewpubs may not bottle their beers, but do allow carryout in growlers.

GROWLER

A growler is a half-gallon glass jug used for taking home draft beer from the brewpub. Not everyone agrees about the origin of the word. Some say it refers to the sound of the beer sloshing in the buckets once used for this purpose, but nobody seems to know for sure. While pubs have sent beer home with their customers for years—sometimes in plastic containers or waxed cardboard boxes and, long ago, in those "growling" galvanized buckets—the glass jug growler is a recent invention. Many brewpubs fill them up for you, or you can buy them prefilled. Growlers are a great way to bring home local, fresh beer. The beer lasts for maybe a week in the refrigerator, so drink up!

Why is the South so light on beer resources? Perhaps because these states were the stragglers—the last region to legalize the brewing of beer after Prohibition and this may have been because this is America's Bible belt. While pockets of enthusiastic beer drinkers and home brewers work hard to improve beer knowledge in the South, they seem to fight a continuing uphill battle. One example of such an effort is the website The Beer Cellar (*www.thebeercellar.com*), devoted to craft beer in the American southeast, and to educating people in the South about the positive aspects of craft beer.

History

While most of the early brewing history in America happened in the Northeast, the Southeast has its share of beer trivia. Virginia resident George Washington did quite a bit for the promotion of beer in America. Washington openly encouraged brewing and the consumption of locally produced beer rather than imported beer. He was a big fan of the Porter brewed by Robert Hare in the 1770s, and made frequent, insistent requests for beer rations for his troops during the Revolutionary War. After the war, Washington was the original promoter of the "buy American" concept.

Thomas Jefferson also enjoyed beer, and brewed it himself. He experimented not only with barley but also with corn and wheat in his home brewing. In 1783, the first brewery in the Deep South, built by Major William Horton, opened on Jekyll Island, Georgia. In Salem, North Carolina, in the heart of the Moravian religious settlement, the Single Brothers Brewery and Distillery opened in 1774.

But the South has been more famous for its bourbon whiskey than its beer. When Tennessee native Andrew Jackson became president in 1828, whiskey's popularity increased. Tennessee and Kentucky are whiskey states. America has always been rich with corn resources, and corn is better for distilling than for brewing beer. Whiskey has a much longer shelf life than beer, especially in the steamy South, and so became a more economically viable product.

While lager became more and more popular in the Northeast and Midwest during the 1800s, the South never really exploded with breweries. Not until after

World War II did the South have any major commercial breweries, except in New Orleans. As early as the mid-1800s, brewing thrived in the Big Easy. After the Civil War, New Orleans boasted a number of brewpubs and larger breweries, including the Dixie Brewing Company and the Jackson Brewery.

Most accounts of the microbrew revolution don't make much mention of southern states, although many knew of Kentucky's giant Oldenburg Brewery. Its beer hall could hold 650 people, and they also had a beer garden and hosted live entertainment. (They closed in 1999.) Today the South still fights for beer recognition, but in beer-friendly pockets, beer lovers and beer advocates cluster and fight the good fight, brewing their own beer and lobbying to bring better beers into their states.

Current Trends

The southern states include West Virginia, Virginia, Kentucky, Arkansas, Tennessee, North Carolina, South Carolina, Georgia, Alabama, Mississippi, Louisiana, and Florida. When Prohibition was repealed, many southern states instituted a law that no beer above 6% alcohol could be sold in the state. This included imports, not just local brews. This law has had a significant impact on how much and what variety of beer people can buy and drink in the southern United States.

Georgia and North Carolina both recently repealed this law, raising their allowed levels to 14%. However, Alabama, Arkansas, Mississippi, and South Carolina are still subject to this limiting law. Citizens groups in these other southern states are working to follow Georgia's example. Pop the Cap!, a beer advocacy group in

North Carolina, was the most recent to successfully achieve this victory in 2005.

While the craft-beer explosion has peaked and leveled out or slowed down in most of the U.S., the South still remains somewhat of a microbrewing frontier. Stay tuned for a future explosion of southern craft beer, if those lobbying for more relaxed beer laws have their way in the rest of the southern states. If Georgia and North Carolina can change the law, say beer aficionados, then so can the rest of the South.

The following state-by-state look at some of the most interesting breweries and brewpubs in the southern United States is, of course, subject to change as breweries open and close with the times and changing regulations (and hurricanes!). Call before visiting!

WEST VIRGINIA

West Virginia isn't exactly famous for its microbrew scene, but it does have several brewpubs producing a variety of ales, lagers, and seasonal brews with a southern flair: West Virginia Brewing Company in Morgantown, Blackwater Brewery Company in Davis, and North End Tavern & Brewery in Parkersburg. River City Ale Works in Wheeling recently went out of business.

VIRGINIA

Old Dominion Brewing Company and Brewpub in Ashburn produces some of the best-known craft beers on the Eastern Seaboard, with a variety of ales, lagers, and seasonal beers, both for the brewpub and bottled for distribution. Because it still gets chilly in the winter in Virginia, you can even find some warming, winter-weight beers, such as their Dominion Millennium, a barley wine. The St. George Brewing Company in Hampton makes several award-winning ales and lagers. Sweetwater Tavern has several Virginia brewpub locations, and the Legend Brewing Company in Richmond is one of Virginia's oldest and largest commercial microbrewers.

KENTUCKY

The Bluegrass Brewing Company in Louisville makes a wide variety of beers, rotating what's on tap and also selling their beer in bottles. Newport also has a brewery licensed by Munich's famous Hofbräuhaus, and brews classic German lagers according to the Hofbräuhaus rules.

ARKANSAS

The Diamond Bear Brewing Company in Little Rock is so named because Arkansas is the only U.S. state with a diamond mine, and the state also used to have a large bear population. Little Rock also has a brewpub called Vino that calls itself "Little Rock's original brewpub."

TENNESSEE

Tennessee is home to the famous Blue Moon brewery in Memphis, although they are actually owned by Colorado-based Coors. Microbrewers include Yazoo, producing interesting handcrafted ales from an old car factory in Nashville; and Big River Grille & Brewing Works in Chattanooga, the fastest-growing restaurant chain in America during 1999, according to the trade publication *Restaurant Business*. They own dozens of locations around the United States but are based in

Chattanooga. The Smoky Mountain Brewery in Gatlinburg is owned by the Copper Cellar Corporation, which operates seven different restaurant brands at fourteen locations around Tennessee. Boscos brewpub has locations in Memphis and Nashville. In Clinton, the Shady Grove Meadery produces only mead.

NORTH CAROLINA

Until summer of 2005, a law in North Carolina stated hat beer could not contain over 6% alcohol. Today, all that has changed, so North Carolina may soon blossom as a source of great beer. Already, the western side of North Carolina has a pocket of microbrewers: the Highland Brewing Company and the French Broad Brewing Company in Asheville; Catawba Valley Brewing Company in Glen Alpine; and Carolina Brewing Company in Holly Springs and Carolina Beer Company in Moorseville. These microbrewers produce styles in the European tradition with some exciting results. The Weeping Radish Brewery and Bavarian Restaurant in Manteo on the Outer Banks brews German beer and serves German food, but also bottles, sells, and distributes their beer in several southern states. Bottling on a smaller but growing scale is the Duck-Rabbit Craft Brewery in Farmville.

SOUTH CAROLINA

Greenville's Thomas Creek microbrewery is a father-son family business creating handcrafted beers in South Carolina, despite the 6% law. The Palmetto brewing company in Charleston has many devotees. The Aiken Brewing Company in Aiken is a brewpub that produces award-winning brews, both regularly and seasonally.

GEORGIA

Most of the brewing activity in Georgia happens in Atlanta, which has Georgia's oldest microbrewery, and its largest microbrewery. Atlanta Brewing Company was the state's first, opening relatively early in the microbrew revolution (especially for the South), in 1993, with roots dating from the 1800s. They make the famous Red Brick Beer. The recent closure of Dogwood Brewing Company in Atlanta saddened Georgia beer lovers. Still going strong, Sweetwater Brewing Company is Georgia's largest microbrewer, and wins lots of awards for its brews. Terrapin Brewing Company is a popular microbrewer in Athens.

Until recently, a law in Georgia limited the sale of any beer above 6% ABV. This included imports. Fortunately for Georgians, the law was repealed, and now residents of the state can enjoy some of the better high-gravity beers the world has to offer.

ALABAMA

The Montgomery Brewing Company and Brewpub in Montgomery was one of the first brewpubs in the South, but closed due to Prohibition in 1919. They reopened (in a different location and obviously with a different owner, but with the old name) in 1995, in an old warehouse just a few blocks from the brewery's original location. Alabama law requires brewpubs to be in counties that had brewing prior to Prohibition, and to be located in a building eligible for National History Register. After some legal wrangling and the discovery of a nearby annexed town, the Olde Auburn Ale House brewpub was able to open legally in Auburn in 1998.

MISSISSIPPI

Hal & Mals in Jackson is one of just a couple of brewpubs in the state. Coast Brewing Company sits within the festive Beau Rivage Resort & Casino in Biloxi, and the casinos were largely responsible for encouraging Mississippi to allow brewing in the state. During Hurricane Katrina, however, casinos suffered major damage. As of this writing, we will have to wait to see how well they recover. Mississippi's only dedicated microbrewer, Lazy Magnolia Brewing Company in Kiln, also suffered heavy hurricane damage but will, we hope, be back on its feet soon. Even aside from hurricane challenges, brewing in Mississippi remains highly regulated.

LOUISIANA

Not surprisingly, brewing in Louisiana centers around New Orleans, or did until Hurricane Katrina. The Abita Brewing Company was among the first microbreweries outside the Northwest, opening thirty miles north of New Orleans in 1986 (technically in Covington). Today they own a brewpub and a stand-alone brewery, producing five flagship brews and five seasonal brews. Abita beers are widely available in the South, Northeast, and Midwest. Abita survived Hurricane Katrina and reopened as soon as power was restored. They brewed Abita Fleur-de-Lis Restoration Ale to raise money for the hurricane victims. Dixie Brewing Company in New Orleans, a microbrewery known for their Blackened Voodoo Lager, didn't weather the storm quite so well, and as of this writing, their future is uncertain. Crescent City Brewhouse is the only microbrewery in the French Quarter, and recently reopened, to the joy of Mardi Gras attendees.

FLORIDA

Because Florida has such a large tourist industry and population, it also has more breweries than many other southeastern states. It is also not subject to the 6% law, so Florida breweries can make a wider range of styles. Some notable Florida microbreweries include the Dunedin brewery in Dunedin, the Indian River Brewing Company in Melbourne, and a U.S. subsidiary of the Cuba-based La Tropical in Coral Gables. The Tampa Bay Brewing Company in Tampa's historical Ybor City district offers twelve beers on tap and three cask-conditioned ales, and is a popular and much beloved brewpub.

Characteristic Types of Beer

The range of beer styles brewed in the southeastern United States is more limited than in other areas, but southern microbrewers still produce some interesting interpretations of classic styles, notably lighter ales and beers good for warm weather.

BELGIAN-STYLE WITBIER
Color: STRAW ▉▉▉▭▭▭▭ BLACK
Flavor: HOPS ▭▭▭▉▉▭▭ MALT
ABV: 4.8–5.2%
Serving temperature: 40–45° F

Because witbier is such a tasty thirst-quencher, many examples come out of southern microbrewers. Blue

Moon, the Belgian-style witbier that popularized this style in the United States, comes from Tennessee (although owned by Coors, so it is hardly a microbrew), but it isn't the only example of this cloudy, pale, yeasty wheat beer. Typically flavored with coriander and orange peel, as in the Belgian tradition, these beers with their moderate alcohol content are the perfect choice for sipping on the veranda on a sultry southern afternoon. Who needs a mint julep when you've got a Belgian-style wit?

SOUTHERN BELGIAN-STYLE WITBIERS TO TRY:

❑ *Blue Moon Belgian White (Tennessee)*
❑ *Dominion Wit (Virginia)*
❑ *5 Seasons Djokker Wit (Georgia)*
❑ *French Broad Laurel Country White (North Carolina)*
❑ *Moon River Wild Wacky Witbier (Georgia)*
❑ *West Virginia White-Out Wit (West Virginia)*

HEFEWEIZEN

Color: STRAW ▮▭▭▭▭▭ BLACK
Flavor: HOPS ▭▭▭▮▭ MALT
ABV: 4.9–5.5%
Serving temperature: 40–45° F

Like Belgian wits, this style is a perfect thirst quencher for the steamy South. In the old German style, this is a cloudy white ale that tastes of wheat, yeast, and fruit. American hefeweizens tend to be more citrusy than their German counterparts, but both share spicy notes of nutmeg and cloves. Drink the yeast sediment.

Southern hefeweizens to try:

☐ *Tampa Bay Wild Warthog Weizen (Florida)*
☐ *Weeping Radish Hefeweizen (North Carolina)*

YUMMY YEAST

If your beer has yeast sediment, don't be appalled by the "floaties." Rejoice! Flavor-active compounds ride on yeast and yeast in suspension intensifies a beer's flavor, so enjoy that cloudy yeasty goodness. It's not only good for your health, but good for your palate.

PILSNER

Color: STRAW ▰▰▱▱▱▱ BLACK
Flavor: HOPS ▱▱▰▱▱▱ MALT
ABV: 4–5.5%
Serving temperature: 40–45° F

American microbrewed pilsners sometimes resemble the original pilsners of Bohemia, and sometimes come closer to the German variation (lighter in color and body), depending on the brewer. Light to deep gold with pleasing hop bitterness and a nice balance of malt, pilsners from America may not have Pilzen's soft water but they do generally have the classic pilsner's pleasant, flowery aroma and easy drinkability, and pair well both with the South's warm climate and its varied cuisine. Try one with jerked chicken or jambalaya or Cuban-influenced beans and rice. As in Europe, pilsners represent the pinacle of the pale lagers.

Southern pilsners to try:

☐ *Crescent City Pilsner (Louisiana)*
☐ *La Tropical (Florida)*
☐ *Legend Pilsner (Virginia)*

❑ *Terrapin All-American Imperial Pilsner (Georgia)*
❑ *Thomas Creek Pilsner (South Carolina)*
❑ *Tuppers Hop Pocket Pils (Virginia)*

DORTMUNDER/HELLES

Color: STRAW ▭▭▭▭ BLACK
Flavor: HOPS ▭▭▭▭ MALT
ABV: 5–6%
Serving temperature: 45–50° F

A light golden lager that is sweeter and fuller than pilsner, in America this is an imitation of the style of beer brewed in Dortmund and often referred to as Dortmunder. It has a mineral flavor and can range from very pale to golden. These are popular in the South because of their refreshing, thirst-quenching nature, as a welcome and more fully flavored change from a basic light lager.

Southern Dortmunder/helles to try:

❑ *Dominion Lager (Virginia)*
❑ *Hofbräuhaus Newport Original (Kentucky)*
❑ *Weeping Radish Corolla Gold (North Carolina)*

PALE/GOLDEN/BLOND ALES

Color: STRAW ▭▭▭▭ BLACK
Flavor: HOPS ▭▭▭▭ MALT
ABV: 3–5%
Serving temperature: Minimum of 45° F

Pale, golden, and blond ales are a very popular style of beer for southern craft brewers, perhaps because they combine the generally lesser-known and seemingly more exotic ale style with the easy, refreshing drinkability so appropriate to a warm climate. While many people distinguish between English-style pale ales and American-style pale ales as well as golden and blond ales, they are all grouped together here because these brews cluster together in the golden ale portion of the beer spectrum. Gold to light bronze and easy to drink with noticeable but not overwhelming hops balanced with subtle malt flavors, this category of ales is easy to drink and low in alcohol.

Southern pale/golden/blond ales to try:

- ☐ *Abita Fleur-de-Lis Restoration Ale (Louisiana)*
- ☐ *Aiken West Coast Pale Ale (South Carolina)*
- ☐ *Bluegrass American Pale Ale (Kentucky)*
- ☐ *Carolina Beer Company Carolina Blonde (North Carolina)*
- ☐ *Carolina Pale Ale (North Carolina)*
- ☐ *Celtic Gold Ale (Florida)*
- ☐ *Diamond Bear Pale Ale (Arkansas)*
- ☐ *Diamond Bear Southern Blonde (Arkansas)*
- ☐ *Dominion Pale Ale (Virginia)*
- ☐ *French Broad 13 Rebels ESB (North Carolina)*
- ☐ *Highland St. Tereses Pale Ale (North Carolina)*
- ☐ *Key West Sunset Ale (Florida)*
- ☐ *Mobjack Pale Ale (Virginia)*
- ☐ *New River Pale Ale (Virginia)*
- ☐ *Old Montgomery Blonde (Alabama)*
- ☐ *Palmetto Pale Ale (South Carolina)*
- ☐ *Pipers Pale Ale (Florida)*
- ☐ *St. George Golden Ale (Virginia)*
- ☐ *Sweetwater Tavern Great American Pale Ale (Virginia)*
- ☐ *Terrapin Rye Pale Ale (Georgia)*

❑ *Tuppers Hop Pocket Ale (Virginia)*
❑ *West Virginia Ned's Pale Ale (West Virginia)*
❑ *Yazoo Amorillo Pale Ale (Tennessee)*

INDIA PALE ALE

Color: STRAW ▭▬▭ BLACK
Flavor: HOPS ▬▭ MALT
ABV: 5–7.5%, up to 20% for double/imperial IPAs
Serving temperature: Minimum of 45° F

Once hopped-up for its preservative qualities, today's IPAs remain high in hop bitterness, making them an excellent foil for strongly flavored southern foods. Light golden, the best examples balance malt and hops but have a fresh, aromatic hop quality and the bitterness many beer connoisseurs have come to know and love. American IPAs tend to be even more dramatically hoppy than their British counterparts, even though the style was born in Britain.

Southern IPAs to try:

❑ *Boscos Bombay IPA (Tennessee)*
❑ *Catawba Valley Fire Water IPA (North Carolina)*
❑ *Cottonwood Endo India Pale Ale (North Carolina)*
❑ *Highland Kashmir IPA (North Carolina)*
❑ *Legend Imperial IPA (Virginia)*
❑ *St. George India Pale Ale (Virginia)*
❑ *Tampa Bay Old Elephant Foot IPA (Florida)*

AMBER/RED ALES

Color: STRAW [▭▬▭] BLACK
Flavor: HOPS [▭▬▭] MALT
ABV: 4.3–5%
Serving temperature: Minimum of 45° F

These copper-colored, malty ales inspired by beers ranging from British copper ales and Irish-style red ales through the altbier of Düsseldorf are balanced and smooth, with a maltier taste than a pale ale but less sweetness than a typical German dunkel. Amber ales follow the pale ales in color, continuing toward the deep copper/red end of the color spectrum.

Southern amber/red ales to try:

- ❑ *Dominion Ale (Virginia)*
- ❑ *Dunedin Red Head Red Ale (Florida)*
- ❑ *French Broad Wee Heavy Scotch Ale (North Carolina)*
- ❑ *Highland Gaelic Ale (North Carolina)*
- ❑ *Palmetto Amber Ale (South Carolina)*
- ❑ *Thomas Creek Amber Ale (South Carolina)*
- ❑ *Thomas Creek Red Ale (South Carolina)*
- ❑ *West Virginia Appalachian Ale (West Virginia)*

BROWN ALE

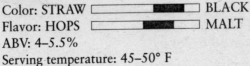

Color: STRAW [▭▬▭] BLACK
Flavor: HOPS [▭▬▭] MALT
ABV: 4–5.5%
Serving temperature: 45–50° F

Bronze to toasty brown, these ales are a medium-weight, malty beer with fruitiness, nuttiness, and a low alcohol content. Brown ales are a popular style in the South, forwardly malty and easy to drink. A darker ale can be a welcome change from all those pale gold beers, even when the weather is hot.

Southern brown ales to try:

☐ *Abita Turbodog (Louisiana)*
☐ *Big River Grille Sweet Magnolia American Brown Ale (Tennessee)*
☐ *Bluegrass Anniversary Nut Brown Ale (Kentucky)*
☐ *Cottonwood Low Down Brown Ale (North Carolina)*
☐ *Dunedin Beach Tale Brown Ale (Florida)*
☐ *Ybor Gold Brown Ale (Florida)*

PORTER

Color: STRAW ▭▬▭ BLACK
Flavor: HOPS ▭▬▭ MALT
ABV: 4.5–6.5%
Serving temperature: 50–55° F

Deep, dark, and full-bodied with reddish jewel tones behind the dark brown to ebony color and flavors of espresso, chocolate, and roasted grain, porter is an excellent beer for sipping after dinner. Following the brown ales on the lighter side and the stouts on the darker side, these brews would perfectly complement a southern pecan pie or a Cuban cigar.

Southern porters to try:

☐ *Bluegrass Dark Star Porter (Kentucky)*
☐ *Duck–Rabbit Porter (North Carolina)*
☐ *Dunedin Highland Games Ale (Florida)*

❑ *Highland Oatmeal Porter (Tennessee)*
❑ *Palmetto Porter (South Carolina)*
❑ *St. George Porter (Virginia)*
❑ *Smoky Mountain Tuckaleechee Porter (Tennessee)*
❑ *Ybor Gold Gaspars Porter (Florida)*

STOUTS AND IMPERIAL STOUTS

Color: STRAW ▭▬ BLACK
Flavor: HOPS ▭▬▭ MALT
ABV: 3–6%; imperial or "extra" stout: 6.5–12% or even higher for certain specialty releases
Serving temperature: Minimum of 50° F

The stout style may have originated in Britain, but southern brewers make it their own, dabbling in the dry Irish style and the sweet stout style, some with truly complex, deep, rich, multilayered flavors.

Southern stouts to try:

❑ *Big River Grille Iron Horse Stout (Tennessee)*
❑ *Dominion Oak Barrel Stout (Virginia)*
❑ *Duck–Rabbit Milk Stout (North Carolina)*
❑ *Dunedin Leonard Croons Old Mean Stout (Florida)*
❑ *Hal & Mals Trophy Buck Stout (Mississippi)*
❑ *Olde Auburn Full Monty Stout (Alabama)*
❑ *Sweetwater Tavern High Desert Imperial Stout (Virginia)*
❑ *Terrapin Wake-N-Bake Coffee Oatmeal Imperial Stout (Georgia)*
❑ *West Virginia Blackwater Stout (West Virginia)*

Bock/Doppelbock/Maibock

Color: STRAW [▮▮▮] BLACK
Flavor: HOPS [▮] MALT
ABV: 5–10%
Serving temperature: 48–54° F

A potent lager, bock is usually dark and strong. Doppelbock is usually darker in color than a bock and is always higher in alcohol, usually over 7%. Some of the southern bocks listed here are seasonal, from Maibocks to holiday incarnations, when the extra-warming quality of a doppelbock is enjoyable—even the South can get chilly in the winter.

Southern bocks to try:

- ❏ *Abita Bock (Louisiana)*
- ❏ *Beau Rivage Bock (Mississippi)*
- ❏ *Hofbräuhaus Newport Maibock (Kentucky)*
- ❏ *Thomas Creek Doppelbock (South Carolina)*
- ❏ *Weeping Radish Christmas Double Bock (North Carolina)*

Barley Wine

Color: STRAW [▮▮] BLACK
Flavor: HOPS [▮] MALT
ABV: 7–12%
Serving temperature: 50–55° F

This high-gravity style works in the South too, where evenings can still be chilly and the winter holidays generate a craving for warmth and deep, complex flavors. These sweet, rich warmers are usually amber to medium brown with suggestions of rich toffee and undertones of port or sherry (this can be accentuated via cask conditioning). You can cellar these for a few years to help them mellow and develop even more complexity.

Southern barley wines to try:

❑ *Bluegrass Bearded Pats Barleywine Style Ale (Kentucky)*
❑ *Dominion Millennium (Virginia)*
❑ *Tampa Bay Moosekiller Barley-Wine Style Ale (Florida)*

SEASONAL AND SPECIALTY BEERS

The brewers in the southern United States don't go particularly wild with their seasonal and specialty beers, but some produce fruit or pumpkin-based brews on a seasonal basis.

Southern seasonal and specialty beers to try:

❑ *Abita Christmas Ale (Louisiana)*
❑ *Abita Purple Haze (a wheat beer flavored with raspberries, Louisiana)*
❑ *Blue Moon Pumpkin Ale (Tennessee)*
❑ *Cottonwood Pumpkin Spiced Ale (North Carolina)*
❑ *Dominion Spring Brew (Virginia)*
❑ *Dominion Winter Brew (Virginia)*
❑ *Dunedin Apricot Peach Ale (Florida)*
❑ *Hurricane Reef Raspberry Wheat Ale (Florida)*
❑ *Vinos Holidaze (Arkansas)*

☕ 17 ☕
United States: Midwest

The Midwest is famous for its beer—its megabrewed commercially produced pale lager, that is. Anheuser-Busch calls St. Louis home, producing Budweiser, Bud Light, Michelob, and Busch beers. Milwaukee spawned the giant Miller Brewing Company, makers of not only Miller Genuine Draft, Miller High Life, and Miller Light, but Milwaukee's Best, Pabst Blue Ribbon, Ice House, Schlitz, and Red Dog. This is football beer, tailgating beer, quintessential midwestern beer . . .

But wait! The Midwest is lager country, for a few reasons. The prodigious ice on the Great Lakes during the winter historically provided plenty of coolant for early German immigrant brewers' lagering needs (remember, lager beer is brewed at a lower temperature for a longer time than ale). The Midwest is also populated with large numbers of Americans of German ancestry, so good lager is a matter of pride in the Midwest. And, although the large commercial brewers admittedly produce most of the region's (and the world's) lager, microbrewers in the Midwest have also made lager a matter of pride and artistry, producing some truly interesting examples of the lager style and foiling even some of those die-hard ale lovers who insist they don't like lager.

But lager isn't the only style available in the subtly experimental Midwest. Craft brewers also produce an impressive range of creative ale styles. So why isn't the Midwest known for its craft-brew scene? In America, people tend to focus on the two coasts, and the two coasts tend to focus (competitively) on each other. The West Coast essentially invented the craft-brew revolution in the late 1970s, and the East Coast responded with its own loud answers to west coast craft beer. The western beers got hoppier, the eastern beers got more experimental, and with all the yelling back and forth, few people noticed that the midwest was listening. In their own sweet time (the way we midwesterners tend to do things), craft brewers in the Midwest began to brew alternatives to the ubiquitous pale lager being brewed and sold all around them.

Another reason the Midwest isn't known far and wide for its brewing prowess is the draconian beer legislation many states still enforce, leveling large taxes on high-alcohol beers or prohibiting their production entirely. The result: some brewers just don't ship their more interesting and experimental beers to these states. Or, arguably worse, they dilute their beers before shipping to these states, so they meet the requirements for that state's legal definition of beer, which is often much lower than the beer style really calls for.

On the other hand, midwestern states like Michigan, Wisconsin, Ohio, Illinois, and Missouri are true beer meccas. Not only do they produce great local beer, but many establishments in these states serve beer from all over the country and the world, for your convenient tasting pleasure—the real versions, not the watered-down versions. In other words, you don't have to live on a coast to get really good American craft beer. But depending on where you are in the Midwest, you might have to cross a state line or two.

History

This isn't a book about the megabrewers, and brewing in the Midwest didn't start with Anheuser-Busch and Miller, but the advent of these corporations certainly put midwestern beer on the map. Long before A-B and Miller existed, however, German lager brewers were setting up shop in Chicago, St. Louis, and Milwaukee. In 1847 Chicago, John Huck and John Schneider began brewing lager to compete with the large ale brewer Lill & Diversey. In 1852, George Schneider began brewing lager and in 1856 opened the Bavarian Brewery, a brewery that would later be run by Eberhard Anheuser, who would then hire his son-in-law, Adolphus Busch.

In Milwaukee, lager brewing has been going strong for more than 150 years. Two lager breweries opened in 1840, to compete with local ale breweries: the German Brewery and Stotz & Krill. Soon after, the Eagle Brewery, Munzinger & Koethe Brewery, and Union Brewery opened. In 1844, Jacob Best founded the Empire Brewery, and his son Charles would later launch a business that would become the Miller Brewing Company. Another of Best's sons, Phillip, later married a girl with the last name Pabst.

Prohibition and the Second World War had their devastating effect on the Midwest as elsewhere in the States. While many breweries closed during Prohibition, the megabrewers survived by producing soda pop, "near beer," and other legal products, and by getting into other fields such as shipping (they already had the distribution infrastructure) and manufacturing. In Chicago, bootlegging was big business. When Prohibition was repealed in 1933 with the election of Franklin Delano Roosevelt, only the larger companies remained to put their brewing operations back together. For decades afterward, breweries like Anheuser-Busch, Pabst, Hamm's, and Schlitz dominated the scene, even throughout the difficult periods of the Great Depression and Second World War.

After a few complacent decades of mediocre lager, microbrews began to open and proliferate. By the mid-1980s, even the Midwest had caught the fever. Today well-established micros in the Midwest continue to produce surprising and wonderful beer, win awards for it, and innovate. While microbreweries may not be opening at the rate America saw in the 1990s—craft-beer sales increased about 40% annually during this "golden era" of craft beer—many of those with devoted followings show no sign of slowing down or giving up (although the occasional surprise closure of a beloved microbrewery is still all too common). Craft-beer sales rose 7% in 2004, and those numbers are also reflected in many of the Midwest's craft-brew sales. While this doesn't seem like much compared to the early 1990s, it is nevertheless an encouraging upswing compared to the past few years. The Midwest has a taste for craft beer now. No turning back.

A positive benefit of a state pumped full of revenue because of a large beer industry is the pressure to enact beer-friendly legislation. Wisconsin and Missouri remain among the most beer-friendly states, due to the presence of large commercial brewers. The smaller craft

brewers who aren't in competition with the likes of
Miller and Budweiser benefit from the environment, although not as much as in some places around the world.
In Belgium, for example, smaller brewers are taxed at a
lower rate than larger ones. No such luck here. At least
craft brewers in Wisconsin and Missouri aren't subject
to the prohibitive beer laws some states must endure.

Current Trends

The midwestern states include Michigan, Ohio, Indiana, Wisconsin, Illinois, Minnesota, Iowa, Missouri,
North Dakota, South Dakota, Nebraska, and Kansas.
In some of these states, really good beer is still hard to
find, but in others, craft beer rules. Some states have
mostly brewpub chains, while others have independ-
ently owned craft brewers gaining fame and praise from
the self-proclaimed beer nerd set.

Michigan's Bell's Brewery (formerly called the Kalamazoo Brewing Company) began to brew the spectacu-
lar Bell's beers (some of these are my absolute personal
favorites), and innovates yearly with new experimental
styles. Don't miss their Sparkling Ale, or in summer, the
popular Oberon. Goose Island and Two Brothers in Illinois make wonderfully drinkable ales and lagers that
can ease even the most die-hard pale lager drinker into
a more interesting taste experience. Boulevard Brewing
Company in Kansas City offers a diverse range of craft-
brewed products. Wisconsin's New Glarus and Indiana's Three Floyds come up with some truly innovative
creations, the latter famous for its super-hoppy but
smoothly balanced ales that will give any West Coast
hop-bomb IPA a run for its money.

THE CHAIN GANG

The novice beer connoisseur should learn to distinguish between the truly local microbrewery, craft brewer, or brewpub versus chain brewpub franchises. Although the latter have their place and some make pretty good beer—and they do, after all, increase beer diversity and its appreciation—chain franchises work in a very corporate mold that is a bit antithetical to the spirit of the small, family-run, local microbreweries. Chain brewpubs are popular in the Midwest. In fact, chains in general are popular in the Midwest—perhaps we cautious midwesterners generally like to know what we are getting before we get it—but part of the excitement of craft beer is finding something truly unique. However, chain brewpubs are popping up all over the country and are a reality of our times and the country's recent love affair with beer. In some places, they are your only option if you want something brewed on-premises or locally, which is another reason that they can be a welcome addition to a community. A chain brewpub is usually better than no brewpub at all, in my opinion, and you could also theorize that a brewpub chain's success in a formerly brewpub-barren town might set the stage for more experimental craft brewers to enter the scene and start brewing something truly great. Rock Bottom and Granite City are each examples of brewpub franchises that successfully pepper the Central States.

August Schell's Minnesota brewery has been in business since 1860 and is one of just a couple of smaller regional breweries to have survived both Prohibition and the Second World War, and they are still crafting beer today. These are just a few of the interesting and innovative craft brewers quietly going about their business in the Midwest. Of course, when midwestern beers win big awards for their innovative creations, those of us living in the Midwest get pretty loud about it.

The following state-by-state look at some of the most interesting breweries and brewpubs in the Midwest is, of course, subject to change as breweries open and close with the times and changing regulations. Call before visiting!

MICHIGAN

The Bell's Brewery, which makes Bell's beer, is well known far beyond the Michigan border as one of the most innovative and adventurous craft brewers on the scene. They began as a home-brewing supply shop in 1983 and began selling beer in 1985. Until recently, this brewery was called the Kalamazoo Brewing Company and is the oldest, and among the most influential, of craft brewers east of Colorado. The operation also includes the Eccentric Café brewpub—the first Michigan brewery to serve beer on tap to the public—and Bell's General Store, where you can buy cases of the their tasty brew—and a T-shirt—as well as brewing supplies.

Other notable Michigan microbreweries include the Michigan Brewing Company in Webberville, Kuhnhenn Brewing in Warren, Dark Horse Brewing Company in Marshall, Arcadia Brewing Company in Battle Creek, Founder's Brewing Company in Grand Rapids, Stoney Creek Brewing Company in Detroit, New Holland Brewing Company in Holland, Dragonmead Brewery in Warren, and the standout Jolly Pumpkin Artisan Ales in Dexter, producing some truly great brews in the past year. Michigan really is a Midwestern craft beer lover's paradise.

Оню

Ohio's first microbrewery, Great Lakes Brewing Company in Cleveland, opened in 1988 and continues to be one of the state's most high-profile and award-winning microbreweries. Their Blackout Stout is one of the country's best stouts. Other good Ohio-based microbreweries/brewpubs include Buckeye Brewing Company in Bedford Heights, Columbus Brewing Company in Columbus, and Thirsty Dog Brewing Company in Copley.

INDIANA

Three Floyds Brewing Company in Munster, Indiana (just over the border from Chicago), is a relatively small operation producing some unquestionably big beers. Their super-hoppy Alpha King Pale Ale made them legendary on the craft beer scene. (Alpha King derives its name from the iso-alpha acids that form the bittering component of the hops plant), and according to the most recent Ratebeer poll of thousands of beer drinkers from sixty-five countries, Three Floyds was named the second best brewer in the *world*, and their Dark Lord Russian Imperial Stout was named second best beer in the world too. Many of their other beers are known far and wide among those who pay attention to the craft brew scene. Talk about midwestern influence! Other notable Indiana breweries include the Upland Brewing Company and brewpub in Bloomington, which serves the college students at the University of Indiana, Oaken Barrel in Greenwood, Barley Island in Noblesville, Mad Anthony Brewery Company in Fort Wayne, Back Road Brewery in LaPorte, and Mishawaka Brewing Company in Mishawaka.

WISCONSIN

The New Glarus Brewing Company in New Glarus makes whimsical and winning beers, from their Fat Squirrel to their Spotted Cow. They have been winning awards since 1995 and have twice been listed as one of the top ten breweries in the United States, according to the World Brewery Championship.

Capital Brewing in Middleton is located in a former egg processing plant and distributes all over the Midwest. Capital Brewing specializes in lagers, an unusual niche for a craft brewer in American today since craft brewers tend to prefer ales. But this is the Midwest, after all. Capital makes a few ales, but lagers are their crowning glory, especially their Capital Amber. Open since 1984, this multiple award-winning brewery shuns tasteless pale lagers in favor of more flavorful, traditional German styles and some Midwestern riffs on the lager theme, like Wild Rice Lager and Blonde Doppelbock.

Central Waters in Junction City makes creative ales and lagers including a popular bourbon barrel stout. Sprecher Brewing Company in Glendale is Milwaukee's original microbrewery and won Small Brewing Company of the Year in 2004 at the Great American Beer Festival. Also in Milwaukee, the Lakefront Brewery microbrews award-winning beers for the region. According to the Joseph Huber Brewery in Monroe, they are the oldest brewery in the Midwest, and the second oldest in the country. The brewery, operating since 1845, survived Prohibition through an employee stock buyout by producing a near beer called Golden Glow. They make Berghoff beer. The Stevens Point Brewery in Stevens Point opened in 1857 and also survived Prohibition by making near beer and soft drinks.

Finally, among more mainstream beers, Wisconsin may be Miller country, but the locals love their Leinies. The Jacob Leinenkugel Brewing Company based in Chippewa Falls is the seventh oldest brewery in the United States and the oldest business in Chippewa Falls. Leinenkugel merged with Miller in 1988, allowing them to distribute more widely but essentially separating them from the grassroots craft-beer scene. They opened a second small brewery to handle the demand for their specialty brews, but mainstream Leinenkugel Red and Leinenkugel Honey Weiss are ubiquitous in the Midwest. They may not be the most unusual of microbrews—and many today wouldn't consider them microbrews at all—but they have a large and devoted midwestern following.

ILLINOIS

Two of Illinois' most prominent and influential microbrewers are Goose Island Beer Company and Two Brothers Brewing Company, the former in the heart of Chicago, the latter just west of the city in Warrenville. Goose Island was founded in 1988, one of the first midwestern microbreweries, and their beer is now widely distributed. Their famous white goose head tap is easy to spot from across a crowded bar. Cubs fans can drink Goose Island beer in bottles inside Wrigley Field. But, while Goose Island beers may have a certain degree of mass appeal they periodically release some amazing special-edition brews that would thrill any connoisseur.

Family-owned and operated Two Brothers opened in 1987. They specialize in bringing lesser-known beer styles to the American palate, such as bière de garde and

high-gravity specialty ales. Their success has captured
the craft-beer community's attention, deservedly.

MINNESOTA

Schell's is the second oldest family-owned brewery in
the country, brewing lagers in the German tradition
(and a few ales too) in New Ulm for the past 150 years.
They are widely available in the Midwest. In 1986, the
Summit Brewing Company opened in St. Paul, and has
a staunch local following. Minneapolis Town Hall
Brewery in Minneapolis brews an incredibly adventurous range of beers for its local taps, and has won
awards for its ales. They also make root beer. The stel-
lar Lake Superior Brewing Company revived brewing in
the Duluth area in 1994 and distributes throughout the
Midwest, lucky for us! Barley John's Brew Pub in New
Brighton is a local favorite.

IOWA

The Millstream Brewing Company in the Amana
Colonies (a former German religious commune and current tourist attraction with Old World–inspired shops,
German restaurants, and their own large Oktoberfest)
has been brewing beer since 1984. Millstream's beer
wins awards and they continue to increase their distribution radius. Iowa also has several chain brewpubs,
and many small-scale brewpubs here and there. Old
Capitol Brewpub in Iowa City produces some interesting experimental ales and lagers, including some good
Belgian-inspired offerings. The Sutliff Cider Company
makes hard cider in Lisbon.

Although this book doesn't typically mention beer retailers, no discussion of beer in Iowa would be complete

without a mention of John's Grocery in Iowa City. This small, family-owned grocery store is the state's best source for take-out beer, and one of the nation's best sources for a diversity of Belgian imports. If not for John's Grocery, Iowans would have a much smaller and less interesting selection of beers available to them. The staff at John's has incredible beer knowledge, and staff consultant Eric Nielsen is the technical editor of this book. No trans-Iowa drive on Interstate 80 by any beer lover would be complete without a stop-in to John's Grocery. Just ask for owner Doug Alberhasky. Bring this book. Maybe he will give you a discount! (I'm not guaranteeing anything.)

Unfortunately, the beer climate in Iowa—as in several other midwestern and southern states—isn't favorable to brewers, or to beer retailers. Some breweries water down their beer before selling it to Iowa, just to stay within the state's legal definition of beer (5% alcohol by weight). Anything over 5% gets taxed as a liquor, at a whopping 25% mark-up. An organization called Lift the Limit (*www.liftthelimit*.org) is currently working to change Iowa's outdated beer laws.

MISSOURI

Just because you live in Missouri doesn't mean you are required to drink Budweiser. Boulevard Brewing Company in Kansas City, founded in 1989, claims it is the largest specialty brewer in the Midwest, with its regular and seasonal offerings available in ten midwestern states. These days, you can find Boulevard Wheat on tap in many tiny midwestern towns. (This seems to me a very good sign that beer tastes are rising in the Heartland.) The St. Louis Brewery, on Anheuser-Busch turf, brews Schlafly beer and also has cask-conditioned ale on draft at their brewpub, The Tap Room. Their nearby Bottleworks is the company's production brewery. The O'Fallon Brewery is a small microbrewery northwest of St. Louis in the town of O'Fallon, and the Springfield Brewery Company is a microbrewery built, operated, and owned by a company that makes brewery equipment in Springfield.

NORTH DAKOTA

When it comes to craft beer, it's slim pickin's in North Dakota. As of this writing, the Great Northern Brewery and Restaurant, the state's only microbrewery, went out of business. Fargo now has a Granite City brewpub, and that's about it for North Dakota.

SOUTH DAKOTA

The Black Hills resort area has brought a wider selection of craft beer to South Dakota than to its northern brother, but brewpubs remain sparse. The Firehouse Brewing Company in Rapid City and the Mount Rushmore Brewing Company in Hill City offer rare oases in the middle of the Great Plains for stopping in and enjoying a freshly brewed beer. South Dakota also has a Granite City brewpub in Sioux Falls. The Sioux Falls Brewing Company has gone out of business.

NEBRASKA

Nebraska's larger cities have a few brewpubs: the Empyrean Brewing Company in Lincoln has made ales and lagers since 1990, and the Upstream Brewing Company in Omaha sells its brews in the restaurant/pub as well as for carry-out in growlers and kegs. Spilker Ales is a microbrewery in Cortland and just began putting their dry-hopped Hopluia beer in sixteen-ounce cans, available in four-packs in Omaha and Lincoln.

KANSAS

Like many midwestern states, Kansas was a brewing hub before Prohibition. Now it has just a handful of brewpubs. The Free State Brewing Company is a brewpub in Lawrence that opened in 1989. It was the first legal brewery in Kansas since Prohibition. Great Plains Brewing Company is the largest microbrewery in Kansas (and a subsidiary of a larger Missouri-based cooperative). Their Pony Express Brewing Company brews beer in Olathe.

Characteristic Types of Beer

While pale lagers still rule the turf due to the mostly midwestern-based megabrewers, this section focuses instead on the smaller and mid-sized microbrewers in the Midwest who are exercising their rights to brew in a wide variety of styles. The range of beer styles brewed in the midwestern United States is vast, just like the Midwest itself. For that reason, some relatively disparate styles are grouped together here, mainly according to their type (ale or lager) and placement on the color spectrum. You wouldn't normally expect to see so many different kinds of wheat beer in one region, but midwesterners love wheat beer, perhaps because wheat is a midwestern crop and just sounds like home. Whether a traditional German-style hefeweizen, a spiced Belgian-style witbier, or a "plain" American wheat, wheat beer is widely available in the Midwest, so be sure to try some midwestern variations on this theme.

PREMIUM PALE LAGER/DORTMUNDER/HELLES/PILSNER

Color: STRAW ▬▬▬□□□□□□□ BLACK
Flavor: HOPS □□▬▬▬▬□□□□ MALT
ABV: 4–5.5%
Serving temperature: 40–45° F

These golden lagers are a step above the pale lagers typical of mainstream American brewing. Whether they resemble the full, malty golden lagers from Dortmund in German, Bohemian pilsners, or American versions of these German classics, these lagers are light to deep gold with pleasing hop bitterness and a nice balance of malt. In general, American versions have a hoppier taste and more forward malt flavors than their European counterparts, but Midwestern examples tend to be fairly true to their Germanic roots.

Midwestern premium pale lagers/Dortmunders/helles/pilsners to try:

❑ *Back Road Millennium Lager (Indiana)*
❑ *Boulevard Bobs 47 Munich-Style Lager (Missouri)*
❑ *Goose Island Pils (Illinois)*
❑ *Great Lakes Dortmunder Gold (Ohio)*
❑ *Great Lakes Locktender Lager (Ohio)*
❑ *Millstream German Style Pilsner (Iowa)*
❑ *Schell Pilsner (Minnesota)*
❑ *Summit Grand (Minnesota)*
❑ *Two Brothers Dog Days (Illinois)*

AMERICAN WHEAT

Color: STRAW 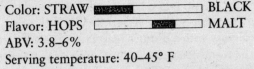 BLACK
Flavor: HOPS MALT
ABV: 3.8–6%
Serving temperature: 40–45° F

Cloudy, straw to dark gold, and fruity, American-style wheat beers should have a subtle fruitiness and a breadlike yeasty flavor. American wheat makes a great summer beer with a more complex flavor than standard pale lager. This is lawn-mowing beer with class.

Midwestern American wheats to try:

- [ ] *Bell's Oberon Ale (Michigan)*
- [ ] *Buckeye Wheat Cloud (Ohio)*
- [ ] *Capital Kloster Weizen (Wisconsin)*
- [ ] *Millstream Wheat (Iowa)*
- [ ] *New Glarus Solstice Weiss (Wisconsin)*
- [ ] *Three Floyds Gumballhead (Indiana)*
- [ ] *Upland Wheat Ale (Indiana)*

HEFEWEIZEN

Color: STRAW 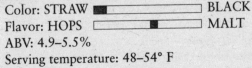 BLACK
Flavor: HOPS MALT
ABV: 4.9–5.5%
Serving temperature: 48–54° F

Perhaps because so many midwesterners have German heritage, traditional German styles are popular and beloved. This style—a wheat beer served with yeast so that it is cloudy with a distinct yeasty flavor—is another perfect thirst-quencher for long midwestern summers. This is the style that inspired the American wheat style. In its more classic German-based incarnation, this is a straw-to-amber ale that tastes of wheat, yeast, and fruit. American hefeweizens tend to be more citrusy than their German counterparts, but both share spicy notes of nutmeg and cloves. Enjoy the complex, layered flavors in the suspended yeast sediment. This style is particularly popular in German-influenced Wisconsin.

Midwestern hefeweizens to try:

- ❏ *Berghoff Hefe-Weizen (Wisconsin)*
- ❏ *Boulevard Unfiltered Wheat (Missouri)*
- ❏ *Buckeye Wheat Cloud (Ohio)*
- ❏ *Capital Kloster Weizen (Wisconsin)*
- ❏ *New Glarus Solstice Weiss (Wisconsin)*
- ❏ *Sprecher Hefe Weiss (Wisconsin)*
- ❏ *Summit Hefe Weizen (Minnesota)*
- ❏ *Two Brothers Ebelweiss (Illinois)*

WINNOWING THE WHEATS

Wheat beer comes in several different incarnations, and it can become confusing telling them apart. "Wheat" (called "weizen" in German) is the most general term, and simply implies that wheat is included as a significant portion of the grist schedule (along with the malted barley). "Hefe" is German for "yeast," and hence implies that the beer should be served cloudy with the yeast sediment included in the correct pour. Wit is a subclass of wheat—also referred to as bière blanch in France or Tarwebier in the Netherlands—which is a uniquely Belgian style and generally implies the use of spices, beyond the basic implication of wheat in the mash. Due to the use of specialty yeasts, even wheat beers without spicing tend to have a clove or nutmeg edge to them from yeast secondary metabolites, so you cannot assume a beer contains spices merely because it tastes spicy. You *can* assume you taste spicy notes, though.

BELGIAN-STYLE WITBIER

Color: STRAW ▨▨▨▭▭▭ BLACK
Flavor: HOPS ▭▭▨▭ MALT
ABV: 4.8–5.2%
Serving temperature: 40–45° F

Belgian-style witbier is lovely in the summer, but best for savoring every complex swallow rather than chugging at the lakeside. Typically flavored with coriander and orange peel, as in the Belgian tradition, these beers with their moderate alcohol content are perfect summer sippers. This style gives craft brewers a chance to

really exercise their creativity, as they strive to capture the unique essence of this Belgian-style favorite. Bell's Brewery also makes a Belgian-style wit for winter, called Bell's Winter White. (They always like to push the envelope.)

Midwestern Belgian-style witbiers to try:

❑ *Bell's Winter White (Michigan)*
❑ *Berghoff Solstice Wit (Wisconsin)*
❑ *Boulevard Zôn (Missouri)*
❑ *Dark Horse Sapient Summer Wheat (Michigan)*
❑ *Great Lakes Holy Moses (Ohio)*
❑ *Jolly Pumpkin Calabaza Blanca (Michigan)*
❑ *Lakefront White Beer (Wisconsin)*
❑ *Michigan Brewing Celis White (Michigan)*
❑ *Millstream John's Generations White Ale (Iowa)*
❑ *New Holland Zoomer Wit (Michigan)*
❑ *Schlafly Wit (Missouri)*
❑ *Two Brothers Monarch Wit (Illinois)*
❑ *Upland Wheat Ale (Indiana)*

Pale Ales/Bitters/ESBs

Color: STRAW  BLACK
Flavor: HOPS  MALT
ABV: 3–5%
Serving temperature: Minimum of 45° F

This is the group of pale to deep gold ales, including pale ales, bitters, and ESBs. These are a popular style in the Midwest, as craft brewers enjoy experimenting with ales and midwestern drinkers tend to like lighter-colored beers. These are all gold to light bronze, and those in the American style will be more aggressively hopped than those in the British style. With noticeable hops balanced with relatively subtle maltiness, this category of pale to golden ales is easy to drink, unless you really don't like the bitter hop flavor. Despite the names "bitter" and "ESB" (extra special bitter), this style isn't always overwhelmingly bitter. It really depends on the brand, so try a few. For even higher hop bitterness, see the IPA category, following this one.

Midwestern pale ales, bitters, and ESBs to try:

- ❑ *Arcadia Lake Super ESB (Michigan)*
- ❑ *Bell's Pale Ale (Michigan)*
- ❑ *Boulevard Pale Ale (Missouri)*
- ❑ *Central Waters Happy Heron Pale Ale (Wisconsin)*
- ❑ *Columbus Pale Ale (Ohio)*
- ❑ *Empyrean LunaSea ESB (Nebraska)*
- ❑ *Free State Copperhead Pale Ale (Kansas)*
- ❑ *Goose Island Honkers Ale (Illinois)*
- ❑ *Great Lakes Burning River Pale Ale (Ohio)*
- ❑ *Lake Superior Special Ale (Minnesota)*
- ❑ *Mad Anthony Ol' Woody Pale Ale (Indiana)*
- ❑ *New Glarus Spotted Cow (a cream ale, Wisconsin)*
- ❑ *Oaken Barrel Gnaw Bone Pale Ale (Indiana)*
- ❑ *Pony Express Rattlesnake Pale Ale (Kansas)*
- ❑ *Schell Pale Ale (Minnesota)*
- ❑ *Schlafly Pale Ale (Missouri)*
- ❑ *Schlafly Winter ESB (Missouri)*
- ❑ *Springfield Pale Ale (Missouri)*
- ❑ *Summit Extra Pale Ale (Minnesota)*
- ❑ *Three Floyds Alpha King Pale Ale (Indiana)*
- ❑ *Three Floyds Big Ups Bitter (Indiana)*
- ❑ *Three Floyds Extra Pale Ale (Indiana)*
- ❑ *Two Brothers The Bitter End Pale Ale (Illinois)*
- ❑ *Upstream Firehouse ESB (Nebraska)*

INDIA PALE ALE

Color: STRAW ▭ BLACK
Flavor: HOPS ▭ MALT
ABV: 5–7.5%, up to 20% for double/imperial IPAs
Serving temperature: Minimum of 45° F

The bitterest of the bitter ales, today's IPAs remain high in hop bitterness, making them an excellent foil for strongly flavored foods—barbecue anyone?—as well as a good appetite stimulant before dinner. Light golden, the best examples balance malt and hops but have a fresh, aromatic hop quality and the bitterness many beer connoisseurs enjoy. The so-called double and imperial IPAs take bitterness to its extreme, but these beers remain justifiably balanced by virtue of the high gravity (alcohol content) and resulting intensity of overall flavors. The best ones remain balanced even while maxing out the hop aroma and flavor.

Midwestern IPAs to try:

❑ *Back Road Midwest IPA (Indiana)*
❑ *Bell's Two Hearted Ale (Michigan)*
❑ *Buckeye Hippie IPA (Ohio)*
❑ *Buckeye Seventy-Six (Ohio)*
❑ *Founders Centennial IPA (Michigan)*
❑ *Goose Island Imperial IPA (Illinois)*
❑ *Goose Island India Pale Ale (Illinois)*

- ☐ *New Glarus Hop Hearty Ale (Wisconsin)*
- ☐ *New Holland Mad Hatter Ale (Michigan)*
- ☐ *Spilker Hopluia (Nebraska)*
- ☐ *Summit India Pale Ale (Minnesota)*
- ☐ *Three Floyds Dreadnaught Imperial IPA (Indiana)*
- ☐ *Town Hall Masala Mama IPA(Minnesota)*
- ☐ *Two Brothers Heavy Handed India Pale Ale (Illinois)*
- ☐ *Upland Dragonfly IPA (Indiana)*
- ☐ *Upstream India Pale Ale (Nebraska)*

BELGIAN-STYLE ALES/STRONG ALES/ABBEY-STYLE TRIPELS

Color: STRAW ▭▬▬▬▭ BLACK
Flavor: HOPS ▭▬▬▭ MALT
ABV: 6.5–12%
Serving temperature: Minimum of 45° F

These are the light- to medium-colored Belgian-style ales. Their cousins are the American strong ales. This style is brewed—to a greater or lesser extent—with influences from the Belgian abbey tradition. Midwestern craft brewers both imitate and tamper with the Belgian abbey styles in interesting ways, in those states where the brewing of high-alcohol beers is allowed. That makes some of these similar to authentic Belgian ales and strong ales, and some mere suggestions of the original style, truly American improvisational interpretations. Usually light-bodied and pleasant to drink yet warming, these styles are generally a brilliant gold color and lightly hopped, with only lightly kilned malts to impart subtle nuances of malt character and color. Sometimes they range toward a darker amber or even edge toward brown, depending on the individual ale. These strong ales are often brewed with Belgian candy sugar, softening any sense of hop bitterness and accentuating this ale's natural fruity and caramelized characters.

Midwestern Belgian-style ales/strong ales/abbey-style tripels to try:

- ❏ *Bell's Sparkling Ale (Michigan)*
- ❏ *Dark Horse Belgian Amber Ale (Michigan)*
- ❏ *Dark Horse Sapient Trip Ale (Michigan)*
- ❏ *Dragonmead Final Absolution Belgian Style Trippel (Michigan)*
- ❏ *Goose Island Demolition 1800 Ale (Illinois)*
- ❏ *Goose Island Pere Jacques (Illinois)*
- ❏ *Great Lakes Grand Cru (Ohio)*
- ❏ *Great Lakes Nosferatu (Ohio)*
- ❏ *New Glarus Unplugged Triple (Wisconsin)*
- ❏ *New Holland Black Tulip Trippel Ale (Michigan)*
- ❏ *Schlafly Belgian Tripel (Missouri)*
- ❏ *Sprecher Abbey Triple (Wisconsin)*
- ❏ *Town Hall Tripel Vision (Minnesota)*
- ❏ *Two Brothers Prairie Path Golden Ale (Illinois)*

AMBER/RED ALE

Color: STRAW ▭ BLACK
Flavor: HOPS ▭ MALT
ABV: 4.3–5%
Serving temperature: 45–50° F

This category includes the copper-colored to reddish, malty ales inspired by a range of European and British beers from Irish reds and Scottish ales to German alt-bier. This style is generally balanced and smooth, with a  maltier taste than a pale ale, and continues the ale color spectrum from copper to deep reddish-brown. As is typical for American microbrewers, this category contains many examples of brewers taking liberties with the classic ale/lager distinction and blurring the line between those categories.

Midwestern amber/red ales to try:

- ☐ Bell's Amber Ale (Michigan)
- ☐ Boulevard Irish Ale (Missouri)
- ☐ Flying Monkey Amber Ale (Kansas)
- ☐ Founders Dirty Bastard Scotch Ale (Michigan)
- ☐ Goose Island Kilgubbin Red Ale (Illinois)
- ☐ Great Lakes Conways Irish Ale (Ohio)
- ☐ Kuhnhenn Fourth Dementia Old Ale (Michigan)
- ☐ Mishawaka Four Horsemen Ale (Indiana)
- ☐ New Glarus Snowshoe Ale (Wisconsin)
- ☐ New Holland Red Tulip (Michigan)
- ☐ New Holland Sun Dog (Michigan)
- ☐ Oaken Barrel Indiana Amber (Indiana)
- ☐ Sprecher Special Amber (Wisconsin)
- ☐ Stoney Creek Stoney Red Ale (Michigan)
- ☐ Thirsty Dog Hoppus Maximum (Ohio)
- ☐ Three Floyds Brian Boru Old Irish Red (Indiana)

❏ *Three Floyds Robert the Bruce Scottish Ale (Indiana)*
❏ *Trinity Red Ale (Illinois)*
❏ *Upland Amber Ale (Indiana)*

OKTOBERFEST-MÄRZEN/VIENNA LAGER/MUNICH LAGER

Color: STRAW ▭▭▭▭▭▭ BLACK
Flavor: HOPS ▭▭▭▭▭▭ MALT
ABV: 4.5–5%
Serving temperature: 45–50° F

These amber-hued lagers include the classic Oktoberfest-Märzen, Vienna, and Munich categories. Like their German counterparts, these American lagers are medium-weight and range from deep golden to a rich bronze with just a suggestion of hoppiness. Lightly caramelized or bready malt dominate the flavor. These have a smooth mouthfeel and make festive choices for fall and that ubiquitous midwestern Oktoberfest party—where almost everyone has German in their ancestry, Oktoberfest celebrations are imminent.

Midwestern Oktoberfest-Märzen, Vienna, and Munich-style lagers to try:

❏ *Berghoff Oktoberfest (Wisconsin)*
❏ *Boulevard Bobs 47 Munich-Style Lager (Missouri)*
❏ *Buckeye Martian Marzen Lager (Ohio)*
❏ *Capital Fest (Wisconsin)*
❏ *Capital Wisconsin Amber (Wisconsin)*
❏ *Dark Horse Oktoberfest (Michigan)*
❏ *Goose Island Oktoberfest (Illinois)*
❏ *Great Lake Eliot Ness (Ohio)*
❏ *Lakefront Oktoberfest (Wisconsin)*

❑ *Lakefront Riverwest Stein (Wisconsin)*
❑ *Millstream Oktoberfest (Iowa)*
❑ *Millstream Schild Brau Amber (Iowa)*
❑ *New Glarus Staghorn Oktoberfest (Wisconsin)*
❑ *Schell Firebrick (Minnesota)*
❑ *Schell Oktoberfest (Minnesota)*
❑ *Schlafly Oktoberfest (Missouri)*
❑ *Sprecher Oktoberfest (Wisconsin)*
❑ *Sprecher Special Amber (Wisconsin)*
❑ *Summit Oktoberfest (Minnesota)*

BROWN ALE

Color: STRAW ⬜▬⬜ BLACK
Flavor: HOPS ⬜▬⬜ MALT
ABV: 4–5.5%
Serving temperature: 45–50° F

Bronze to toasty brown, these ales are a medium-weight, malty beer with fruitiness, nuttiness, and a low alcohol content, darker than amber ales and leading, on the color spectrum, toward the porters and stouts. These are forwardly malty with a fruity tang or a nutty richness, and easy to drink.

Midwestern brown ales to try:

❑ *Bell's Best Brown Ale (Michigan)*
❑ *Empyrean Third Stone Brown (Nebraska)*
❑ *Goose Island Hex Nut Brown Ale (Illinois)*
❑ *New Glarus Fat Squirrel (Wisconsin)*

BOCK/DOPPELBOCK

Color: STRAW ▭ BLACK
Flavor: HOPS ▭ MALT
ABV: 7–10%
Serving temperature: Minimum of 45° F

These potent lagers in the bock style include the (approximately) double-strength doppelbock, the light but potent Maibock, the concentrated high-alcohol eisbock, and the occasional chocolate-flavored bock. The Midwest's German-influenced heritage tends to make midwesterners particularly receptive to this rich, full-bodied style.

Midwestern bocks to try:

- ❏ *Bell's Consecrator Doppelbock (Michigan)*
- ❏ *Capital Autumnal Fire (Wisconsin)*
- ❏ *Capital Blonde Doppelbock (Wisconsin)*
- ❏ *Millstream Schokolade Bock (Iowa)*
- ❏ *New Glarus Uff-da Bock (Wisconsin)*
- ❏ *New Glarus Unplugged Eisbock (Wisconsin)*
- ❏ *Sprecher Doppel Bock (Wisconsin)*
- ❏ *Summit Maibock (Minnesota)*

SCHWARZBIER

Color: STRAW ▭ BLACK
Flavor: HOPS ▭ MALT
ABV: 3.8–5%
Serving temperature: 48° F

The darkest of the dark lagers, these range from dark brown to black. Some are so dark that they are nearly opaque, others have a ruby-colored or purplish edge.

American dark lagers tend to be quite different in character than German-style schwarzbiers—lighter bodied and more lightly flavored than the classic, self-confident German-style schwarzbier, but American microbrewers, yet again, like to blur the lines. Not aggressively bittered and possessing a delicate and easy-drinking mouthfeel, this traditional dark beer takes lager to a whole new level. If you think you don't like dark beer, or you think all dark beers are bitter, try one of these to foil your own expectations.

Midwestern schwarzbiers to try:

- ☐ *Goose Island Schwarzbier (Illinois)*
- ☐ *Great Lakes Eliot Ness (Ohio)*
- ☐ *Schell Dark (Minnesota)*
- ☐ *Schlafly Schwarzbier (Missouri)*
- ☐ *Sprecher Black Bavarian (Wisconsin)*

PORTER

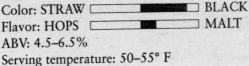

Color: STRAW ▭ BLACK
Flavor: HOPS ▭ MALT
ABV: 4.5–6.5%
Serving temperature: 50–55° F

Deep, dark, and full-bodied with reddish jewel tones behind the dark brown to ebony color and flavors of espresso, chocolate, and roasted grain, porter is an excellent beer for sipping after dinner. Midwestern craft brewers also like to experiment with this style, augmenting the natural suggestions of coffee and chocolate with added flavors, from real vanilla to smoked malts. This style generally bridges the brown ales and the stouts, both in color and in flavor.

Midwestern porters to try:

- ☐ *Barley Island Bourbon Barrel-Aged Porter (Indiana)*
- ☐ *Barley Johns The Dark Knight (Returns) (Minnesota)*
- ☐ *Bell's Porter (Michigan)*
- ☐ *Boulevard Bully! Porter (Missouri)*
- ☐ *Central Waters Mud Puppy Porter (Wisconsin)*
- ☐ *Empyrean Dark Side Vanilla Porter (Nebraska)*
- ☐ *Great Lakes Edmund Fitzgerald Porter (Ohio)*
- ☐ *O'Fallon Smoked Porter (Missouri)*
- ☐ *Stoney Creek Original Vanilla Porter (Michigan)*
- ☐ *Summit Great Northern Porter (Minnesota)*
- ☐ *Thirsty Dog Old Leghumper (Ohio)*
- ☐ *Upland Bad Elmers Porter (Indiana)*

STOUTS AND IMPERIAL STOUTS

Color: STRAW ▭▬ BLACK
Flavor: HOPS ▭▬▭ MALT
ABV: 3–6%; imperial or "extra" stout and strong ale: 6.5–12% or even higher for certain specialty releases
Serving temperature: Minimum of 50° F

In general, stout is dark, rich, and similar to porter (they are often lumped together), with a strong, toasted grain flavor nuanced by roasted coffee and bittersweet chocolate flavors. This is another category with which midwestern craft brewers like to experi-

ment by adding different flavors or amping up the gravity in the brewhouse. You'll find a lot of midwestern-brewed stouts with added flavors of coffee, chocolate, or both, and plenty of examples of high-alcohol imperial stouts, as well as more traditional oatmeal and cream stouts.

Midwestern stouts to try:

- ❑ *Arcadia Imperial Stout (Michigan)*
- ❑ *Barley Island Bourbon Barrell-Aged Oatmeal Stout (Indiana)*
- ❑ *Bell's Expedition Stout (Michigan)*
- ❑ *Bell's Java Stout (Michigan)*
- ❑ *Bell's Kalamazoo Stout (Michigan)*
- ❑ *Bell's Special Double Cream Stout (Michigan)*
- ❑ *Boulevard Dry Stout (Missouri)*
- ❑ *Central Waters Brewers Reserve Bourbon Barrel Stout (Wisconsin)*
- ❑ *Central Waters Satin Solstice Imperial Stout (Wisconsin)*
- ❑ *Firehouse Smoke Jumper Stout (South Dakota)*
- ❑ *Founders Breakfast Stout (Michigan)*
- ❑ *Founders Imperial Stout (Michigan)*
- ❑ *Free State Oatmeal Stout (Kansas)*
- ❑ *Free State Owd Macs Imperial (Kansas)*
- ❑ *Goose Island Oatmeal Stout (Illinois)*
- ❑ *Great Lakes Blackout Stout (Ohio)*
- ❑ *Lake Superior Sir Duluth Oatmeal Stout (Minnesota)*
- ❑ *Millstream Colony Oatmeal Stout (Iowa)*
- ❑ *Mishawaka Founders Stout (Indiana)*
- ❑ *New Glarus Coffee Stout (Wisconsin)*
- ❑ *New Glarus Unplugged Imperial Stout (Wisconsin)*
- ❑ *Schlafly Oatmeal Stout (Missouri)*

❏ *Springfield Mueller Mudhouse Stout (Missouri)*
❏ *Thirsty Dog Siberian Night Imperial Stout (Ohio)*
❏ *Three Floyds Dark Lord Russian Imperial Stout (Indiana)*
❏ *Town Hall Black H20 Oatmeal Stout (Minnesota)*

BARLEY WINE

Color: STRAW ▭▬▭ BLACK
Flavor: HOPS ▭▬▭ MALT
ABV: 7–12%
Serving temperature: 50–55° F

This high-gravity style makes a perfect evening warmer on a winter night. What could be cozier than a barley wine in front of the fire while a midwestern blizzard rages outside? Why not take some with you while ice fishing? These sweet, rich warmers are usually amber to medium brown with suggestions of rich toffee and undertones of port or sherry (which can be accentuated via cask conditioning). You can cellar these for many years to help them mellow and develop even more complexity.

Midwestern barley wines to try:

❏ *Back Road No. 9 Barleywine (Indiana)*
❏ *Barley Johns Barrel Aged Rosies Ale (Minnesota)*
❏ *Free State Old Backus Barley Wine (Kansas)*
❏ *Lake Superior Old Man Winter Warmer (Minnesota)*
❏ *Three Floyds Behemoth Barleywine (Indiana)*
❏ *Upland Winter Warmer (Indiana)*

SEASONAL AND SPECIALTY BEERS

Midwesterners love to celebrate the profound changes of the seasons in this region with fresh fruit-spiked summer beers and warming holiday brews. Some of the "winter warmers" from the Midwest only contain about 5–6% alcohol, not a lot compared to strong  ales from other regions, but such are the laws in many midwestern states. Many midwestern brewers experiment with seasonals and specialty brews, doing with spices and alternative flavorings what they can't do with ABV levels. These vary too much in color, flavor, etc. to scale, so try these with a sense of adventure!

Midwestern seasonal and specialty beers to try:

- ☐ *Bell's Eccentric Ale (mysteriously spiced, Michigan)*
- ☐ *Bell's Winter White Ale (brewed with wheat, Michigan)*
- ☐ *Boulevard Nutcracker Ale (Missouri)*
- ☐ *Dark Horse Fore Smoked Stout (Michigan)*
- ☐ *Empyrean Burning Skye Scottish Ale (Nebraska)*
- ☐ *Goose Island Christmas Ale (Illinois)*
- ☐ *Goose Island Summertime (Illinois)*
- ☐ *Great Lakes Christmas Ale (Ohio)*
- ☐ *Great Northern Saison (North Dakota)*
- ☐ *Kuhnhenn Devil's Horn (a red raspberry strong ale, Michigan)*

- ❏ *Kuhnhenn Raspberry Eisbock (Michigan)*
- ❏ *New Glarus Belgian Red (over one pound of Door County cherries in every bottle, Wisconsin)*
- ❏ *New Glarus Raspberry Tart (flavored with Oregon raspberries, Wisconsin)*
- ❏ *Oaken Barrel Razz Wheat (brewed with Oregon raspberries, Indiana)*
- ❏ *Schlafly Winter ESB (Missouri)*
- ❏ *Summit Winter Ale (Minnesota)*
- ❏ *Three Floyds Alpha Klaus Christmas Porter (Indiana)*
- ❏ *Two Brothers Domaine DuPage French Style Country Ale (a bière de garde, Illinois)*

🍺 18 🍺

United States: Northwest and West Coast

The Northwest and West Coast gave birth to craft brewing in its modern incarnation, and this region of the country remains the heart, soul, and center of craft beer in the United States. While talented craft brewers certainly produce amazing beer in other regions, no one can deny the deep underlying influence of the Pacific Northwest and California in the way craft brew has emerged, developed, and matured in the United States. This is truly the land of craft beer. Whenever craft beer seems to settle into a definition, northwestern craft brewers push that definition out of shape again. Experimentation, innovation, and a true, deep appreciation for handmade beer with real flavor define this region of the United States.

Northwestern craft brewers have a few distinct characteristics, not the least of which is to defy having any characteristics. Experimenting with styles, blurring boundaries, tinkering with definitions, and adding all manner of flavorings, the Northwest continues to set the standard for craft beer. Yet, one long-standing trend in the Northwest is, undoubtedly, hoppiness. While not every northwestern brewer produces big hop bombs, many of them do, and this is a characteristic for which the Northwest is famous. Stereotypes, after all, come from somewhere! One reason the Northwest may be so enamored with the hop plant is that this is the country's source for growing hops, with a climate that best suits the hop plants. One obvious sign of this is that virtually every northwestern craft brewer of note makes a version of the hop-heavy India pale ale (IPA) style. (Note the exceptionally long list of northwestern IPAs to try in this chapter.)

Northwestern brewers also like to experiment with flavors. Any style may be subject to such experiments— mandarin oranges in a wheat beer, hazelnuts in a brown ale, chipotle chilies in a golden ale, or juniper berries in a pale ale, not to mention the more obvious chocolate and coffee stouts. And, while American microbrewers in general tend to be unique (in a worldwide and historical scope) for brewing both ales and lagers in the same brewery, northwestern microbrewers take it a step further. Many craft brewers in these regions, even those who run relatively small operations, brew a huge number of styles. The wide variety of ale styles are certainly an emphasis in the Northwest, as opposed to, for example, the lager-intensive Midwest. Yet many northwestern craft brewers also produce excellent, even experimental lagers.

Northwestern craft brewers like to foil beer assumptions of all kinds. Don't expect the label to necessarily tell you what kind of beer you're getting. The Rogue brewery in Oregon, for example, is famous for bending the rules about what they call their beers and how they brew them. Dead Guy Ale is actually brewed in the German Maibock style, but with an ale yeast. Rogue's Half-e-Weizen sounds like a Hefeweizen, is advertised as being "brewed in the Belgian style," but comes closest to a quirky American wheat beer. Go figure. The one thing you can definitely say about northwestern craft brewers: they aren't afraid to break the rules.

On the other hand, breweries like Sierra Nevada have set the standard and the benchmarks for assessing many styles. Craft brewers and beer judges generally consider Sierra Nevada Pale Ale to be that style's classic example, in its American incarnation. California accomplishes some pretty big beers all on its own. In 2004, according to Ratebeer, three of the top ten brewers in the world were located in southern California: AlesSmith Brewing Company in San Diego was number one, and Stone Brewing Company in San Marcos and Pizza Port in Solana Beach came in third and eighth, respectively.

Because the northwestern United States has hundreds and hundreds of creative and committed craft brewers, space requirements prohibit including them all in this chapter. Instead, below you will find more a summary or overview of craft brewing in the Northwest today, with apologies to all those microbrewers and brewpubs not mentioned in these pages. (Contact me and let me know about you!) For more detailed, extensive, and up-to-the-minute information on microbrewers and brewpubs in the Northwest and West Coast, consult the travel sections on Ratebeer (*www.ratebeer.com*) and Beer Advocate (*www.beeradvocate.com*). Even so, the beer lists in this chapter are long, especially for certain styles northwestern craft brewers favor, like India pale ale and strong ale/old ale. Have fun tasting and training your palate to recognize the big, loud, often unusual, always interesting northwestern and western-brewed craft beers.

History

Before 1850, hardly anybody even lived on the West Coast, and California didn't become a state until 1850. Oregon achieved statehood in 1859. But something happened in 1849 that changed the West Coast forever . . . the discovery of gold. Gold in the Sierra Nevada foothills sparked a huge migration to the West, as everyone had great dreams of great riches—the nineteenth century's own lotto. San Francisco blossomed into a huge boomtown, and with a vigorous, active, thirsty population comes a great need for beer. Brewing thrived in San Francisco throughout the last half of the 1800s. Some accounts state that bottled, imported beer was already widely available in San Francisco even before the Gold Rush. By the mid-1850s, San Francisco was booming with breweries, including the Empire Brewery, the California Brewery, Schuppert's, the Bavarian Brewery, the San Francisco Brewery, the Eagle Brewery, the Eureka Brewery, and the Seidenstrecker & Rathe Washington Brewery.

When lager became popular all over the country, California brewers began producing a unique local brew called steam beer, sometimes also called California common beer. Beer historians have various ideas about what this beer was and how it was originally produced.

One predominant theory is that California brewers were faced with the challenge of not having access to cold temperature for lagering, but had customers who wanted lager. Importing ice from Alaska or the mountains was expensive and impractical, so California brewers began brewing beer using lager yeast but under warmer "ale conditions," resulting in this unique beer style. Some believe the carbon dioxide build-up resulted in a burst of steam upon tapping the kegs, hence the name. Another theory is that steam beer was actually beer brewed using steam engine technology. The world may never know for sure.

STEAM BEER TODAY

While many small breweries and brewpubs make a beer they call steam beer or California common, Anchor Brewing Company makes the only widely available version of this old classic. Try their Anchor Steam Beer, not listed in any of the categories in this chapter because of its unique nature. Is it a lager? Is it an ale? Have a taste, and form your own opinion.

Meanwhile, up in Oregon, Portland was also becoming a brewing hub. When gold was discovered in Alaska in 1881, Juneau became a small hub of brewing activity too. But then the Great Depression, Prohibition, and their resulting conditions forced many small breweries to close. Brewing on the West Coast shriveled . . . until Prohibition was repealed.

After Prohibition, breweries cautiously began to re-open on the West Coast. That included the Anchor Brewery in San Francisco, a company that specialized in Anchor Steam Beer, reclaiming California's original beer style. Anchor was just one of many northwestern breweries to change ownership, location, and status throughout the early years of the twentieth century, but it also played a pivotal role in the subsequent formation of microbrews all over this region.

Brewing historians often credit Fritz Maytag with sparking the microbrew revolution, not by opening a microbrewery but by reviving and improving the failing Anchor Brewery way back in 1965. At this time, smaller breweries were either consolidating, getting bought up by the large brewers, or going out of business. Maytag—of the family that makes the appliances and the famous Maytag Bleu Cheese from their dairy farm in Newton, Iowa—used to patronize the Anchor Brewing Company in San Francisco during his college days at Stanford. Open since 1895, the Anchor Brewing Company, like so many others, was going under. Maytag hated to see that happen. Fresh out of college, he bought the brewery, rescuing it from closure.

At a time when beer was largely homogenized to be low in flavor, light in color, and appealing to the masses—inevitably with the help of flavorless cheap adjuncts like corn and rice to cut production costs and lighten taste—Maytag took a different approach. He decided to commit to the process of brewing beer with flavor and high-quality ingredients. After a lot of trial and error, Maytag not only got Anchor back on its feet but began bottling its Anchor Steam Beer. The brewery also began producing other styles: porter, barley wine, seasonal summer wheat beer, and seasonal Christmas beer with an annually changing recipe. Anchor was small, it focused on quality handcrafted beer, and it worked.

Just north of Anchor Brewing in Sonoma, New Albion Brewing opened in 1976 and was technically the first microbrewery to open as a new small brewery. This brewery lasted only a few years, but people began to notice what was happening in California: breweries could open, produce small batches of tasty handcrafted beer, and people would actually buy it. A few years later, in 1980, River City Brewing in Sacramento and Sierra

Nevada Brewing in Chico both opened. Today Sierra Nevada is one of the continent's largest microbreweries, and their brews—especially the famous and much beloved Sierra Nevada Pale Ale—converted thousands (millions?) of Americans to craft beer.

Also in 1980, microbreweries opened in Colorado and New York, but throughout the 1980s, most new microbreweries proliferated in the Northwest, spreading all over Washington state (Red Hook Ale Brewery and Bert Grant's Yakima Brewing & Malting, to name two of the most famous), Oregon (Hillsdale, Rogue Brewery), and of course, California (Anchor Brewing, Sierra Nevada, Mendocino Brewing, Buffalo Bill Owens's brewpub, San Francisco Brewing, to name just a few of the early ones). In Alaska, the Alaskan Brewing Company opened in 1986, and was the only brewery in the entire state at the time, brewing an amber ale from a recipe popular during the Gold Rush days.

These microbreweries did something important for American beer drinkers: they introduced us to a huge range of styles most Americans had forgotten about, or may never have even known existed. Amber ales, brown ales, pale ales, India pale ales, stouts, porters, wheat beers, strong ales, old ales, and ales flavored with local produce from huckleberries to honey—beer had a brand-new face, and the public embraced it enthusiastically.

The Microbrew Revolution peaked in the Northwest in the mid-1990s, but many of the well-established microbreweries continue to do extremely well today. Anchor Steam Beer has never advertised and relies on word of mouth, but is available in all fifty states, testament to America's enduring affection for beer with flavor, character, and a nod to history.

Current Trends

The northwestern states include Washington, Oregon, and California (even if it isn't completely in the Northwest), and for our purposes, we will also include Montana, Wyoming, Idaho, and Alaska.

Brashness, if not a trend, is certainly a characteristic of northwestern brewers. Above all, the Northwest sets the trends, rather than being subject to them. Northwestern craft brewers keep setting the standard for the rest of the country, even if other brewers decide to argue with that standard. Whether inventing the double IPA, reinventing barrel-aging systems, or being the first to use the new aluminum bottle, the Northwest is always trying something new.

For those of us who don't live in the Northwest, one great advantage of northwestern craft beers is their wide distribution. While some of the most interesting eastern and midwestern craft beers are only available regionally, many of the original microbrewers in the Northwest became so popular that they have managed to distribute their wares all over the United States. For example, you can't buy Bell's beer or Dogfish Head beer in Iowa, but you can easily get Rogue, Sierra Nevada, Pyramid, Anchor, or Redhook. Others are more regionally distributed—the smaller microbrewers and those in less beer-intensive states like Montana and Wyoming—but still widely known among craft beer enthusiasts.

The following state-by-state look at some of the most interesting breweries and brewpubs in the northwestern United States is, of course, subject to change as breweries open and close with the times and changing regulations. Because of the huge number of microbrewers and brewpubs, we can't possibly list them all, or every great example of each brewery's beers, but here are a sampling of some of the best known and most heralded, as well as a few of my personal favorites.

WASHINGTON

Seattle is a brewing hub in Washington. Seattle-based Pyramid opened in 1984 and today brews eight year-round beers and four seasonals, with a complete portfolio of more than twenty ales, lagers, and wheat beers. Some of their most popular varieties are flavored fruit beers, widely available all over the United States. Other Seattle microbrewers of note—many with their own brewpubs and even restaurants—include Seattle's Pike Brewing Company, Elysian Brewing Company, Hales Ales Brewery & Brewpub, and Big Time Brewery & Alehouse.

Elsewhere in Washington, Redhook Brewery is probably the most widely known and distributed microbrew. Redhook started small in 1981 with their Redhook Ale followed by their Blackhook Porter. When they released Ballard Bitter in 1984, their popularity skyrocketed. In 2002, they were purchased by Anheuser-Busch, and today they brew in three locations: their original city of Ballard, from a second brewery in Woodinville, and also on the East Coast in Portsmouth, New Hampshire, assuring fresh Redhook for both coasts (and a lot of states in the middle too). As is often the case, a buyout by a megabrewer allowed a previously small brewery to drastically broaden its distribution.

The Yakima Brewing & Malting Company in Yakima makes Grant's ales, also popular and widely distributed across the United States. Fish Brewing Company in Olympia is a small craft brewer that makes the certified organic Fish Tale Ales and was recently named twenty-third best brewer in the world. Other notable Washington microbrewers and brewpubs include La-Conner Brewing Company in LaConner—they also own a specialty beer shop in Seattle called Bottle-works—Diamond Knot Brewery in the Puget Sound area, which opened in 1993 in Mukilteo, and Dicks Brewing Company in Centralia.

OREGON

In Oregon, no microbrewer has gained more fame or had more influence than Rogue. Founded in 1988 in Ashland, they have since moved to Newport. Their widely popular and widely distributed Dead Guy Ale sets the standard for this brewery's quirky styles—a Maibock in style but brewed with an ale yeast. Rogue updates product names, rereleases them in slightly different versions on occasion, and also likes to change the bottle art. Never a dull moment with this brewery's exciting beers! Rogue consistently produces high-quality brews in a baffling variety of styles and never hesitates to do things big or try something new. Luckily for craft-brew fans all over the United States, you can buy at least a few of Rogue's exceptional brews in most states. They also have Rogue Pubs scattered throughout Oregon, with one outpost in San Francisco. I've never tried a Rogue beer I didn't like, although some of them are pretty unusual.

Portland is home to the largest concentration of microbrewers in the entire world. Bridgeport Brewing Company advertises itself as Oregon's oldest craft brewer, opening in 1984. Widmer Brothers Brewing

Company also opened in 1984. Other Portland fixtures include Hair of the Dog Brewing Company (recently voted fifth best brewer in the world), Full Sail Brewing Company, MacTarnahan's Brewery/Portland Brewing Company, Alameda Brewing Company, and Laurelwood Public House & Brewery, the latter Oregon's only certified organic brewery. Other Oregon microbrewers producing traditional and experimental craft beers: Deschutes Brewery in Bend and the Pelican Pub & Brewery in Pacific City.

CALIFORNIA

California is practically peppered with great craft brewers, but the Anchor Brewing Company in San Francisco is generally considered the first microbrewer and the progenitor of the craft brew scene in America. Anchor still makes its Anchor Steam Beer, its most popular style. Sierra Nevada Brewing Company in Chico was also among the first microbreweries, and today has grown to be one of the country's largest.

California has so many wonderful microbreweries and brewpubs that this book simply doesn't have the space to list them all, but a few of the most well known and those producing the very best include AleSmith Brewing Company in San Diego, recently listed in Ratebeer's huge public survey as the number one brewery in the world. (Not just America. The world!) Other great California breweries include Stone Brewing Company in San Marcos, the Pizza Ports in Solana Beach and Carlsbad, Ballast Point Brewing Company in San Diego, Bear Republic Brewing Company in Healdsburg, Russian River Brewing in Santa Rosa, North Coast Brewing Company in Ft. Bragg, Anderson Valley Brewing Com-

pany in Anderson Valley and also in Boonville, Mendo-
cino Brewing Company in Hopland, Lagunitas Brewing
Company in Petaluma, Left Coast—Oggi's Pizza and
Brewing Company in Del Mar, Lost Coast Brewery &
Café in Eureka (the owners are two women, unusual for
the microbrewery business), Alpine Beer Company in
Alpine, Speakeasy Ales & Lagers in San Francisco,
Drake's Brewing Company in San Leandro, Buffalo
Bill's Brewery in Hayward, Firestone Walker Fine Ales
in Paso Robles, and Moylan's Brewery and Restaurant
in Novato.

MONTANA

Montana can't compete with its western neighbors
when it comes to sheer volume of craft brewers, but it
does have a few. Big Sky Brewing Company in Missoula
is the most celebrated, and their Moose Drool brown
ale is by far Montana's best-selling beer among those
brewed in the state. Big Sky claims to be the first brewery in America to use the revolutionary new aluminum
bottle. (Time will tell if this catches on.)

Also in Missoula, Bayern Brewing makes lagers in
the German tradition, with a couple of ales thrown in
for good measure. Big Hole Brewing Company in Bel-
grade, Yellowstone Valley Brewing Company in
Billings, and Great Northern Brewing Company in
Whitefish also produce good craft beers in the pioneering spirit one would expect from the Land of the Big
Sky. The Lang Creek Brewery in Marion advertises itself
as "America's Most Remote Brewery," and has an
airstrip on the premises.

WYOMING

The Snake River Brewing Company in Jackson Hole is the state's most well-known microbrewery and brewpub. They have received many awards for their beers, their brewery, and their brewer. Other Wyoming microbrewers include Bottoms Up Brewery in Pinedale and a handful of brewpubs in Laramie, including the Library Restaurant & Brewing Company and Altitude Chophouse and Brewery.

IDAHO

Grand Teton Brewing Company in Victor and the Coeur d'Alene Brewing Company in Coeur d'Alene are two of Idaho's most prominent craft brewers, the latter founded in 1908 and revived, post-Prohibition, in 1987. In Boise, Sockeye Brewing serves their craft beers in their beer pub.

ALASKA

Canada may separate Alaska from the Pacific Northwest, but the brewing styles in this American outpost resemble those in Washington and Oregon—hoppy and with a rebellious, pioneering spirit. The Alaskan Brewing Company in Juneau opened in 1986, and was at the time Alaska's only brewery. They now distribute their beer to the Pacific Northwest. Other Alaskan microbrewers of note include Midnight Sun in Anchorage, opened in 1995, and Silver Gulch Brewing and Bottling Company just north of Fairbanks, opened in 1998. Alaska also has a handful of brewpubs in Anchorage: Glacier Brewhouse, Mooses Tooth, and Sleeping Lady Brewing Company. Other small microbrewers include

Haines Brewing Company in Haines and Homer Brewing Company in Homer.

THE GERMAN INFLUENCE

The West Coast and Pacific Northwest tend to favor ales, but the Alaskan Brewing Company in Juneau makes several lagers popular in this region. They aren't listed elsewhere in this chapter because this region doesn't have enough entries for lager categories, but if you can get them, try the Alaskan Amber, in the German altbier style, and the Alaskan Summer Ale, a classic kölsch.

Characteristic Types of Beer

Hops, hops, hops. And more hops. If it's a hoppy style, or it can be made more hoppy, it tends to be popular in the Northwest. English-style strong ales and old ales also proliferate here, but are relatively rare in other areas of the country. Northwestern craft brewers also tend to favor pale ales (hoppy ones) and a wide array of unusual stouts and imperial stouts. The range of beer styles brewed in the northwestern United States mainly centers around a wide variety of ales, with just a few favorite lager styles. In this chapter, you'll find styles grouped together mainly according to their general characteristics and placement on the color spectrum.

HEFEWEIZEN/AMERICAN WHEAT

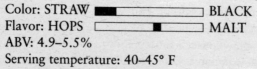

Color: STRAW ▭ BLACK
Flavor: HOPS ▭ MALT
ABV: 4.9–5.5%
Serving temperature: 40–45° F

Experimental Northwestern craft brewers like to play around with this style, so that many of their brews with variations of "hefeweizen" in the name are really American-style wheat beers. Because of the blurry lines, they are grouped together in this category as all the pale sedimented wheat beers loosely in the German hefeweizen style. In general, this style is a cloudy, straw-colored ale that tastes of wheat, yeast, and fruit. This style generally has spicy notes and complex, layered flavors in the suspended yeast sediment.

Northwestern hefeweizens/wheat beers to try:

- *Anchor Summer Beer (California)*
- *Great Northern Wheatfish Hefeweizen (Montana)*
- *North Coast Blue Star (California)*
- *Pyramid Hefeweizen (Washington)*
- *Redhook Hefeweizen (Washington)*
- *Sierra Nevada Wheat (Oregon)*
- *Widmer Brothers Hefeweizen (Oregon)*

PALE ALES/BITTERS/ESBS

Color: STRAW ▬▬▬▬▭ BLACK
Flavor: HOPS ▭▬▭ MALT
ABV: 3–5%
Serving temperature: Minimum 45° F

In the Northwest, pale ales, bitters, ESBs, and all their cousins tend to be hoppier with even bigger flavors than pale ales from other regions in the United

States. This is the group of pale to deep gold ales, including pale ales, blond ales, golden ales, bitters, and ESBs. Easy to drink, usually with ample hops balanced with a judicious malt character, this category of pale to golden ales is low in alcohol and perfect for drinking several over the course of an evening.

Northwestern pale ales, bitters, and ESBs to try:

- ❏ *Acme California Pale Ale (California)*
- ❏ *Alaskan ESB (Alaska)*
- ❏ *Alaskan Pale (Alaska)*
- ❏ *AleSmith Amber ESB (California)*
- ❏ *AleSmith X (California)*
- ❏ *Anchor Liberty Ale (California)*
- ❏ *Anchor Small Beer (California)*
- ❏ *Anderson Valley Poleeko Gold Pale Ale (California)*
- ❏ *Bayern Montana Trout Slayer Ale (Montana)*
- ❏ *Bert Grant's Fresh Hop Ale (Washington)*
- ❏ *Big Hole Headstrong Pale Ale (Montana)*
- ❏ *Big Sky Powder Hound Winter Ale (Montana)*
- ❏ *Big Sky Scapegoat Pale Ale (Montana)*
- ❏ *Bridgeport Blue Heron Ale (Oregon)*
- ❏ *Deschutes Bachelor ESB (Oregon)*
- ❏ *Deschutes Mirror Pond Pale Ale (Oregon)*
- ❏ *Firestone Double Barrel Ale (California)*
- ❏ *Full Sail Pale Ale (Oregon)*
- ❏ *Full Sail Rip Curl (Oregon)*
- ❏ *Grand Teton Bitch Creek ESB (Idaho)*
- ❏ *Hair of the Dog Ruth (Oregon)*
- ❏ *MacTarnahans Highlander Pale Ale (Oregon)*
- ❏ *Mendocino Blue Heron Pale Ale (California)*
- ❏ *Pike Naughty Nellie's Ale (Washington)*
- ❏ *Pike Pale Ale (Washington)*

- ❏ *Pyramid Pale Ale (Washington)*
- ❏ *Redhook Blonde Ale (Washington)*
- ❏ *Redhook ESB (Washington)*
- ❏ *Rogue Brutal Bitter (Oregon)*
- ❏ *Rogue Oregon Golden Ale (Oregon)*
- ❏ *Rogue Youngers Special Bitter (Oregon)*
- ❏ *Sierra Nevada Harvest Ale (California)*
- ❏ *Sierra Nevada Pale Ale (California)*
- ❏ *Snake River Pale Ale (Wyoming)*
- ❏ *Stone Pale Ale (California)*

INDIA PALE ALE

Color: STRAW ▭▬▭ BLACK
Flavor: HOPS ▬▭ MALT
ABV: 5–7.5%, up to 20% for double or imperial IPAs
Serving temperature: Minimum of 45° F

Once hopped-up for its preservative qualities, today's IPAs remain high in hop bitterness, especially in the Northwest. Light golden with a fresh, aromatic hop quality and the bitterness many beer connoisseurs have come to know and love, IPAs really are hoppy everywhere in America, but the style is most popular here. Northwestern craft brewers and beer drinkers love that hop bitterness, perhaps because this region of the country grows hops so they are available right there in the neighborhood. This region spawned the so-called double or imperial IPA, taking hop bitterness to its extreme. The best ones remain balanced even while maxing out the hop aroma and flavor. You'll even see some holiday-themed IPAs from this region. While everyone else is drinking warming barley wines and strong ales during the Yuletide season, northwesterners are reaching for that crisp, bright, hoppy holiday IPA. (After all, Christmas along the Pacific Ocean can get pretty balmy.)

SUPER HOP AROMA VIA DRY HOPPING

Dry hopping is a technique in which hops are added to beer after the wort is cooled. While hops added to the boiling wort contribute hop bitterness to the resulting beer, dry hopping adds an extra punch of hop aroma to the final product, and can also contribute additional layers of hop flavor. Many West Coast brewers use dry hopping to amp up the hop quotient in their brews.

Northwestern IPAs to try:

- ☐ *Acme California IPA (California)*
- ☐ *AleSmith IPA (California)*
- ☐ *AleSmith YuleSmith India Pale Ale (California)*
- ☐ *Anderson Valley Hop Ottin IPA (California)*
- ☐ *Bear Republic Racer 5 (California)*
- ☐ *Bert Grant's Hopzilla IPA (Washington)*
- ☐ *Bert Grant's India Pale Ale (Washington)*
- ☐ *Big Time Bhagwans Best IPA (Washington)*
- ☐ *Bridgeport IPA (Oregon)*
- ☐ *Deschutes Quail Springs IPA (Oregon)*
- ☐ *Diamond Knot IPA (Washington)*
- ☐ *Elysian The Immortal IPA (Washington)*
- ☐ *Fish Tale Organic India Pale Ale (Washington)*
- ☐ *Full Sail Wreck the Halls (Oregon)*
- ☐ *Grand Teton Sweetgrass India Pale Ale (Idaho)*
- ☐ *Hales Aftermath Imperial IPA (Washington)*
- ☐ *Hales Mongoose IPA (Washington)*
- ☐ *LaConner India Pale Ale (Washington)*

- ❏ *Lagunitas India Pale Ale (California)*
- ❏ *Lagunitas Maximus (California)*
- ❏ *Library Bantam IPA (Wyoming)*
- ❏ *Lost Coast Indica India Pale Ale (California)*

- ❏ *MacTarnahans Woodstock IPA (Oregon)*
- ❏ *Mendocino White Hawk IPA (California)*
- ❏ *Midnight Sun Cohoho Imperial IPA (Alaska)*
- ❏ *Midnight Sun Sockeye Red IPA (Alaska)*
- ❏ *Pelican India Pelican Ale (Oregon)*
- ❏ *Pike IPA (Washington)*
- ❏ *Pizza Port Frank Double IPA (California)*
- ❏ *Pyramid India Pale Ale (Washington)*
- ❏ *Redhook IPA (Washington)*
- ❏ *Rogue Imperial Pale Ale (Oregon)*
- ❏ *Russian River Pliny the Elder (California)*
- ❏ *Sierra Nevada Celebration Ale (California)*
- ❏ *Sierra Nevada India Pale Ale (California)*
- ❏ *Sockeye Dagger Falls IPA (Idaho)*
- ❏ *Speakeasy Big Daddy IPA (California)*
- ❏ *Stone India Pale Ale (California)*
- ❏ *Stone Ruination IPA (California)*

BELGIAN-STYLE ALES/STRONG ALES/ABBEY-STYLE TRIPELS

Color: STRAW ▭▬▬▭ BLACK
Flavor: HOPS ▭▬▬▭ MALT
ABV: 6.5–12%
Serving temperature: Minimum of 45° F

These are the light- to medium-colored Belgian-style ales with a heavier alcoholic content, brewed in the abbey tradition. Some northwestern craft brewers specialize in this style, but even those who don't like to experiment with it, in the true spirit of Belgian beer. Light-bodied and pleasant to drink, yet warming, these styles are generally a brilliant gold in color and less delicately hopped in the Northwest than in some other regions. Lightly kilned malts impart subtle nuances of malt character and color.

Northwestern Belgian-style ales/strong ales/abbey-style tripels to try:

- ❑ *AleSmith Grand Cru (California)*
- ❑ *Big Hole Mythical White Grand Cru (Montana)*
- ❑ *Hair of the Dog Rose (Oregon)*
- ❑ *Lagunitas Censored (Kronik) (California)*
- ❑ *MacTarnahans Gran Luxe Tripel Ale (Oregon)*
- ❑ *Midnight Sun Épluche-Culotte (Alaska)*
- ❑ *Midnight Sun La Mâitresse du Moine (Alaska)*
- ❑ *North Coast PranQster Belgian (California)*
- ❑ *Pizza Port Cuvee de Tomme (California)*
- ❑ *Russian River Damnation (California)*
- ❑ *Stone 04.04.04 Vertical Epic Ale (California)*

AMBER/RED ALE

Color: STRAW ▭▬▭ BLACK
Flavor: HOPS ▭▬▭ MALT
ABV: 4.3–5%
Serving temperature: 45–50° F

Many small northwestern craft brewers consider their versions of amber or red ale to be their flagship beers. These copper-colored, malty ales inspired by beers ranging from the UK copper ales through the altbier of Düsseldorf are balanced and smooth, with a less aggressively hopped—and hence maltier—taste than a pale ale. Also included in this category are the Irish-style red ales and the caramely Scottish-style ales. This category is meant to continue the ale color spectrum from copper to deep reddish-brown. As is typical for American microbrewers, this category contains many examples of brewers taking liberties with the classic ale/lager

distinction and fiddling with new ways of blurring the line between those categories. These ales are darker in color than the pale ales, and lower in alcohol than the Belgian-style strong ales. As is also typical for the Northwest, these amber and red ales tend to have a slightly more prominent hop profile than elsewhere in the states.

Northwestern ambers/red ales to try:

☐ *Anderson Valley Boont Amber Ale (California)*
☐ *Bert Grant's Scottish Style Ale (Washington)*
☐ *Bottoms Up Adventure Amber (Wyoming)*
☐ *Deschutes Cinder Cone Red Ale (Oregon)*
☐ *Full Sail Amber Ale (Oregon)*
☐ *Grand Teton Teton Ale (Idaho)*
☐ *Lang Creek Tri-Motor Amber Ale (Montana)*
☐ *MacTarnahans Amber Ale (Oregon)*
☐ *Mendocino Red Tail Ale (California)*
☐ *North Coast Red Seal Ale (California)*
☐ *Pike Kilt Lifter Scotch Ale (Washington)*

❏ *Pyramid Broken Rake (Washington)*
❏ *Pyramid Tilted Kilt (Washington)*
❏ *Rogue American Amber (Oregon)*
❏ *Rogue Saint Rogue Red (Oregon)*
❏ *Speakeasy Prohibition Ale (California)*
❏ *Stone Levitation Ale (California)*
❏ *Yellowstone Valley Wild Fly Ale (Montana)*

BROWN/MILD ALE

Color: STRAW ▭▬▭ BLACK
Flavor: HOPS ▭▬▭ MALT
ABV: 4–5.5%
Serving temperature: 45–50° F

Bronze to toasty brown, these ales are a medium-weight, malty beer with fruitiness, nuttiness, and a low alcohol content, darker than amber ales and leading, on the color spectrum, to the porters and stouts. These are forwardly malty with a fruity tang or a nutty richness, and easy to drink.

Northwestern brown ales to try:

❏ *Acme California Brown Ale (California)*
❏ *Bear Republic Pete Brown Tribute Ale (California)*
❏ *Coeur d'Alene Lakeside British Ale (Idaho)*
❏ *Dicks Danger Ale (Washington)*
❏ *Lost Coast Downtown Brown (California)*
❏ *Midnight Sun Kodiak Brown Ale (Alaska)*

☐ *Pelican Doryman's Dark Ale (Oregon)*
☐ *Redhook Nut Brown Ale (Washington)*
☐ *Rogue HazelNut Brown Nectar (Oregon)*
☐ *Sierra Nevada Brown (California)*

STRONG ALE/OLD ALE

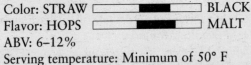

Color: STRAW ▭ BLACK
Flavor: HOPS ▭ MALT
ABV: 6–12%
Serving temperature: Minimum of 50° F

This style hasn't captured the attention of most craft brewers in the United States, but in the Northwest, many brewers try their hand at these traditional British styles. Rich, darkish, and warming, strong ales and old ales are smooth with varying degrees of bitterness. Strong ales get their name from a higher ABV, while old ales get their name from the aging process. Whereas some beers can be ready for consumption in a couple of weeks or might potentially age for a few months, both strong ales and old ales can age for years, which just makes them smoother and more complex. When old ales are aged in casks that once held port, whiskey, or other liquors, they take on some of the flavor characteristics of the cask's previous contents. Some old ales rival wine in alcohol content, and hence lead into the strongest ale category of barley wine. Let old ales and strong ales come up in temperature before the pleasure of that first complex, soul-warming sip. American versions in general and northwestern versions in particular tend to have bold flavors and a discernible hop bitterness to balance the rich malt flavors and warming alcohol content of beers in this style.

Northwestern strong/old ales to try (many of these are seasonal winter beers):

- ❑ *AleSmith Horny Devil (California)*
- ❑ *Arrogant Bastard Ale (California)*
- ❑ *Bear Republic Hop Rod Rye Ale (California)*
- ❑ *Bear Republic Red Rocket Ale (California)*
- ❑ *Bert Grant's Deep Powder Winter Ale (Washington)*
- ❑ *Big Hole Diablo (Montana)*
- ❑ *Bridgeport Ebenezer Ale (Oregon)*
- ❑ *Deschutes Jubelale (Oregon)*
- ❑ *Double Bastard Ale (California)*
- ❑ *Fish Tale Old Woody English Old Ale (Washington)*
- ❑ *Full Sail Wassail Winter Ale (Oregon)*
- ❑ *Hair of the Dog Adam (based on a traditional dark ale from Dortmund, Germany, called Adam, Oregon)*
- ❑ *Hair of the Dog Fred (Oregon)*
- ❑ *Lagunitas Hairy Eyeball Ale (California)*
- ❑ *Mendocino Eye of the Hawk Select Ale (California)*
- ❑ *Portland Benchmark Old Ale (Oregon)*
- ❑ *Pyramid Snowcap Ale (Washington)*
- ❑ *Redhook Winterhook (Washington)* ·
- ❑ *Rogue Santa's Private Reserve (Oregon)*

BOCK/DOPPELBOCK

Color: STRAW 〔━━━━〕 BLACK
Flavor: HOPS 〔━━━━〕 MALT
ABV: 7–10%
Serving temperature: Minimum of 45° F

While lagers aren't a particular focus in the Northwest, brewers do enjoy experimenting with the flexible bock style. As is characteristic of northwestern craft brewers, those versions of bocks that crank up the normal aromas, flavors, and alcohol content are particularly popular: the "double" doppelbocks and Maibocks. Potent lagers in any form, bocks are usually dark in color and always high in alcohol, usually over 7%.

Northwestern bocks to try:

☐ *Fish Tale Detonator Doppelbock (Washington)*
☐ *MacTarnahans Mac Frost Winter Ale (Oregon)*
☐ *Saxer Bock (Oregon)*
☐ *Saxer JackFrost Winter Doppelbock (Oregon)*
☐ *Sierra Nevada Pale Bock (California)*

PORTER

Color: STRAW ▭▬▭ BLACK
Flavor: HOPS ▭▬▭ MALT
ABV: 4.5–6.5%
Serving temperature: 50–55° F

Deep, dark, and full-bodied with reddish jewel tones behind the dark brown to ebony color and flavors of espresso, chocolate, and roasted grain, porter is an excellent beer for sipping after dinner. Northwestern craft brewers also like to experiment with this style, cask aging it in liquor casks or augmenting the natural suggestions of coffee and chocolate with added real coffee, chocolate, vanilla, or other flavorings.

Northwestern porters to try:

☐ *Anchor Porter (California)*
☐ *Bert Grant's Perfect Porter (Washington)*
☐ *Deschutes Black Butte Porter (Oregon)*

❑ *Elysian Perseus Porter (Washington)*
❑ *Full Sail Half Pipe Porter (Oregon)*
❑ *Full Sail Imperial Porter (Oregon)*
❑ *MacTarnahans Blackwatch Cream Porter (Oregon)*
❑ *MacTarnahans Bourbon Cask Aged Blackwatch Cream Porter (Oregon)*
❑ *Redhook Blackhook Porter (Washington)*
❑ *Rogue Mocha Porter (Oregon)*
❑ *Sierra Nevada Porter (California)*

STOUTS AND IMPERIAL STOUTS

Color: STRAW ▭▭▭▭▭ BLACK
Flavor: HOPS ▭▭▭▭▭ MALT
ABV: 3–6%; imperial or "extra" stout and strong ale: 6.5–12% or even higher for certain specialty releases
Serving temperature: Minimum of 50° F

Dark, rich stout is similar to porter, especially in this region of the country where brewers are so likely to experiment and blur the lines between similar categories. As with porters, northwestern craft brewers like to experiment by adding different flavors or amping up the ABV.

Northwestern stouts and imperial stouts to try:

❑ *Alaskan Stout (Alaska)*
❑ *AleSmith Speedway Stout (California)*
❑ *Anderson Valley Barney Flats Oatmeal Stout (California)*
❑ *Bear Republic Big Bear Black Stout (California)*
❑ *Bert Grant's Imperial Stout (Washington)*
❑ *Big Sky Slow Elk Oatmeal Stout (Montana)*

- ❏ *Deschutes Obsidian Stout (Oregon)*
- ❏ *Dick's Imperial Stout (Washington)*
- ❏ *Hales Pikop Andropovs Rushin Imperial Stout (Washington)*
- ❏ *Lost Coast 8 Ball Stout (California)*
- ❏ *MacTarnahans Thunderheat Stout (Oregon)*
- ❏ *Mendocino Black Hawk Stout (California)*
- ❏ *Moylan's Ryan O'Sullivans Imperial Stout (California)*

- ❏ *North Coast Old No. 38 Stout (California)*
- ❏ *North Coast Old Rasputin Russian Imperial Stout (California)*
- ❏ *Pelican Tsunami Stout (Oregon)*
- ❏ *Pike Street XXXXX Stout (Washington)*
- ❏ *Rogue Chocolate Stout (Oregon)*
- ❏ *Rogue Imperial Stout (Oregon)*
- ❏ *Rogue Shakespeare Stout (Oregon)*
- ❏ *Sierra Nevada Stout (California)*
- ❏ *Snake River Zonker Stout (Wyoming)*
- ❏ *Stone Imperial Russian Stout (California)*

BARLEY WINE

Color: STRAW ▭▬▭ BLACK
Flavor: HOPS ▭▬▭ MALT
ABV: 7–12%
Serving temperature: 50–55° F

This high-gravity style makes a perfect evening warmer on a winter night, even in sunny California.

These sweet, rich, almost-liquors are usually amber to medium brown with suggestions of rich toffee and undertones of port or sherry, which can be accentuated via cask conditioning. You can cellar these for a few years to help them mellow and develop even more complexity.

Northwestern barley wines to try:

- *AleSmith Old Numbskull (California)*
- *Anchor Old Foghorn Ale (California)*
- *Bridgeport Old Knucklehead (Oregon)*
- *Full Sail Old Boardhead Barley Wine (Oregon)*
- *Moylan's Old Blarney Barleywine (California)*
- *North Coast Old Stock Ale (California)*
- *Rogue Old Crustacean Barley Wine (Oregon)*

FRUIT, VEGETABLE, SPICED, AND OTHER FLAVORED BEERS

In the Northwest, where fresh fruits, spicy chilies, and all kinds of produce are available most of the year, flavored beer is a natural fit. Northwestern brewers take full advantage of the Northwest's bounty by trying hundreds of flavors and flavor combinations. This is also the place where all the Rogue brewery's most adventurous mixed styles go, when they don't fit anywhere else. For that reason, I haven't included a scale for these wildly various brews.

Northwestern flavored beers to try:

- *Alaskan Smoked Porter (Alaska)*
- *Alaskan Winter Ale (brewed with spruce tips, Alaska)*
- *Amber Valley Winter Solstice (California)*
- *Bert Grant's Mandarin Hefeweizen (Washington)*
- *Big Sky Summer Honey Seasonal Ale (Montana)*

- *Buffalo Bill's Orange Blossom Cream Ale (California)*
- *Buffalo Bill's Pumpkin Ale (California)*
- *Great Northern Wild Huckleberry (Montana)*
- *Lang Creek Huckleberry N Honey (Montana)*
- *Pyramid Apricot Ale (Washington)*
- *Redhook Sunrye Ale (made with rye, Washington)*
- *Rogue Buckwheat Ale (Oregon)*
- *Rogue Dead Guy Ale (a bock-style beer brewed with ale yeast, Oregon)*
- *Rogue Half-e-Weizen (flavored with coriander and ginger, this one floats somewhere between a hefeweizen, a Belgian-style wit, and an American wheat beer, Oregon)*
- *Rogue Honey Cream Ale (Oregon)*
- *Rogue Mexicali (sometimes called Rogue Chipotle Ale, a golden ale flavored with chipotle chilies, Oregon)*
- *Rogue Smoke (Oregon)*
- *Stone Smoked Porter (California)*

♔ _19_ ♔
United States:
West and Southwest

The southwestern and western United States may not be as beer-intensive as the Northwest and West Coast, but they do have Colorado (which really could have been in the previous chapter, too). Home to Coors, one of the country's mega-brewers, Colorado is a beer-friendly state, but they aren't exclusive about pale lager in mountain country. In fact, Colorado played a significant part in the craft-beer revolution, right along with California, Oregon, and Washington. Some of the country's first and most enduring microbreweries began in Colorado, and Denver is a craft-beer hub. Every fall, Denver hosts the Great American Beer Festival, arguably the country's biggest celebration of craft beer and the source for many beer awards.

The rest of this region, however, remains relatively limited in craft brewers, often due to prohibitive legislation, like limiting beer to products with alcohol percentages of 3.2% and lower. This discourages craft brewers who like to experiment with styles characterized by higher alcohol levels. Just try making a good barley wine or imperial stout with an ABV of 3.2%. Not really possible.

Despite the difficulties for craft brewers in many

southwestern states, people in this region of the country like to drink beer—with the exception of the largely Mormon teetotaling population of Utah. The Southwest can get hot in the desert, and even the skiers in the mountains like to relax with a warming brew after a long day on the slopes. So, despite state-by-state difficulties, craft beer is alive and available—more or less—in the western and southwestern states.

THE GREAT AMERICAN BEER FESTIVAL

If you love beer and you want to make just one beer pilgrimage each year, the Great American Beer Festival is the one to choose. This three-day event held in Denver every fall hosts more than 28,000 attendees who get to sample more than 1,400 different beers from more than 300 different brewers—the biggest selection of American beers available for tasting in one location. Many consider this the best beer festival in the world, located in what some have called the Napa Valley of Beer. The festival also features the nation's most prestigious beer judging competition. For more information on the next Great American Beer Festival, check out the Brewer's Association web page with the most current information: www.beertown.org/events/gabf/index.htm.

History

The southwestern United States may actually have been one of the continent's original sources of beer. Mexican natives brewed a fermented corn beverage, and evidence suggests that this practice radiated north and throughout what would later be the southwestern United States. As is typical for ancient cultures, they brewed according to the products they had. Barley didn't grow here, but corn did, and formed an integral part of the diet for the people living in this region.

NATIVE BEER IS STILL HERE

Tesguino, consisting of a range of native corn-brewed alcoholic beverages, is still brewed by the Tarahumara Indians in northern Mexico. The Tarahumara still live in much the same way as they have for centuries, hunting and gathering for food and farming corn. Tesguino is integral to the culture, and much of the Tarahumara's corn is used for making this intoxicating beverage, which is used in social rituals—"tesguino parties."

When barley-brewed beer first came to the eastern shores of the continent, it took a while for it to reach all the way to the West Coast . . . until the Gold Rush. During this time of prolific western growth, beer came right along with the settlers hoping for their big break. Colorado was one mining hub, and brewers opened to serve the booming population during the mid-1800s.

Denver quickly became a brewing hub. Their Rocky Mountain Brewery opened in 1858, but didn't survive Prohibition. Brewer John Good, who took over the Rocky Mountain Brewery in 1861, took over Milwaukee Brewery in Denver in 1900. He renamed it the Tivoli Brewery, which became Western Products Company during Prohibition. The brewery survived Prohibition, becoming Tivoli-Union in 1934, and Tivoli again in 1953.

In 1873, Adolph Coors and Jacob Schueler opened the Golden Brewery in Golden City. A German immigrant, Adolph Coors, bought out Schueler in 1880, and the company grew dramatically as it supplied gold miners with liquid refreshment. During Prohibition, Coors survived under the name Mannah, producing near beer and malted milk.

Even before the Civil War, Texas had several large, influential breweries, mostly in San Antonio, due to its large population of German immigrants. Adolphus Busch opened the Lone Star Brewery in 1884. After Prohibition, brewers revived the Lone Star Brewery in the 1930s. Another influential Texas brewery was the Spoetzl Brewery in Shiner, which started as the Shiner Brewing Association in 1909. Spoetzl managed to make it through the lean Prohibition years and holds the honor of being the oldest independent brewery in Texas.

After Prohibition and the Depression, not many breweries remained in the Southwest, but that all changed in 1980, when microbreweries began to open in California and, right on their heels, in Colorado. The first-ever independent post-Prohibition microbrewery, New Albion Brewing, was founded in 1976 in Sonoma, California, and Sierra Nevada Brewing opened in Chico in 1980. Also in 1980, Boulder Brewing Company opened, changing to Rockies Brewing in 1993, the name they still hold today. They set the stage for craft brewers in Colorado and elsewhere in the Southwest.

Today, Coors definitely owns the market share of beer sales in Colorado, but any craft-beer fan can find satisfaction in Denver and beyond, not to mention in Texas, Arizona, New Mexico, and even Hawaii. Other southwestern states, such as Utah, Nevada, and Oklahoma, have strict regulations governing the brewing and sale of beer, but every southwestern state has at least one brewpub.

Current Trends

The western and southwestern states include Colorado, Nevada, Utah, Arizona, New Mexico, Oklahoma, Texas, and (just because this is the region to which it is the closest) Hawaii.

The California microbrewery influence is obvious in the beer-friendly states, especially Colorado. In states with more punitive beer laws like Utah, Nevada, and New Mexico, microbreweries are less common, but a few still hold their own. This is also the only region of the country—the world, even—where you can find beer with hot chilies added to it (except for the Rogue brewery, which dabbles in the spicy stuff from Oregon). You will also find beers with names reminiscent of the dramatic southwestern landscape, evocative of the desert, the Rocky Mountains, the casinos of Nevada, the ocean surrounding Hawaii, and the pioneering spirit inherent in this last bastion of wide-open spaces: Breckenridge Avalanche Amber from Colorado, Monte Carlo High Roller Red from Nevada, Sonora Burning Bird Pale Ale from Arizona, Wasatch Polygamy Porter from Utah, and Kona Fire Rock Pale Ale from Hawaii. The American Southwest is intimately characterized by its landscape, and that landscape shapes the people. As beer ultimately reflects the consciousness of the people in a region, so it goes in this place of geographical extremes and rugged individualism.

The following state-by-state look at some of the most interesting breweries and brewpubs in the Southwest is, of course, as elsewhere, subject to change as breweries open and close with the times and changing regulations.

COLORADO

Colorado, home to Coors, is a booming beer state with lots of great microbreweries and brewpubs. The existence of Coors opens up the door to craft brewers, whereas neighboring states like Utah and Nevada have highly restrictive beer regulations. Despite being flanked by these beer-challenged states, Colorado was one of the hubs of the Microbrew Revolution. Denver is the center of it all, hosting the Great American Beer Festival (GABF) every year.

Colorado's first microbrewery opened in 1979. Boulder Brewing Company changed its name to Boulder Beer Company in 1990 and Rockies Brewing Company in 1993. In 1994, they opened The Pub at Rockies Brewing Company, a brewpub and restaurant. In 1992, they made a deal with the brewpub franchise, Rock Bottom, and their Singletrack copper ale is now served in some of Rock Bottom's chain of brewpubs.

The Flying Dog brewery opened in Aspen in 1983, the first brewery in the city for one hundred years. In 1994, the brewery—having outgrown their Aspen location—moved to a larger space in Denver, then moved again to open a brewery and brewpub in 2000. Flying Dog is known for its 1995 lawsuit against the Colorado Liquor Enforcement for pulling their Road Dog Scottish Ale because it had the words "Good beer, no shit," on the label. In 2001, Flying Dog prevailed and was able to restore the notorious phrase on the label.

In 1994, after traveling in Europe and coming home to experiment with brewing Belgian-style beers, homebrewer Jeff Lebesch began to brew commercially. His New Belgium brewery in Fort Collins, which operated out of his basement until moving to a larger location, brews many different kinds of Belgian-style and Belgium-inspired ales, and is Colorado's primary source of Belgian-styled beer. Their Fat Tire amber ale is a favorite among craft beer lovers, and the brewery is wind-powered.

Originally two small breweries in Longmont, Tabernash Brewing Company and Left Hand Brewing Company, merged in 1998. Avery Brewing Company in Boulder opened in 1993. Founded in 1989 in Fort Collins, Odell Brewing Company specializes in English ales. Also in Fort Collins is Coopersmith Pub & Brewing.

Great Divide Brewing Company in Denver opened in 1994 and specializes in producing some of the more challenging beer styles for adventurous Colorado beer drinkers. Also in Denver, the Breckenridge Brewing Company has two locations, in addition to their original Breckenridge location, first open in 1990. Founded in 1988, the Wynkoop Brewing Company is Colorado's oldest brewpub. The Tommyknocker Brewery is just twenty-five miles west of Denver in former mining boomtown Idaho Springs, and Durango is home to SKA Brewing.

NEVADA

In Nevada, brewpubs mostly revolve around (or are located within) casinos, the state's most famous entertainment industry. Most of these brew for the premises only. The Monte Carlo Pub & Brewery in the Monte Carlo Resort & Casino in Las Vegas is one of the most spacious brewpubs in the country. The only microbrewery in Nevada that packages and sells its beers for sale off-premises is the Ruby Mountain Brewery in Clover

Valley. This microbrewery opened in 1994 on a cattle ranch at the base of the East Humboldt range of Nevada's Ruby Mountains.

UTAH

Utah is, well . . . pretty dry, and that's not just the salt flats. A conservative legislature consisting mostly of tee-totaling Mormons doesn't look with much interest or indulgence on the state's brewing industry. Park City is one of the few cities in Utah where one can even purchase beer. Schirf Brewing Company/Wasatch Brewpub is Utah's first and most enduring microbrewery—and also its most notorious. In April 2003, founder Greg Schirf dressed up as Ben Franklin and staged a protest of the state's increasing beer taxes by dumping several kegs of his First Amendment Lager into the Great Salt Lake. Schirf continues to needle the Mormon-controlled legislature with beers like Polygamy Porter ("Why have just one?") and slogans like "Utah's Other Religion." His Evolution Amber Ale is "Darwin approved" and "created in 27 days, not 7." Because most of Utah's population doesn't drink, Schirf sees the excessive beer taxation as an unfair minority tax.

Uinta Brewing Company in Salt Lake City is 100% wind-powered. In 1993, they began brewing craft beer and distributing it to local pubs and restaurants. In 1996, they began bottling. Their Cutthroat Pale Ale is, according to Uinta, Utah's top-selling craft beer.

ARIZONA

Black Mountain Brewing Company in Cave Creek, Arizona, opened in 1989 and began putting Serrano chilies into their beers to encourage people *not* to "spoil" their beer with a lime wedge. The chili beer was a novelty but soon became so popular that Black Mountain began bottling it. Cave Creek Chili Beer is now available in twenty states. The brewery also makes other styles, but they are most famous for their chili beer.

Arizona's largest microbrewery is Nimbus Brewing Company in Tucson—they make it a point to mention that they do *not* produce chili beer. Tucson is also home to the cozy Gentle Ben's brewpub. Sonora Brewing Company in Phoenix has its brews available in local restaurants and pubs, or by the keg. Other Arizona microbrewery and brewpub standouts include Oak Creek Brewing Company in Sedona, Papago Brewing Company in Scottsdale, and Four Peaks Brewing Company in Tempe. Also in Tempe, Rio Salado Brewing Company specializes in German-style lagers and ales.

New Mexico

New Mexico isn't a craft-brewing hub, but the state does host a few microbrewers. In cultural mecca Santa Fe, the Santa Fe Brewing Company is New Mexico's oldest microbrewery, brewing since 1988. Their beers are distributed statewide and beyond. Sierra Blanca Brewing Company in Carrizozo takes advantage of local lore with Roswell Alien Amber. Rio Grande Brewing Company in Albuquerque produces its own version of chili beer. In Pecos, the Abbey Beverage Company is potentially the only monastery-affiliated U.S.-based brewery. It is operated by the Pecos Benedictine Monastery of Christ in the Desert. They have entered their beers in contests, and have won awards, but they aren't open to the public yet, so stay tuned.

OKLAHOMA

Coach's Restaurant and Brewery has three locations, in Norman, Edmond, and Oklahoma City, which also has Bricktown Brewery Restaurant and Pub and Huebert Brewing Company. Pete's Place is a brewpub in Krebs known for their wheat beer, called Choc Beer. Belle Isle Brewpub is in Oklahoma City and Royal Bavaria Restaurant and Brewery is in Moore. Strict beer regulations in Oklahoma have so far kept this state from booming with microbreweries.

TEXAS

Texas is home to the well-known Shiner Bock, from the Spoetzl Brewery in Shiner. "The Little Brewery in Shiner" is a commercial brewery but still remains relatively small, although its beers are distributed in twenty states. The oldest post-Prohibition microbrewery in Texas is the Saint Arnold Brewing Company in Houston, brewing since 1994. Real Ale Brewing Company is a brewpub in Blanco, and Great Grains Brewing opened in Dallas in 1997. TwoRows Restaurant & Brewery is also in Dallas.

Austin has many notable brewery/brewpubs, including Bitter End Bistro & Brewery, Live Oak Brewing Company, North by Northwest Restaurant and Brewery, Copper Tank Brewing Company, Lovejoy's Taproom & Brewery, Draught House Pub & Brewery, and Independence Brewing Company. Other notable Texas breweries include Blue Star Brewing Company in San Antonio, Rahr & Sons Brewing in Fort Worth, Jaxsons Restaurant & Brewing Company in El Paso, and Fredericksburg Brewing Company in Fredericksburg.

HAWAII

Microbrewing didn't really gear up in Hawaii until the 1990s, but now a few devoted craft brewers call Hawaii home. The Kona Brewing Company in Kailua Kona opened in 1994, and began bottling and distributing throughout Hawaii in 1995. Their brews are now also available in some of the southwestern states and Japan. The Mehana Brewing Company opened in 1995 in Hilo and also distributes their beers to states in the southwest and Japan. Other Hawaii brewpubs/microbrewers: Keoki Brewing Company and Whalers Brewpub, both in Lihue, Kuhai; Fish & Game Brewing Company in Lahaina, Maui; and in Honolulu, Brew Moon Restaurant & Microbrewery and Big Aloha Brewery.

Characteristic Types of Beer

The southwestern beer styles can probably best be summed up as individualistic, like the Wild West itself. While some breweries take their cue from the seminal brewers of the Northwest producing huge, hoppy beers, others specialize in classic German lagers or experiment with classic ale styles to come up with their own unique inventions. Call it cowboy beer, call it frontier beer, call it what you like, but southwestern brewers continue to defy categorization. The best way to get a feel for southwestern beer styles is to start trying them. In this chapter, you'll find styles grouped together mainly according to their general characteristics and placement on the color spectrum.

PREMIUM PALE LAGER/PILSNER

Color: STRAW ■■■■■■□□□□□□□□ BLACK
Flavor: HOPS □□□■■■□□□□□□□ MALT
ABV: 4–5.5%
Serving temperature: 40–45° F

These golden lagers are a step above the pale lagers typical of mainstream American megabrewing, but make good transitional beers for people not yet accustomed to the more forward tastes of darker or hoppier styles. American versions of this classic light amber German-Czech-Austrian range of beers are light to deep gold with pleasing hop bitterness and a nice balance of malt.

Southwestern/western premium pale lagers/pilsners to try:

- ❏ *Hueberts Old Tyme Lager (Oklahoma)*
- ❏ *Kona Longboard Lager (Hawaii)*
- ❏ *New Belgium Blue Paddle Pilsner (Colorado)*
- ❏ *Tabernash Pilsner (Colorado)*
- ❏ *Tommyknocker Alpine Glacier Lager (Colorado)*

AMERICAN WHEAT/HEFEWEIZEN

Color: STRAW ■■■■■□□□□□□□□□ BLACK
Flavor: HOPS □□□□□□■■□□□□□ MALT
ABV: 4.9–5.5%
Serving temperature: 40–45° F

Wheat beers make good thirst-quenchers for the arid Southwest, and brewers like to experiment with the style, combining traits of classic German hefeweizens with their own uniquely American ideas about what a wheat beer should be. Because of the blurry lines, American wheat and hefeweizen are grouped together in this category as all the pale, yeast-containing wheat beers loosely in the German hefeweizen style. In general, this style is a cloudy straw-colored ale that tastes of wheat, yeast, and fruit.

Southwestern/western American wheats/hefeweizens to try:

- ❑ *Breckenridge Hefe Proper Ale (Colorado)*
- ❑ *Flying Dog In-Heat Wheat (Colorado)*
- ❑ *Odell Easy Street Wheat (Colorado)*
- ❑ *Pete's Place Choc Beer (New Mexico)*
- ❑ *Rockies Brewing Sweaty Betty Blonde (Colorado)*
- ❑ *Shiner Hefeweizen (Texas)*
- ❑ *Tabernash Weiss (Colorado)*
- ❑ *Tommyknocker Jack Whacker Wheat Ale (Colorado)*

Pale Ales/Bitters/ESBs

Color: STRAW ▬▬▬▬▭▭▭▭ BLACK
Flavor: HOPS ▭▭▬▭▭▭▭▭ MALT
ABV: 3–5%
Serving temperature: Minimum of 45° F

In the Southwest, pale ales, bitters, ESBs, and all their cousins range from West Coast hyper-hoppy to relatively mild, depending on the tendency of the individual brewer. In general, however, you can count on some noticeable hop bitterness as well as the potential for hop delicate aromas in this style. This is the group of pale to deep gold ales, including pale ales, blond ales, golden ales, bitters, and ESBs. This category of pale to golden ales is low in alcohol and perfect for drinking several over the course of a warm desert evening.

Southwestern/western pale ales, bitters, and ESBs to try:

- ☐ *Avery 14er ESB (Colorado)*
- ☐ *Flying Dog Doggy Style Pale Ale (Colorado)*
- ☐ *Flying Dog Tire Bite Golden Ale (Colorado)*
- ☐ *Great Divide Denver Pale Ale (Colorado)*
- ☐ *Kona Big Wave Golden Ale (Hawaii)*
- ☐ *Kona Fire Rock Pale Ale (Hawaii)*
- ☐ *Left Hand Jackmans Pale Ale (Colorado)*
- ☐ *Left Hand Sawtooth Ale (Colorado)*
- ☐ *Mehana Mauna Kea Pale Ale (Hawaii)*
- ☐ *Monte Carlo Jackpot Pale Ale (Nevada)*
- ☐ *Nimbus Palo Verde Pale Ale (Arizona)*
- ☐ *Real Ale Full Moon Pale Rye Ale (Texas)*
- ☐ *Rockies Brewing Hazed & Infused (Colorado)*
- ☐ *Santa Fe Pale Ale (New Mexico)*
- ☐ *Shiner Blonde (Texas)*
- ☐ *Sierra Blanca Pale Ale (New Mexico)*
- ☐ *Sonora Burning Bird Pale Ale (Arizona)*
- ☐ *Uinta Anglers Pale Ale (Utah)*
- ☐ *Uinta Cuthroat Pale Ale (Utah)*

INDIA PALE ALE

Color: STRAW ▭ BLACK
Flavor: HOPS ▭ MALT
ABV: 5–7.5%, up to 20% for double/imperial IPAs
Serving temperature: Minimum of 45° F

Southwestern IPAs are high in hop bitterness—this is a category where southwestern brewers tend to emulate their northwestern neighbors. Light golden with a fresh, aromatic hop quality, IPAs really are hoppy everywhere in America but no less so here. While you won't find the vast offerings of IPAs in the Southwest that you will find in California (most examples in this category come from Colorado), the style is popular here. The best examples are balanced even as they maximize hop aroma and flavor.

Southwestern/western IPAs to try:

- ❏ *Avery Eleven (Colorado)*
- ❏ *Avery IPA (Colorado)*
- ❏ *Coach's India Pale Ale (Oklahoma)*
- ❏ *Flying Dog Snake Dog IPA (Colorado)*
- ❏ *Great Divide Hercules Double IPA (Colorado)*
- ❏ *Great Divide Titan IPA (Colorado)*
- ❏ *Rockies Brewing Mojo IPA (Colorado)*
- ❏ *Saint Arnold Alissa IPA (Texas)*
- ❏ *Sonora IPA (Colorado)*

A BIT OF BELGIUM IN COLORADO

The Southwest doesn't tend to produce a lot of Belgian-style beers, but the New Belgium brewery in Fort Collins and the Avery Brewing Company in Boulder specialize in a few of the Belgian styles. Most known for their Fat Tire Amber Ale, New Belgium also brews many unusual Belgian styles not easy to find from any other brewery in this region. Avery also specializes in English ales. For more on these individual styles, refer back to Chapter 5 on Belgium and the Netherlands. If you can find some authentic imported Belgian beers, try them alongside similar American products that they have inspired so that you can understand the (sometimes substantial) differences. A few Belgian-inspired brews from New Belgium and Avery that are worth a try:

☐ *Avery Salvation (Belgian strong ale)*
☐ *Avery the Beast Grand Cru (Belgian strong ale)*
☐ *Avery the Reverend (quadrupel)*
☐ *New Belgium 1554 Brussels Style Black Ale (a historic recreation)*
☐ *New Belgium Abbey (dubbel)*
☐ *New Belgium Bière de Mars (bière de garde)*
☐ *New Belgium La Folie (Flemish sour ale)*
☐ *New Belgium Loft (Belgian ale)*
☐ *New Belgium Saison (saison)*
☐ *New Belgium Sunshine Wheat (witbier)*
☐ *New Belgium Trippel (tripel)*

OKTOBERFEST-MÄRZEN

Color: STRAW [▭▬▭▭▭] BLACK
Flavor: HOPS [▭▭▬▭▭] MALT
ABV: 4.5–5%
Serving temperature: 45–50° F

While these somewhat denser lagers are less common in the Southwest than in the Midwest, some brewers produce this style, popular in the fall. Like their German counterparts, these American lagers are medium-weight and range from deep golden to a rich bronze with just a suggestion of hoppiness. Lightly caramelized or bready malt dominates the flavor. These have a smooth mouth-feel and are easy to drink, a nice flavorful change from pale lagers for those fans of the lager family.

Southwestern/western Oktoberfest-Märzens to try:

☐ *Avery the Kaiser Imperial Oktoberfest (Colorado)*
☐ *Flying Dog Dogtoberfest (Colorado)*

❑ *Rio Salado Monsoon Maerzen Amber Lager (Arizona)*
❑ *Tabernash Oktoberfest (Colorado)*
❑ *Wynkoop Railyard Ale (an Oktoberfest style brewed with an ale yeast, Colorado)*

AMBER/RED ALE

Color: STRAW [▭▭■▭▭] BLACK
Flavor: HOPS [▭▭■▭▭] MALT
ABV: 4.3–5%
Serving temperature: 48° F

These copper-colored, malty ales are linked by color and a malty character but are only loosely based on copper, red, and Scottish ales you might find in Britain. Southwestern amber ales tend instead, generally, to echo those from the Northwest with a slightly more prominent hop profile than elsewhere in the States—certainly more so than in Britain.

Southwestern/western amber/red ales to try:

❑ *Avery Redpoint Ale (Colorado)*
❑ *Breckenridge Avalanche Amber (Colorado)*
❑ *Bricktown Copperhead Premium Amber Ale (Oklahoma)*
❑ *Four Creeks Kiltlifter Scottish Amber (Arizona)*
❑ *Monte Carlo High Roller Red (Nevada)*
❑ *New Belgium Fat Tire (Colorado)*
❑ *Odell 90 Schilling (Colorado)*
❑ *Ruby Mountain Angel Creek Amber Ale (Nevada)*
❑ *Saint Arnold Amber Ale (Texas)*
❑ *Sierra Blanca Roswell Alien Amber Ale (New Mexico)*
❑ *Sonora Desert Amber (Arizona)*
❑ *Walnut Brewery Single Track Copper Ale (Colorado)*

BROWN ALE

Color: STRAW ⬜▭▬▭⬜ BLACK
Flavor: HOPS ⬜▭▬▭⬜ MALT
ABV: 4–5.5%
Serving temperature: 45–50° F

This mid-range class of beers sports elements of fruits and nuts, generally with a distinct maltiness to the profile as well. Popular in the Southwest, perhaps because they offer an alternative to lighter-colored, hoppier beers but are still light enough in body to drink in the heat, brown ales can be wedged along the color spectrum somewhere between the amber/red ales and the porters.

Southwestern/western brown ales to try:

- ☐ *Avery Ellies Brown Ale (Colorado)*
- ☐ *Coach's Downtown Brown (Oklahoma)*
- ☐ *Copper Tank Big Dog Brown Ale (Texas)*
- ☐ *Left Hand Deep Cover Brown Ale (Colorado)*
- ☐ *Nimbus Brown Ale (Arizona)*
- ☐ *Oak Creek Nut Brown Ale (Arizona)*
- ☐ *Oasis Tut Brown Ale (Colorado)*
- ☐ *Real Ale Brewhouse Brown Ale (Texas)*
- ☐ *Saint Arnold Brown Ale (Texas)*
- ☐ *Sierra Blanca Nut Brown Beer (New Mexico)*
- ☐ *SKA Busternut Brown (Colorado)*
- ☐ *Tommyknocker Maple Nut Brown Ale (Colorado)*

STRONG ALE/OLD ALE

Color: STRAW [▭▬▬▭] BLACK
Flavor: HOPS [▭▬▬▭] MALT
ABV: 6–12%
Serving temperature: Minimum of 50° F

Rich, darkish, and warming, strong ales and old ales are smooth with varying degrees of bitterness and flavors that mature and deepen with aging. This style isn't as popular in the Southwest as in the Northwest, where the weather gets colder, but a few brewers experiment with the style, particularly in mountainous Colorado where warming becomes pretty important in the middle of January.

Southwestern/western strong/old ales to try:

❑ *Avery Old Jubilation Ale (Colorado)*
❑ *Breckenridge Christmas Ale (Colorado)*
❑ *Flying Dog K-9 Cruiser (Colorado)*
❑ *Great Divide Hibernation Ale (Colorado)*

BOCK

Color: STRAW [▭▬▭] BLACK
Flavor: HOPS [▭▬▭] MALT
ABV: 7–10%
Serving temperature: 48–53° F

Southwestern versions of the bock style feature the customary aromas, flavors, and alcohol content of classic bock, a style that is decidedly robust in any of its incarnations. Bocks are generally dark in color and dependably high in alcohol, usually over 7%.

Southwestern/western bocks to try:

❏ *Breckenridge Pandoras Bock (Colorado)*
❏ *Flying Dog Heller Hound Bock (Colorado)*
❏ *Saint Arnold Spring Bock (Texas)*
❏ *Shiner Bock (Texas)*
❏ *Tabernash Rye Bock (Colorado)*
❏ *Tommyknocker Butt Head Bock (Colorado)*

PORTER

Color: STRAW ☐▭▬☐ BLACK
Flavor: HOPS ☐▬☐ MALT
ABV: 4.5–6.5%
Serving temperature: 50–55° F

Porter's complexity invites experimentation, and southwestern brewers—like many other craft brewers in other regions—tend to play with this style to make it their own.

Southwestern/western porters to try:

❏ *Avery New World Porter (Colorado)*
❏ *Flying Dog Road Dog Scottish Porter (Colorado)*
❏ *Great Divide St. Bridget's Porter (Colorado)*
❏ *Left Hand Black Jack Porter (Colorado)*
❏ *Papago El Robusto Porter (Arizona)*
❏ *Uinta Kings Peak Porter (Utah)*
❏ *Wasatch Polygamy Porter (Utah)*

STOUTS AND IMPERIAL STOUTS

Color: STRAW ☐▬▬ BLACK
Flavor: HOPS ☐▬☐ MALT
ABV: 3–6%; imperial or "extra" stout and strong ale: 6.5–12% or even higher for certain specialty releases
Serving temperature: Minimum of 50° F

Southwestern brewers also take a cue from the Northwest by favoring the high-powered (high-alcohol) and intensely flavored imperial stouts, but they also experiment with this style, brewing dry Irish-style versions, British-style sweet versions, and smooth oatmeal stouts. In general, stout is dark, rich, and similar to porter (these styles can be considered to be two endpoints of "dark" spectrum), with deep roasted grain and bittersweet cocoa and coffee overtones.

Southwestern/western stouts and imperial stouts to try:

- *Avery Out of Bounds Stout (Colorado)*
- *Avery The Czar Imperial Stout (Colorado)*
- *Breckenridge Oatmeal Stout (Colorado)*
- *Great Divide Yeti Imperial Stout (Colorado)*
- *Left Hand Imperial Stout (Colorado)*
- *Left Hand Milk Stout (Colorado)*
- *Left Hand Oak Aged Imperial Stout (Colorado)*
- *Sonoran Inebriator Stout (Arizona)*

BARLEY WINE

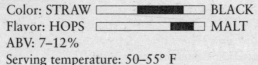

Color: STRAW ⬛ BLACK
Flavor: HOPS ⬛ MALT
ABV: 7–12%
Serving temperature: 50–55° F

This high-gravity style resembles a sweet, rich liqueur. Amber to medium-brown with suggestions of rich toffee and undertones of port or sherry (sometimes accentuated via cask conditioning), barley wines typically have a high alcohol content, so many southwestern states aren't allowed to brew or sell them—and probably wouldn't mind, since they are more suited to cold weather.

Southwestern/western barley wines to try:

❑ *Avery Hog Heaven (Colorado)*
❑ *Flying Dog Horn Dog Barley Wine (Colorado)*
❑ *Real Ale Sisyphus (Texas)*
❑ *Sonoran Old Saguaro Barley Wine (Arizona)*
❑ *Uinta Anniversary Barley Wine (Colorado)*

FRUIT AND VEGETABLE FLAVORED BEERS

While fruit isn't exactly a bumper crop in the desert, the Southwest's more mountainous regions have berries, and Colorado brewers like to include berries in their flavored beers. The desert Southwest prefers to experiment with spicy chilies. New Belgium, with its Belgian-style specialty beers, also makes its own versions of the classic Belgian frambozen (raspberry) and kriek (cherry) styles, albeit somewhat Americanized. These styles vary too much to include scales for color, flavor, etc.

Southwestern/western flavored beers to try:

❑ *Cave Creek Chili Beer (Arizona)*
❑ *Coach's Green Chili Wheat (Oklahoma)*
❑ *Copper Tank River City Raspberry Ale (Texas)*
❑ *Great Divide Wild Raspberry Ale (Colorado)*
❑ *Kona Big Island Ginger Beer (Hawaii)*
❑ *New Belgium Frambozen Raspberry Brown Ale (Colorado)*
❑ *New Belgium Transatlantique Kriek (Colorado)*
❑ *Rio Grande Pancho Verde Chile Cerveza (New Mexico)*
❑ *Tommyknocker Tundrabeary Ale (flavored with raspberries and blueberries, Colorado)*

🍺 20 🍺

Tips for Home Brewers

The typical evolution of a beer connoisseur goes something like this: a fondness for pale lager turns into a curiosity about mainstream darker styles and ales. Suddenly pale lager isn't so interesting. This inevitably leads to the discovery of local microbrews and the wonderful knowledge that people brew stouts and pale ales and Oktoberfest beers and pilsners and even some quirky Belgian-inspired styles and flavored beers at a brewery not so far away.

This in turn blossoms into a broader worldview, as the developing beer connoisseur samples beers from other regions and other countries, developing the beer palate and gaining a deeper and more complex appreciation for the art and science that is brewing. Finally, the beer drinker—once contented with that bottle of pale lager—embarks on a lifelong search for the world's best craft beers, sometimes finding a favorite country or region or style and learning everything about it, sometimes becoming an exuberant generalist, curious to try anything and everything craft brewers have to offer. Yes, it can happen to you. You are reading this book, aren't you! This is just the beginning.

But something else happens to many a beer connoisseur as he or she discovers the different beer styles the world has to offer. The question eventually arises, like a small voice from deep inside the beer lover's brain: Could I make this stuff myself?

Of course you can. Home brewing, while not exactly the simplest of hobbies, is a fun and interesting pursuit that has as a payoff the ultimate reward: a whole lot of beer, potentially of very reasonable or even superlative quality, on the cheap. In fact, cost is one reason many people begin home brewing. Some come to it before they have much experience with different beer styles, just to save money on the weekly beer bill. And, although cost may be an initial motivation, the control over the precise nuances of style, options of adding your own quirky flavorings, and so on, often become a strong allure for the home brewer as well.

Another great reason to brew your own beer is that it can put you into contact with lots of other people doing the same thing. Home-brew clubs and societies abound. Most cities have one. Search the Internet for local clubs, or ask around at local beer shops that stock good craft beer. Brewing is fun. Brewing with friends is even more fun, and you'll learn faster if you have experienced home brewers to consult as you go.

Many people have written entire books on home brewing, so consider this chapter just the beginning of your home-brew education. This fun hobby has much in store for you to learn and experience. This chapter just briefly outlines the necessary equipment, ingredients, and steps for making your first batch of beer using a simple beginner's home-brewing kit. As you advance, you can start working from recipes, brewing from grains instead of extracts, adding your own ingredients, and trying all kinds of techniques you discover as you learn more, to tweak your brewing and fermentation process. But when you first begin home brewing, it pays to be successful so you can feel rewarded enough to keep going. The easiest way to be successful is to start simply.

Begin by reviewing these basic guidelines, so you know what is in store for you, then start looking into sources for equipment and kits. Follow the directions, and before you know it, you'll be brewing. And the adventure begins!

LEARN MORE

To learn more about homebrewing, check out these resources:

- American Homebrewers Association (AHA) website. This organization sponsors the National Homebrewer's Conference and the National Homebrewer's Competition. Check them out at *www.beertown.org/homebrewing/*.
- Zymurgy, AHA's magazine dedicated to homebrewing.
- *The Complete Joy of Homebrewing* by Charlie Papazian, 3rd edition (HarperResource, 2003).
- *All About Beer* magazine, and its online home brewing page at *www.allaboutbeer.com/homebrew/*.
- Ratebeer's online weekly magazine with a homebrewing department and a homebrewing chat forum. Look around at *www.ratebeer.com*.
- Beeradvocate's home-brewing information and home-brewing chat forum at *www.beeradvocate.com*.
- How to Brew at *www.howtobrew.com*, which provides a quite comprehensive online guide to hombrewing, from beginner to advanced.

How Long, How Much?

If you started brewing your very first batch of home-brewed ale today, you should have beer to drink in about three to four weeks. That includes about an hour of organizing, cleaning, and sanitizing your equipment, about two to four hours to mix up the beer and ready it for fermentation, about a week of fermentation, an hour or two of bottling, and two or three more weeks of bottle conditioning. Stick those bottles in the fridge for a day, and then all you have to do is crack open a cold one. Your *very own* cold one.

While experienced brewers sometimes like to do as much as possible from scratch, beginning home brewers can learn a lot and get good results using a beer kit. These kits have almost everything you need to brew beer, and tell you exactly what they don't include, so you can buy any remaining ingredients separately. Home-brew kits make brewing simple and clear, and allow you to choose from a number of different beer styles. The resulting quality of a well-executed kit is likely to be better than that of a poorly executed scratch brew. Beginners usually start with ales because these are easier to make and are ready to drink sooner. Wheat beers are arguably the quickest to mature, and also make an excellent and forgiving starter batch if you are at all drawn to that style. Lagers—which require extensive aging at reduced temperatures—are generally reserved for more advanced home brewers.

Typically, you will brew a five-gallon batch of beer. This translates into a little over two cases of beer. While the initial investment in equipment can be somewhat pricey, consider how many five-gallon batches you could make. Also, if involved with a group or club, it is often possible to borrow the equipment for the initial brewing process, since that equipment spends 99% of its life in storage. This is a hobby that quickly pays for itself if you drink a lot of beer and decide to start brewing regularly.

HOME-BREW ECONOMICS

Speaking in terms of rough averages, you might be able to make $65 worth of ale from a kit costing around $30. With experience, you might become able to make around $190 worth of a Belgian clone (the term for a home-brew kit that is designed to imitate a brand or style) from a $45 kit. These estimates vary regionally, and don't include shipping costs. Saving yeast from one batch to start the next is easy, and shaves $5–6 off the price tag per batch.

What You Need

Before you attempt to brew your own beer, you might review the first chapter of this book, explaining how beer is brewed. Be sure you understand how the essential unit operations of brewing beer fit together. Then start collecting your basic equipment and supplies. Some of these things you probably already have around the house. Others you will need to purchase or borrow. Take this checklist to your local home-brew supply store, or purchase your supplies and ingredients from one of the many great Internet brewing supply sources in your region.

BEER SUPPLIES ONLINE

Many people don't have homebrewing supply shops nearby, but luckily, you can get a great selection and reasonable prices from online merchants. Here are a few online resources for homebrewing equipment and other supplies:

- www.homebrewing.org
- www.midwestsupplies.com
- www.breworganic.com
- www.ebrew.com
- www.assemblyrequired.com
- www.bacchus-barleycorn.com
- www.beerathome.com
- www.northernbrewer.com
- williamsbrewing.com

EQUIPMENT

We'll assume you have access to a stove and source of brewing-quality water. Beyond that, you need a certain amount of hardware. Much of this can be purchased in all-in-one brewing equipment kits. These can range from about $100 to $500, depending on what you get. Or purchase individual pieces separately if you already have a fair number of the required items. Here are the basics you need for brewing with a beginning home-brew kit (check your kit directions too, in case it includes anything in addition to this list):

- Five-gallon (minimum volume) cooking pot; enamel or stainless steel—no aluminum!
- Six- to eight-gallon food-grade plastic fermentor or bucket with semisealable lid.

- Thermometer—one immersion style plus one of the liquid-crystal style ones to stick on the outside of your fermentor.
- Hydrometer (which measures the gravity, that is, the density of the wort).
- Sanitizer or unscented household bleach.
- One- or two-cup glass measuring cup.
- Plastic pipe and compatible flexible tubing for siphoning/transferring beer.
- Food-grade transfer bucket for bottling.
- Bottle filler.
- Bottle capper.
- Bottles—about sixty.
- Bottle caps—about sixty.
- Bottle-cleaning brush.
- If you're working alone, nothing beats a few clamps that can be used to hold bottling tubes in place without the help of a buddy. Plastic withstands sanitizers better than metal.

One of the most important aspects of home brewing and the key to a quality finished product is undoubtedly sanitation. Clean, sanitized equipment is crucial to successful home brewing, so don't skip this important step! Anything that comes into contact with your home brew *must* be sanitary. If you miss anything and your beer becomes contaminated, it won't make you sick. No known pathogens that affect humans have been shown to survive in brewed beer. But they can make your beer taste bad enough to make you *think* you are sick, and who wants to spend a whole month working on a batch of beer only to discover it is spoiled? (It happens to everyone on occasion, but the cleaner your equipment, the greater your chance for success.)

THE BUCKET VERSUS THE CARBOY

Many home brewers brew in some sort of carboy (a large glass or plastic bottle), which allows a near-perfect seal using a device called a fermentation lock in the mouth of the carboy. The argument for this style of fermentor is that it keeps the beer more sterile and free of bacteria and ambient yeast that could spoil the beer. However, bucket-style fermentors are much easier to clean, and they allow the novice brewer ample opportunity to agitate the wort to add oxygen. This step is critical to the yeast as it starts the fermentation process, and is regularly screwed up by beginning homebrewers. Don't skimp on the fermentor. Be sure to get a food-grade bucket with a lid of moderate tightness from a restaurant supply house. If you have adequate fermentation, the ongoing discharge of CO_2 will create ample positive pressure inside the bucket to assure that no spoilage occurs. Historically, brewers long used open vats—no lids at all, let alone a perfect seal—for fermentation, and some still do. A bucket with a lid will do nicely, thank you.

INGREDIENTS

Next, you need the ingredients to make the beer. If you buy a brewing kit, this should contain most of what you need, but you might need to buy yeast separately (check the label). Kits typically contain malt extract, some form of hops, and yeast. Kits might also contain specialty ingredients like small bags of adjunct or flavoring grains, fresh hops instead of pellets, or additives like priming sugar and flavoring. Every company is different, so read the label carefully. Kits will also include a recipe, but the more you learn about beer, the more you can begin to experiment with other recipes you find.

BEGINNING BREWING

Brewing beer consists of many subtleties, and this section is by no means a complete treatise on everything the beginner must know to brew beer. The more you read and talk to other homebrewers, the more you will learn. This is, however, a very basic overview of the steps involved in brewing your first batch of beer using a beginner's brewing kit, so you know what to expect.

Always read the instructions on the kit carefully, all the way through, before you begin. Have everything ready before you begin. Keep everything clean. And don't be afraid to start. Home brewing is fun, and brewing from a kit is pretty easy if you are careful and follow the instructions precisely. Special attention has been paid to details that may be oversimplified in beginning brewing instructions, with the sincere hope that you will amaze yourself with your first batch of beer.

1. First, assemble your equipment and ingredients so you have everything you need in one place: equipment and brewing kit. Affix the surface thermometer to the outside of your fermentor. Double check that you have all the equipment and ingredients you need before you start. If your kit includes priming sugar, set this and all bottling-specific equipment aside for bottling day.

2. Clean and sanitize every piece of equipment, from the fermentor to the smallest plastic spoon. That includes the fermentor and lid, glass measuring cups, and the

immersion-style thermometer. First, rinse all pieces of equipment, scrubbing to remove surface grunge to expedite the sanitation process if necessary for borrowed/used equipment. Then, fill the fermentor with the hottest possible tap water, adding two ounces of bleach and a couple of tablespoons of baking soda. The pH increase caused by the baking soda makes your sanitizer much more lethal to microorganisms. Soak all the relevant equipment in the sanitizer for at least ten minutes.

3. As you need each piece of equipment, take it out of the fermentor and rinse it. When you are ready to use the fermentor, dump the sanitizer and rinse it thoroughly. Never wipe down equipment; this only introduces additional potential for contamination. Better to let it air-dry on a sanitized wire dish rack.

NOTE: Every step before this one could be done the day before. Leave everything immersed in sanitizer, but note that if you are sanitizing with bleach, this could corrode metal objects.

4. Fill your five-gallon pot with three gallons of clean, good-quality, purified (dechlorinated) water. Heat on high until the water comes to a boil.

5. Follow the instructions on the kit or the beer recipes. This will typically include adding malt extract to the boiling water, then adding hops and boiling for at least one hour. You are reconstituting the wort from its concentrated form.

6. After you add kit ingredients according to the recipe and boil, the wort must be cooled as rapidly as possible. This is usually done by moving the boiling kettle into a sink or larger container with cold running water (on the outside). After the wort has cooled to below 100 degrees Fahrenheit (or so), the cooling can

be completed by the addition of two to three gallons of cool, sterile (bottled or scalded and previously cooled) water directly to the boiling pot. Kits that direct you to fill the plastic fermentor with about two to three gallons of cold water are attempting to simplify the process to an extent that endangers the quality of your beer.

7. Next, pour the cooled wort into the fermentor, mixing it with as much oxygen as possible. This can easily be accomplished by transferring the cool wort back and forth between the brew pot and the fermentor, say half a dozen times, with as much agitation as possible. It is not necessary to transfer the entire contents with each pour. The point is just to incorporate air. Add more sterile cold water if necessary until you have five full gallons, although be sure to leave at least six to eight inches of head space at the top of the fermentor.

8. Take a wort sample from the fermentor using your sterile glass measuring cup and transfer it to the hydrometer tube. Check temperature to make sure it is roughly 70 degrees Fahrenheit. Float the hydrometer in the wort to check the original gravity of the wort. This will be relevant later, but make a note of both temperature and gravity.

9. Add yeast from starter culture to the wort. Don't stir it.

10. Snap the lid onto the fermentor.

11. Optional step: Pray to whatever beer-friendly deities seem appropriate.

12. Store the fermentor in a cool place, under 75 degrees Fahrenheit but not much cooler than 65 degrees. After about a week, the beer will be fermented.

Be sure to check the temperature of the fermentation at least once if not twice each day, and write it down.

Monitor the progress of fermentation by using your sanitized measuring cup to sample the gravity of the wort every two to three days. It can be helpful to keep a fermentation log, where you record all this information. If necessary, the temperature of a small five-gallon fermentor can be stabilized by suspending it, for example, in a clean thirty-gallon trash can full of water. The water creates a much more thermally stable environment.

COMMON HOME-BREWING MISTAKES

Everyone makes mistakes, but you don't have to make these. When home brewing, be sure you do *not*:

- Skimp on safety. Five gallons of boiling wort packs a *lot more* heat than five gallons of water, and turns into a sticky mess when it hits flesh. Wear sandals for drinking beer, but not for brewing it! If using caustic chemicals for cleaning, label removal, and so on, don't skimp on the gloves and goggles either.
- Use chlorinated municipal water. Either use bottled water, well water, or reverse osmosis water. Alternatively, run your municipal tap water through an activated charcoal filter.
- Skimp on quality and freshness of ingredients. If your local home-brew shop seems in the least limited in selection, it may not be moving enough inventory to keep it fresh. In this case, it is definitely worth considering an order to an online home-brew supply shop.
- Underestimate the importance of yeast:
  - Dry is vastly inferior to yeast in liquid culture. When you gain some experience, try using yeast starter instead of those dry packets.
  - Don't be afraid of yeast either. It's easy and economical to save yeast for your next batch. Simply pur-

chase a half dozen disposable, presterilized urine sample containers from your local clinic (really!), transfer yeast slurry into them until half-full from what remains in your fermentor (using your sanitized glass measuring cup), and save them in the fridge for up to two months.

- ■ It is best to make yeast starter a few days before brewing. Clean and scald a one-quart mason jar. Make about 0.5 liter average wort by mixing dry malt extract and boiling water. When cool, add contents of your already started yeast slurry (see above) and gently screw down the lid so it stays sterile but CO_2 can escape. When brewing day comes around, you have a beautiful active rollicking big yeast culture that will crank into your beer with abandon. Perfect!

- Fail to cool and adequately aerate wort prior to fermentation. This cannot be overstressed! This is a hallmark failure of newbie home brewers. Overoxygenation is impossible, so keep transferring that cooled wort between fermentor and brew kettle, just a few extra times more than you think is necessary.

- Boil less than the maximum amount your kettle will hold—the greater the proportion of the beer that is boiled, the better it is, as a general rule. Watch out for boil overs, though, as they make for nasty cleanup.

- Take inadequate notes. Be ruthless with yourself on this one. This is the only way you learn from your mistakes, not to mention the best way to re-create your successes! It may not seem like much, but all of a sudden, there you are with three batches of beer bottled up, asking yourself, "Now which hops did I use to dry-hop this one, because it tastes really good?" Take good notes!

- Fail to maintain consistent/appropriate fermentation

temperature. Fermentation temperature needs to be both appropriate and consistent. Your yeast culture will come with documentation indicating appropriate temperature; it's your job as the novice brewer to make it happen.

- Skimp on the minor expense of keeping a couple of pounds of dry malt extract on hand. It is much handier than the syrup if you need to bring the gravity of a brew up a little bit, and to make your yeast starter cultures.

Bottling Day

After a week (or so) of anticipation and two or three sequential hydrometer readings confirming a constant finishing gravity to make sure that fermentation is complete, you get to put that precious brew in bottles. For this process, you will need your bottling equipment, which you should sanitize: the measuring cup, small pan, bottling bucket, plastic cane and tubing, and bottle filler. You will also need your hydrometer again, as well as about sixty twelve-ounce bottles, sixty bottle caps, some form of priming sugar—dextrose or dry malt extract made for brewing—and a bottle capper. Six good beers to split and a willing friend to split them with and to add extra hands when needed isn't a bad idea at all here either.

Here's what happens next:

1. Twenty-four to forty-eight hours prior to bottling, move your fermentor to the place you will want it to be for bottling so that it will have time to let the majority of yeast settle out prior to bottling. Since fermentation should be complete, temperature is no longer quite as critical.

2. Wash, sanitize, and rinse your bottles using the bottle brush, hot water, and your sanitizer or bleach solution (two ounces bleach to five gallons water). If the bottles are new, they should already be clean, but rinse them and sanitize them anyway.

3. Wash, sanitize, and rinse all your other equipment, including the plastic bottling cane and tubing, the measuring cup, pan with lid for scalding priming sugar solution, bottling bucket, bottle caps, and bottle filler.

4. You will need to be able to start a sanitized siphon with your bottling cane and tubing. To do this, you should fill the entire tube with tap water, clamp it so no fluid can flow, and practice running a sanitizer through it a few times. With the tube full, place the open end into the sanitizer, lower the filler tip well below the sanitizer level, and practice filling a few bottles with sanitizer. It's an acquired skill, so you'll want to practice for a bit before trying to do it with your precious brew. Be sure to rinse tubing, filler, and bottles to remove sanitizer before trying to transfer beer.

NOTE: Steps prior to this can happen the day before. Cover bottles collectively with clingwrap or individually with small pieces of foil, or leave them full of sanitizer.

5. Prep the priming sugar and leave it covered on the stove so that it is ready to be added to the transfer bucket in a timely fashion. Measure out three-quarters of a cup of priming sugar or dry malt extract. Don't use regular granulated sugar. Add the sugar to a cup of boiling water to sanitize the sugar and scald briefly; store covered on stove until needed.

6. Now you are ready to put the beer into the bottling bucket so you can fill those bottles. Put the fermen-

tor on a high surface, like a table or counter, and block one edge up so it has a bit of a tilt. Put the bottling bucket right in front of the fermentor, but on a lower surface like a chair.

7. Put the cane in the fermentor and the tube into the bucket below, close to or touching the bottom.

8. Release the hose clamp so the beer begins to flow through the tube into the transfer bucket. The goal here is to get as much clear beer as possible into the bottling bucket, while leaving behind the spent yeast. Add the priming sugar solution to the transfer bucket while beer is being siphoned in. The movement from the siphoning will mix in the priming solution. Turn off the clamp before all the beer has siphoned out, so you still have beer inside the entire length of the cane and tube. Cover the fermentor during remaing steps if you want to save the yeast.

9. You might notice that the beer has no bubbles. That is the way it is supposed to be. Adding sugar at this stage will give the yeast needed raw materials to create CO_2 to form carbonation in your final product.

10. Put the bottling bucket on a counter, high enough that the beer can siphon into the bottles, once again blocking up one edge so it has a bit of a tilt.

11. Line up the clean, sanitized bottles significantly lower than the level of the bottling bucket to drive the siphon flow. If forced to work on the floor, put down a clean towel to work on.

12. Put the bottle filler on the end of the tube and practice using it a few times, with the end of the tube in the sanitized measuring cup, just to get the hang of it. Draw off about half a cup, and save this wort to take a

hydrometer reading on the final gravity after you finish the bottling process. (Don't add this beer back into your mix, but you can drink it to see how it tastes. Just remember, it will be room temperature and not carbonated.)

13. Put the bottle filler into a bottle, press the bottle filler against the bottom of the bottle, and fill it. When the bottle is full all the way to the top, release pressure on the filler to stop the flow. When you take out the filler, the liquid level will go down leaving about two inches of headspace.

14. Fill the rest of the bottles in this same way. When the beer in the bucket gets low, make sure the supply side of the tube is at the lowest point in the bucket so you can get it all.

15. Once you've used up all the beer, use the bottle capper to put caps on all the bottles. Better yet, you fill and a friend runs the capper. Bottling is easier and more fun with two people.

16. Store the beer at room temperature, between 65 and 75 degrees Fahrenheit, for about three weeks (as short as two weeks, as long as four weeks). Try a beer after two weeks to see if it is carbonated and tastes good. If it still tastes flat, give it another week or two, possibly increasing the storage temperature as well.

17. Finally, your beer is finished! Put it in the refrigerator and invite your friends over. They will be so impressed with you! Or don't tell anybody (except the person who helped you bottle it, of course). You might just want to keep your very first batch of home brew to yourself.

BOOM!

Every so often, a bottle of homebrewed beer will explode. This is rare, but it can happen. While your beer is waiting in its bottles, consider keeping them at least in cardboard with a lid. If a bottle explodes, the mess and broken glass will be easier to clean up.

Home brewing is truly an adventure, and the more you do it, the more you may begin to feel like part mad scientist, part artist, part gourmet chef. This is a hobby people can practice for years and still learn new things. Just like learning to taste and appreciate good beer, home brewing has a bit of a learning curve, but what lessons could be more fun?

Many home brewers have gone on to become professional craft brewers, turning hobby into profession. Could this be you? No way you'll know until you try. Whether you make just one batch of home brew or start winning awards for your fantastic beer creations, remember always to have fun.

In fact, having fun is a part of what it means to drink beer. Beer encourages camaraderie, warm conversation, friendship, and an appreciation of all that tastes good and makes life sparkle. It nourishes and sustains us. It can lighten your mood and strengthen your body. What we take in helps to make us who we are, and when we drink beer, we become part of a community far exceeding our homes, neighborhoods, or even cities. Beer is about aesthetic pleasure, aroma, and taste, a link to the ancient world and a bridge to the future. It is also about sharing the human experience. Drink better beer, brew better beer, enjoy beer with friends, and be happy. That's what the world of beer is really all about.

About the Author

Eve Adamson is an award-winning freelance writer and the author or coauthor of more than forty books. She is a member of the International Association of Culinary Professionals and has been interested in beer for two decades, beginning (as many do) with a fondness for pilsner that grew into an appreciation for all beer styles. Favoring the British ales (from IPAs to stouts) and Belgian abbey ales (from wits to quadruples), and anything experimental craft brewers have to offer, Eve is an adventurous beer taster and a self-taught home cook, often including beer in her culinary inventions. In her spare time, she tastes and records beers on *www.ratebeer.com*. She has written recipes for many different books and publications, and has an MFA in creative writing from the University of Florida. She lives—and drinks and cooks—in Iowa City with her family.

About the Technical Editor

Eric Nielsen has been involved with the beer industry—
in some capacity—for roughly the last twenty-five
years. Isolated in the California outback as a stay-at-
home house-dad in the early nineties, Eric found ample
time and impetus to construct a sizable, elaborate, pro-
ductive, and tasty home-brewing operation. Combining
this experience with a bachelor's degree in quantitative
biological sciences, Eric successfully completed the
Master Brewer's certification program jointly adminis-
tered by the University of California at Davis and the
Institute of Brewing, London. His teaching experience
at literally all grades one to Ph.D. couples with his beery
knowledge to create an excellent springboard for his
work with the renowned beer department at John's
Grocery of Iowa City, Iowa (*www.johnsgrocery.com*),
where he served as international liaison and codirector
of staff and consumer education programs. When not in
Belgium ferreting out intriguing new beers (and beer
spots . . . and beer people . . .), Eric also teaches regular
beer connoisseur's classes. Cooking, gardening, and the
study of French and Dutch languages easily fill any free
hours.